CELEBRATING 200 YEARS

OF

ST COLMAN'S CHURCH, CLOYNE

Margaret Hartnett

Patricia Lyons

Kevin Terry

Cloyne Parish

Published by Cloyne Parish 2015

© Cloyne Parish

While every care is taken with the publishing
of the material in this journal, the editor cannot be held responsible
for the opinions expressed by the authors, or for any errors of fact.

Printed and bound in Ireland by
Carraig Print Inc. Litho Press,
Carrigtwohill, Co. Cork, Ireland.
Tel: 021 4883458

PRINT
IRISH
CLÓBHUAILE
IN ÉIRINN

Paperback
ISBN: 978 0 9934728 1 7

Hardback
ISBN: 978 0 9934728 0 0

Contents

List of Illustrations

Acknowledgements

We would like to thank Canon Donal O'Mahony, former parish priest of Cloyne, and the Cloyne Bicentenary Committee, under the chairmanship of Billy Walsh, for their encouragement and support in writing this account of the 200 year history of the parish church in Cloyne. Many people helped in this task. We wish also to thank Fr Jim Moore, Diocesan Secretary, and Eileen O'Connell, Diocesan Archivist, for their help and support.

Many people provided help in various ways. These included: Michael Cuddigan, Donal & Bunny Cusack, Helen Lynch, Kathleen Walsh, Bunty Cahill, Geraldine O'Brien, Betty Dorgan, Marie Walsh, Patrick O'Keeffe, Maurice Griffin, Dominic Neville, Philomena Hurley, Catherine Hurley, Hannah Ring, Mrs P. McCarthy, Eddie Tucker, Nora Brett, Alice Crowley, Mary Ellen Maguire, Kitty Cahill, Jim Mc Murtry, Denis and Betty Cronin, Marion Cassidy, Martha Wall, Amanda Wallace, Maeve Myers, Sr Bernard, Kilkenny, Phil Lynch, Eileen O'Connell, Daphne & John Potter Cogan, James Quain, Johanne Williams, Mrs Sheehan, Doneraile, Adrienne Morrissey, Micheál McGrath, Mary Steele, Mae & Moíre Fitzpatrick, Adrienne Forbes, Canon Colman O'Donovan, P.E., Fr G. Coleman, C.C. Berrings, Mr Fitzgerald, Macroom, Fr Robin Morrissey, P.P., Aisling Lyons, John Garde, Ann Walsh, Mr & Mrs Simon Kelly. Thanks to Veronica O'Donoghue, Principal, for facilitating the taking of photographs of the portraits of the bishops in St Colman's College, and to Noel Barry and Joan Hunter.

The photographs in the book, unless otherwise stated, are by Kevin Terry. Particular thanks to Oliver Lyons and Anne McAuliffe, who proofread the draft.

FOREWORD

It is with a great sense of thanksgiving, gladness and joy that we have celebrated the bicentenary of St Colman's Church, Cloyne – the mother Parish of the Diocese. Two hundred years ago was a period of general church building in the area. Last year we celebrated the bicentenary of the Church in Shanagarry.

Bishop William Crean, the people of the parish and from a wider area have rejoiced in this time of celebration. Fr Joe Rohan C.C. and I have been particularly glad to have a role in it. I think of all the happy occasions like baptisms, first confessions, first holy communions and weddings that took place in it over its long history. Many people came here to celebrate and give thanks for happy moments in their lives and in the lives of the wider community. School celebrations have taken place in the Church over the decades since it was built, including during the Bicentenary Year. Prayers were said for good weather for the harvest, for safe passage for people making long journeys (particularly in times past), for the safe return of people engaged in dangerous work such as rescue work at sea, peacekeeping in war zones, or in past wars and other events. Prayers were also said for the success of big religious events such as two Vatican Councils and conclaves to elect new Popes.

I am reminded also of the many times people came to this place of worship in the hope of being consoled and to pray with faith and hope for deceased loved ones. Many funeral Masses have been said in this Church, some, perhaps, more in celebration of a very long life – though still a very sad time for family members; but others very sad and tragic occasions involving the loss of a young person or a baby. The Month's Mind Mass, First Anniversary and other anniversaries have also been very important moments of prayer and consolation. The Great Famine and subsequent waves of emigration from Cloyne must have been a very testing time for the Church here.

At this time, we should remember with deep affection all those who have gone before us 'marked with the sign of faith' and have courageously handed on the faith through the generations, in tranquil and turbulent times. May the mercy of God be extended to all and may they be blessed with seeing the Lord face to face.

Many priests have served in Cloyne over the years. This book will shed some light on their work. I am sure you share with me a sense of gratitude for their efforts, past and present. May the Eternal Priest and Saviour give to all a share in his divine peace and glory.

I wish to take this opportunity to thank the Bicentenary Committee for all its work in ensuring that the year of celebration was a great success and the authors of this book and all those who contributed to it. In particular, I wish to acknowledge and thank my predecessor, Canon Donal O'Mahony, for initiating and supporting the work of writing this book. A special word of gratitude is due to Patricia Lyons, Margaret Hartnett and Kevin Terry for the enormous amount of research that was carried out to produce this volume and for the huge task in editing it.

Finally, I want to give thanks to God for all the present generation who pray and celebrate with us on the Lord's Day and even some on a daily basis - and also the faithful sons and daughters of Cloyne who reside near or far in Ireland and all over the world. The contributions to the parish have enabled the Church to be suitably maintained and decorated and to be kept open for worship and the glory of God. May the worship and praise of God continue in St Colman's Church for generations to come.

Yours in Christ,
Pat Linehan, P.P.

PREFACE

As part of the bicentenary celebrations, the parish priest of Cloyne, Canon Donal O'Mahony, asked the authors of this work to write a history of the church. We had our first meeting on how to set about our task in Lisanley in February, 2014. We worked fairly continuously from that time to the summer of 2015 on the history. Notices were put in the Cloyne and Midleton Parish Newsletters seeking old news items and photographs. A good response was received and items sent to the Parish Office have been used in the book.

In researching a book such as this, one could spend much longer than we have done. However it has to be completed in a reasonable time. For this reason there is, perhaps, relevant material which remains undiscovered.

With modern technology it is possible to update or reprint a book edition much more easily than in the past. As a result this edition can be very much a dialogue between the reader and the authors. We are open to incorporate any new material received in the Parish Office, or make corrections to errors in the book, in a future reprint.

It was a privilege to be asked and a labour of love to undertake this work.

INTRODUCTION

During Penal times the Catholics of the parish of Cloyne did not have a fixed place of worship. Mass was probably celebrated in private houses, in the open and on sites of ruined churches. By the mid 18th century there was a mass house in Cloyne. Mass Houses were described by a person at the time as 'thatched cabins open at one end'. Later there was a chapel.

According to a history of the parish of Cloyne, written in the late 1940s, a chapel stood between the site of the current church and the roadway. This source further states that in 1363 an earlier chapel stood on the site of the existing church.

At the beginning of the 19th century the chapel was in poor condition and totally inadequate for the needs of the parish. Under the stewardship of the then parish priest and with the support of the community, work got underway on building a new chapel. This book is a history of this chapel, or church, as it is now known.

In the visitation of 1828, the then bishop states that the chapel was built by the late Rev. John Scanlon. He states that it is one of the most respectable and commodious in the diocese. The altar is handsome and richly decorated. Over time the Church was further embellished. It was in 1862 that the statue of St Colman was erected on the front gable. *The Cork Examiner* reported, *It is pleasant to observe the anxiety and zealous care of the people of Cloyne in ornamenting their house of worship...*

The book covers the activities of the clergy and others in enhancing its appearance and function over the years.

Following the new liturgy introduced in 1965, the altar facing the people in the church was erected in 1969. The reredos that was backing the altar when the priest celebrated mass with his back towards the congregation is now mounted on the east boundary wall in front of the church.

In the early 1980s the church got a facelift. The front wall of the church was altered with two towers being demolished and replaced by weather slating.

A Foras Forbartha report from 1975 says that the church is a building of outstanding merit. Cloyne is a very good example of a barn church, a type which was built at the end of the 18th and beginning of the 19th century. It says that the tower of the church could have been built earlier than the rest of the building.

The National Inventory of Architectural Heritage states that the interior is particularly fine and features are a testament to the skill of 19th century craftsmen. It states that the church provides the locality with a spiritual and physical focus.

As the town of Cloyne was the seat of the Catholic diocese in former times and the church of St Colman has been referred to as the mother church of the diocese, a chapter of the book is devoted to some bishops of the diocese and those with parish connections. Other chapters include:
- Christian Heritage, demography and religion
- Building of Church
- Parish priests and other religious
- People
- Church plate, vestments and records
- Timeline
- Devotional practice

Finally a chapter is devoted to some photographs of bicentenary celebration events during 2014/2015.

CHAPTER 1

Christian Heritage, Demography and Religion

Cloyne's patron saint, after whom the church is named, Colmán mac Léinín, flourished during the second half of the 6th century. A monastic complex was founded by the saint in the town probably sometime between 563 and 580.[1] MacCotter states that Cloyne was an important episcopal see in the 9th century and probably for some centuries before this.[2] The town became the ecclesiastical centre of the diocese of Cloyne. The current cathedral was built from 1250 on the site of older buildings.[3] Up to as late as 1649 Catholic mass was celebrated here, but from that time to the building of the present church, the Catholics of the town and surrounding area had to make do with places of worship that were not adequate for their needs.

The 1766 Religious Census indicates a population of 303 families in Cloyne; this does not include Churchtown South. About 85% were Catholic and 15% were Protestant. In the bishop's visitation to the parish of Cloyne in 1785 he states that it contains 643 habitations.[4] This does not include Kilteskin, then in Cloyne parish or Churchtown South. This

---

1 Paul MacCotter, *A History of the Medieval Diocese of Cloyne*, Columba Press, 2013, p6.

2 Ibid, p7.

3 John K.S. Ridley Barker, "Cloyne Cathedral", in *The Book of Cloyne*, (ed. Padraigh O Loingsigh), Cloyne Historical and Archaeological Society, 1977.

4 Eric A. Derr, "Episcopal visitations of the diocese of Cloyne and Ross, 1785-1828 [with index]", *Archivium Hibernicum*, LXVI 2013, The Catholic Historical Society of Ireland, 2013. In the bishop's visitation of 1785 he records the Union belonging to Cloyne containing the five parishes, Aghada, Rostellan, Garrane, Inch and Corkbeg.

is over twice the number shown in the 1766 Religious Census just some twenty years earlier. In the bishop's visitation of 1828, it is stated that the population of the parish was about 8,000. This figure may refer to the Catholic parish as it then was, as in Lewis's topographical dictionary the population of the parish - probably the civil parish - is recorded as 6,410 with 2,227 of this in the town.[5] The parish was *one of the finest, richest districts* in the county. On that occasion the bishop confirmed 620 children. The population of the parish peaked around 1830 some fifteen years before the famine. In 1841, the population of the civil parish was 5,456.[6] The slump in demand for agricultural produce, following the defeat of France by Britain in 1815, meant that the days of rapid economic development and dramatic population growth were coming to an end in Cork generally and in Cloyne also. For 1851 the population of the civil parish of Cloyne was 4,545.[7] The capacity of the church was 500 in 1841, and with an attendance of thirty-three per cent, it would take three Sunday Masses to cater for the parish.[8] One third of the population was under 15 years of age. The number of families was 887 and there were 817 houses. The average household size was five. A very high proportion of the people were classified as ministering to food – presumably engaged in agriculture. More than half the people over five years of age could neither read nor write.

5   *Lewis' Cork, A Topographical Dictionary of the Parishes, Towns and Villages of Cork City and County*, The Collins Press, 1998, p120.

6   Sean Horgan, *Famine and Politics in Midleton Poor Law Union 1845-1851*, Litho Press 2012, p4.

7   1851, *Census of the population of Ireland*, National Archives, Dublin.

8   Mass attendance before the Famine nationally was about 33%; Gillian M. Doherty & Tomás O'Riordan, Ireland: Culture & Religion, 1815-1870, U.C.C. Multitext Project in Irish History.

Of the population in 1830, about 95% were Catholic and about 5% Protestant.[9] In 1871, the population of the civil parish was 3529, about 95% Roman Catholic, with an additional 3,000 for Ballycotton and Churchtown.[10] While there was significant population decline owing to the effects of the Famine and emigration, Mass attendance by the end of the 19th century was over 90%. At this time then, the church must have been overflowing on Sunday mornings.

The Parish

Dr McKenna, Bishop of Cloyne, arranged the parochial boundaries of Cloyne within the diocese in 1785, and under this arrangement, Kilmahon was part of the parish of Ballymacoda.[11] A map prepared for the Rev. John Scanlon shows the parishes of Cloyne, Ballintemple and Kilteskin. It also depicts a church. Was this the limit of the jurisdiction of the Cloyne parish priest at that time and did the drawing of the church show the predecessor to the current church? The bishop in reporting on his visitation to Cloyne in 1828 refers to Cloyne as one of the bishop's mensals.[12] Now it is Cobh and Fermoy that are the bishop's mensal parishes.

9   Report of the Commission of Public Instruction, Ireland, for 1835.

10   AIRO. (All Island Research Observatory)/ Maynooth University.

11   Fr Bertie Troy, "A History of the Immaculate Conception Church, Shanagarry and its people 1814-2014", in *A History of the Immaculate Conception Church, Shanagarry and its people 1814-2014*, compiled by Tom Morrison & Helen Kearney, Carraig Print, 2014, p5.

12   Eric A. Derr, op. cit.; the revenues of the parish were for the Bishop.

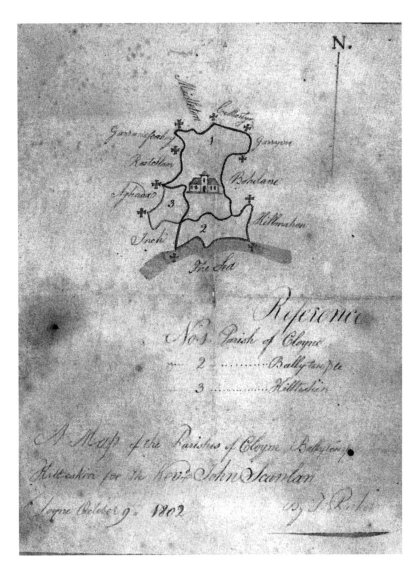

1.1 1802 Map of Cloyne, Ballintemple and Kilteskin
(Courtesy CDA)

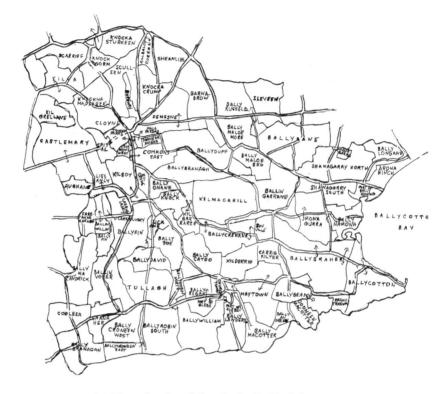

1.2 Townlands of the Catholic Parish

(Courtesy Margaret Hartnett)

The parish of Cloyne is the head of a Roman Catholic union or district, comprising the parishes of Cloyne, Churchtown, Kilmahon, and part of Kilteskin.[13] The townlands in the Catholic parish of Cloyne are shown on Figure 1.2.

The townlands of the civil parish are shown in the following table.[14]

---

13   Lewis' Cork, op.cit. p125.

14   www.billdorgan.com/page6.html

Ballingarrane	Ballyknock	Killinagh
Ballinvoher (part)	Ballymacand-rick	Kilmacahill Kilva
Ballinwillin	(part)	Knockacrump
Ballybane	Ballyonane	Knockasturke-en
Ballybraher	Ballyregan	Knockgorm
Ballybranagh	Ballyroe	Knocknamadderee
(part)	Ballyrussell	Lickane
Ballycotton	Barnabrow	Malapardas
Ballycotton Island	Burgary	Monearaniska
Ballycotton	Carrigatogher	Rathcuppoge (part)
Island, small	Carriglusky	Scarriff
Ballycottin town	Cloyne Town	Sculleen
Ballycrenane	Commons East	Sheanliss
Ballycroneen East	Commons West	Sleveen
Ballycroneen	Demesne	Spital
West	Farrannamana-gh	Sunville
Ballydavid	Gurteenina (part)	Tead Beg
Ballyduff	Kilballycurrane	Tead More
Ballyfin (part)	Kilbarraree	Townparks
Ballygeany	Kilboy	Tullagh (part)
	Kilcrone	
	Kilgrellane	

1.3 Townlands of the Civil Parish of Cloyne

Additional townlands, with the civil parish names in brackets, in the Catholic parish are:

Ardnahinch (Kilmahon)	Ballylongane (Kilmahon)	Ballywilliam (Ballintemple)
Aughane (Rostellan)	Ballymacotter (Ballintemple)	Carrigkilter (Ballintemple)
Ballyandreen (Ballintemple)	Ballymaloe (Kilmahon)	Castlemary (Inch)
Ballybranagan (Titeskin)	Ballynamona (Kilmahon)	Churchtown (Ballintemple)
Ballycatoo (Ballintemple)	Ballyrobin (Ballintemple)	Coolbea (Inch)
Ballylanders (Ballintemple)	Ballytrasna (Kilmahon)	Dooneenmacotter (Kilmahon)
Kilderrig (Ballintemple)	Lissanley (Inch)	Maytown (Ballintemple)
Monagurra (Kilmahon)	Shanagarry (Kilmahon)	Shanahee (Inch)
Ballingarrane (Kilmahon)	Ballinvoher (part; Ballintemple)	Glebe (Ballintemple)
Ballyfin (part; Inch)	Ballymacandrick (part; Inch)	Carriglusky (Inch)
Tullagh (part; Inch)	Rathcuppoge (part; Titeskin)	

1.4 Townlands of Cloyne R.C. parish in Adjacent Civil Parishes

The population of Cloyne District Electoral Division in 1911 was 2,042.[15] One hundred years later it was 3,862 with about half the increase occurring in the period 2001-2011. The population of the town was about 1,600 in 2011.[16] The town comprises only part of the district electoral area.

Those who carried out Griffith's valuations in the mid 19th century classified types of centres by the settlement population. Villages contained between 250 and 500 people; small market-towns between 500 and 2000 people; and large market-towns between 2000 and 19000 people. They considered the sphere of influence for land values to be three miles radius for larger villages and smaller towns. Larger market-towns, up to a population of 15000, influenced an area of up to seven miles radius.[17] Using this classification, then, Cloyne was on the verge of establishing itself as a large market-town in the fourth and fifth decades of the 19th century, prior to the Famine. The Famine, coupled with emigration, had a devastating effect on the town and for much of the 20th century it was heading for a village status. However, relative to Castlemartyr and, particularly, Midleton, Cloyne town had been losing out from the mid 18th century.[18] The wider parish was experiencing growth above the levels for East Cork generally up to about 1830.[19] In the past decade or so the

15   *Census of the population of Ireland, 1911*, National Archives, Dublin.
16   en.wikipedia.org/wiki/Cloyne, September, 2014.
17   Patrick O'Flanagan, *Three hundred years of Urban Life; villages and towns in County Cork. 1600-1901*, in Cork History and Society, (Editors: Patrick O'Flanagan and Cornelius G. Buttimer), Geography Publications, 1993, pp 429-430.
18   William J. Smyth, *Social, Economic and Landscape Transformations in County Cork from the mid-eighteenth to the mid-nineteenth century*, in Cork History and Society, (Editors: Patrick O'Flanagan and Cornelius G. Buttimer), Geography Publications, 1993, p665
19   See Figure 16.8, William J. Smyth, *op. cit*, p682.

population has doubled and it would seem timely to redefine Cloyne as a growing and prosperous area. In conclusion, it can be said that the population of the parish was experiencing rapid expansion at the time the church was built, some two hundred years ago. In addition, the percentage of Catholics in the population was also increasing. The population declined continuously from about 1831 until 1986 with a significant reversal of this trend in the past fifteen years. In terms of religious affiliation, the proportion of Catholics is now about the same as that indicated in the religious census some 250 years ago: 85%.

1.5 The Church and its rich hinterland

The parish of Cloyne is a rich agricultural area. In the late

18th century, landlords were discovering the potential of land to grow a variety of crops other than grass. The main crops grown in the area were turnips, cabbage and potatoes.[20] Dairies were also numerous in the area. In the early 19th century, Midleton became the largest barley market in the region outside of Cork, and Ballinacurra was a busy trans-shipment point.[21] Over the past several decades the trend is towards larger land holdings. In 1980, about one quarter of the land in the parish was given over to corn, over a quarter to hay and silage and one quarter to pasture. About 13% was given over to sugar beet. In the past, mixed farming was the norm but now farms are much more specialised.[22] Fishing is an important activity in Ballycotton.

There was also some industrial activity in Cloyne in the period since the building of the church. A proposal to build a railway line linking Cobh, Cloyne and Ballycotton in 1906 never materialised.

The mining of clay took place at Aughane and Lisanley. Pottery is produced at Shanagarry. It has significant resources relating to tourism, in terms of the natural beauty of the area, and in hospitality with the world-renowned Ballymaloe House and Cookery School.

20   J. J. Harty, *Agriculture*, in The Book of Cloyne,
       edited by Padraig O Loingsigh, p148.
21   David Dickson, *Old World Colony Cork and South Munster 1630-1830*, Cork
       University Press, 2005, p285.
22   J. J. Harty, *Agriculture*, op, cit., p152.

CHAPTER 2

The Building of the Church

B etween 1644 and 1649, the Cathedral in Cloyne was in the possession of the Catholic Church, with mass being celebrated there.[23] In 1649 the Cathedral became Anglican and, from that time to the 1720s, the Catholics of the parish did not have a fixed place of worship. Mass was probably celebrated in private houses, in the open and on sites of ruined churches. With the relaxation of the application of the penal laws in the 1720s, the Catholic Church began to build chapels or mass houses as they were called. These were described by a contemporary as 'mean thatched cabins open at one end'. The Catholics of Cloyne attempted to build one of these places of worship in 1728 within view of the existing Cathedral (exactly where, we do not know) but were prevented from completing it by the local magistrate, John Longfield of Castle Mary. A similar situation existed in Midleton.[24] The Lord's Committee appointed to inquire into the State of Popery in the Kingdom in 1731 includes the following detail concerning Cloyne:
- Mass House begun but not finished.

The late Canon Troy states that in 1731 the only chapel in the Diocese of Cloyne was in Carrigtwohill.[25] With the defeat of Prince Charles at Culloden in 1746, the danger of a Stuart ascending to the English throne receded and the application of the penal laws was further relaxed. By 1764 the mass house

---

23 The Catholic Church since the Reformation, Thomas Kelleher, Chapter 16-
    Book of Cloyne-2nd Edition.
24 Midleton parish bulletin, 11th February, 1996.
25 Ibid.

in Cloyne appears to have been completed and there were also chapels in Ballintemple (Churchtown) and Kilmahon (Shanagarry). The Hearth Tax returns this year give the following chapels in good order: Cloyne, Ballintemple, and Kilmahon.

However, in the mid 18th century, the Catholic Archbishop of Dublin warned that the Church, 'grievously afflicted with misfortunes and persecutions' faced a real threat of extinction in the country.[26] This is not so far-fetched when one considers that Norway almost completely converted to Lutheranism within a couple of decades of 1536.[27] Towards the end of the century the situation began to improve. The Catholic Relief Act of 1778 allowed Catholics to take 999 year leases and to inherit lands on the same terms as Protestants. The Irish Catholic Relief Act of 1782 allowed Catholics who took the oath of allegiance to buy and lease freehold land, and relaxed laws concerning the registration of priests, the carrying of arms, and education.[28]

During the period 1750-1850 Irish Catholics were presented with the Tridentine agenda of the Counter-Reformation. They took this reformed faith to their hearts and, eventually, came to equate this Catholicism with their post-Gaelic national identity and to form the most convincingly Catholic people in Western Europe.[29]

In the bishop's visitation to Cloyne in 1785, it is stated that it comprises three parishes: Cloyne, Churchtown and

---

26 Michael A. Mullett, Catholics in Britain and Ireland, 1558-1829, St. Martin's Press Inc., New York, 1998, p180.
27 en.wikipedia.org/wiki/Religion_in_Norway
28 Michael A. Mullett, op. cit., pg181.
29 Ibid, p185.

Kilteskin.[30] There are two chapels in good order. It does not say where these chapels are but Kelleher identifies one of them as Cloyne.[31] According to a history of the parish of Cloyne, written in the late 1940s, this chapel stood between the site of the current church and the roadway.[32] This source further states that in 1363 a chapel stood on the site of the existing church.

Revolution had broken out in France in 1789 and in a few years the security of Britain and Ireland was threatened. In return for clerical support against the spread of revolutionary ideas, the authorities granted concessions to the Catholic Church. Consciousness of this increasing power led to an increase in church building from this time on. In a great many cases, sites were donated by Protestant landlords, many of whom also gave money. The increased prosperity in the country, resulting from high prices for agricultural produce because of the Napoleonic Wars, may also have helped to finance them.[33]

Around 1794, the Church of Ireland bishop of Cloyne granted Roman Catholics of Cloyne ground to build a chapel on.[34] His nephew also contributed money for the building of the chapel. In 1796, the Cathedral Chapter gave 10 guineas to the Catholics of the town for repair and maintenance of their church, (presumably the chapel constructed 70 years before).

---

30 Eric A. Derr, op. cit.

31 Ibid.

32 History of the Parish of Cloyne, Cloyne Diocesan Archives, Cobh, *c.* 1947, unpublished.

33 Thomas Kelleher, op. cit.

34 Hibernian Journal, 17th February, 1794.

2.1 Grand Jury Map 1811
(www.corkpastandpresent.ie)

The grant of land to build a chapel was referred to by Bishop Coppinger. In a letter to the Royal Dublin Society in 1811, he refers to the princely munificence of the Church of Ireland bishop to the Roman Catholic chapel in Cloyne.[35] In his visitation to Cloyne in 1818 there is no recorded mention of the chapels or a church under construction. In the visitation of 1828, the bishop states that the chapel was built by the late Rev. John Scanlan. He states that it is one of the most respectable and commodious in the diocese, about 90 by 46 feet. The altar is handsome and richly decorated.[36]

---

35   http://archive.irishnewsarchive.com/Olive/OMA/INA/SharedArticle.
aspx?href=SST%2F2000%2F10%2F14&id=Ar02401
36   Eric A. Derr, op. cit.

2.2 St Colman's Church, Cloyne 1937
(Courtesy: *The Irish Examiner*)

It seems probable that it was around this time that the construction of the present church began. It was built on land leased by Bishop Bennet to the parish priest, Fr John Scanlon.

2.3 Masonry around door opening in the tower

A memorial plaque to Fr John Scanlon in the church indicates that construction had begun but it had not been completed on his death in 1820. The inscription states that his remains were buried beneath.[37] The tablet may have been relocated at some point.

2.4 Memorial Plaque to Fr Scanlon

37   Translation by Canon Sean Cotter.

Lewis' Topographical Dictionary of Ireland, first published in 1837, states that the chapel at Cloyne is a large, plain, old edifice. The survey work for this directory was carried out in 1833. The size of the church, from an ordnance survey map, circa 1841, is about one and a half times the size indicated by Bishop Coppinger in his 1828 visitation. So it may well be that it was extended at an early stage. This is the same size as it is today with a capacity of about 500 people.

2.5 Church layout (O.S.l. Map c. 1841)

The statue of St Colman was erected on the front gable of the church in 1862.

2.6 Statue of St Colman

2.7 One of the West Windows

In 1869, on the disestablishment of the Church of Ireland, Cardinal Cullen privately petitioned Gladstone to give the Catholics some of the old cathedrals.[38] When researching for this book, two questions arose at an early stage. One was: when did the 'chapel' become a 'church' and the other was, when did 'Spital Lane' become 'Chapel Street'? In the Ordnance Survey map of Cloyne in *c.* 1840 it is shown as an R.C. chapel situated on Spital Lane. In the map in 1935 it is shown as St Colman's Catholic Church situated on Chapel Street. So the chapel became a church and that part of the street from Cloyne cross as far as the church became Chapel Street. Based on the article in *The Cork Examiner* in 1862, on the erection of the statue of St Colman, it was a fitting place to be referred to as a church. I think, until recent decades, people generally referred to it as a Chapel.

---

38 Holograph letter from Cardinal Cullen to Dr. Kirby, 24 March, 1869, Irish College Rome Archives.

2.8 The West stained glass window

2.9 The East stained glass window

2.10 Cloyne Church
(Lawrence Collection, National Library of Ireland)

A Foras Forbartha report from 1975 says that the Church is a building of outstanding merit.[39] Cloyne is a very good example of a barn church. This design was popular at the end of the 18th and beginning of the 19th century. It says that Cloyne is a late 18th century construction and that the tower could be earlier.

2.11 Cloyne Church

In its appraisal, The National Inventory of Architectural Heritage, states that it is a fine early 19th century church, built by Rev. J. Scanlon, presenting a strong and notable façade. The ogee arch and giant order engaged columns are unusual features, which distinguish it from other ecclesiastical structures. The finely carved porches add artistic interest to the altered entrance front. The interior is particularly fine and features such as the giant order Corinthian columns with carved plinths and reredoses are a testament to the skill of 19th century craftsmen. The tower to the rear is a notable early feature and is indicative of the multiphase construction of the building. Situated adjacent to a graveyard, the church provides the locality with a spiritual and physical focus.[40]

---

39 Transcribed from Liber Chronicus, Cloyne (unpublished)
40 National Inventory of Architectural Heritage

CHAPTER 3

The Bishops of Cloyne
1748 - 2015

John O'Brien (1701 – 1769)

John O'Brien was born at Ballyvaddy near Kildorrery in North Cork, son of Thomas O'Brien and Eleanor McEniry. His family was related to Count Peter de Lacy, one of the most successful imperial commanders in the Russian service, who later became governor of Latvia. He was also related to Bishop Terence O'Brien, the Limerick martyr, who was beatified by Pope John Paul II. As with many more of that time, we have no information about his early education. Presumably, it was in hedge schools.

A large part of his young life was spent on the continent in France and Spain. He was a clerical student in Toulouse in 1725 and 1726, and worked as a priest in that area from 1727 to 1731. He went on to do further studies in Toulouse and in the Sorbonne in Paris. No record of his actual ordination seems to exist. He may have been ordained before he left Ireland. Many young priests postponed their return to Ireland at that time to avoid the rigours of the Penal Laws. One of the options open to them was to remain on the continent as a tutor in an aristocratic household. John O'Brien spent some years in the house of Arthur Dillon, who was the agent of James III, the Old Pretender, in Paris. There is a record of his having got a degree in theology in Toulouse in 1733, and that same year saw him in Spain as tutor to the son of the Connock family, an important expatriate Irish family. He was subsequently retained by other noble families in a similar capacity, travelling with them on the continent. In 1737 he was appointed tutor to the son of Thomas Geraldino (Fitzgerald), Spanish ambassador to the Court of St James in London.

On returning to Ireland in 1738, his first posting was as parish priest of Castlelyons and Rathcormac. The arrangement made was that he would only get half the normal income, the other half going to his predecessor. This division of income was made by Christopher Butler, archbishop of Cashel. While O'Brien agreed initially, he subsequently changed his mind. Fr Coombes in his book *A Bishop of Penal Times* suggests that this 'probably marks the beginning of a lifelong feud between John O'Brien and the Butlers of Cashel'. Over the years they were constantly at odds over such things as parish boundaries, the precise limits of authority of archbishops, bishops and pastors, and relations between diocesan and regular clergy. He was archdeacon of Cloyne and vicar general before being appointed bishop of Cloyne and Ross in 1748. The exiled Jacobite court in Rome still retained influence in the appointment of Irish bishops, and this is considered to have helped John O'Brien's case. The clergy of the diocese, who were either related to or friendly with Archbishop Butler or Bishop Creagh of Waterford and Lismore, were not pleased with the appointment. Most of the bishops at this time came from aristocratic Irish Catholic families, and some snobbishly felt that a farmer's son was not good enough for the job.

O'Brien may not have helped his own case in that he had the reputation of being a difficult person to deal with. He lived in Ballinterry near Rathcormac and the road up to his house was known as 'Bóithrín an Chrá' or 'The road of Vexation' as his priests were reputed to dread their encounters with him. In a broadsheet dated 24 June 1750, said to have been written by a Catholic gentleman, O'Brien is accused of having ordered the closure of twelve mass-houses in Castlelyons and surrounding area, and refers to the 'domineering arrogance' of O'Brien. He received support at that time from his friend, Seán Ó Murchú na Ráithineach, in a poem written to comfort him –

> Le feitheamh nach fada 's le feartaibh chirt Rí na nGrás,
>
> Tillfid na ceathanna scamall so arís gan tábhacht;
>
> Beidh i gcumas dár neasbogaibh tagradh an dlí gan scáth,
>
> Gan urraim, gan acharann Sasanach céim ná ceard.

He became embroiled in the late 1750s in a dispute between expatriate factions of the O'Brien family, rival claimants to the title 'Earl of Thomond'. Pleading the case of one side was the Chevalier Thomas O'Gorman, friend of Louis XV, and on the other side was Charles O'Brien who had commanded the Irish Infantry at Fontenoy in 1745. In the mix was one Lady Lismore and O'Gorman is reputed to have said that O'Brien and his vicar general McKenna, 'would sign the alcoran [the Koran] to please her'.

Bishop O'Brien took over the running of the diocese at a time when the Penal Laws had wreaked havoc on church discipline and practice. Priests and bishops had been absent, churches had fallen into disrepair, and attendance at Mass and the sacraments was a thing of the past. In 1755, he issued his statutes outlining how he expected people, clergy and laity, to practise their religion from now on. This started the diocese of Cloyne and Ross on a journey of renewal which did not start in other places for another generation. Ten years later in 1765, he was in a position to choose fifteen highly capable priests to conduct missions around the diocese. It is believed that these were the first missions held by the Catholic Church in Ireland in the 18th century. The results were reported to be very edifying. Matthew McKenna, later Bishop McKenna, was a member of that mission team.

Bishop O'Brien spent the time from September 1756 to May 1757 visiting the Irish Colleges in Toulouse, Bordeaux and Louvain. He was on the continent again in 1764, and in September 1767 he travelled to Paris via Dublin and London. O'Brien appears to have spent at least eighteen years in France and Spain during his lifetime. He spoke and wrote English, Irish, Latin, French and Italian. It is reasonable to assume also that he had a working knowledge of Spanish, and Greek and Hebrew words are sprinkled liberally through his writings.

In August 1758, he put Mitchelstown and surrounding area under interdict because of the way they treated Bishop Creagh of Waterford and Lismore. 'Creagh was dragged through the streets, beaten with sticks and pelted with stones. He was rescued by a Mr James Butler before the mob could carry out their declared intention of hanging him. The women pelted him with mud as Butler escorted him to a place of safety.'

From 1759, Irish cattle were admitted to the English market, which led to a situation where pasturage was more profitable than tillage. Some landowners cleared whole villages to make way for bullocks. This led to Whiteboy activities in many places. In a pastoral letter in March 1762, O'Brien threatened with excommunication anyone accused of such involvement.

Although there is some confusion between him and other writers of the same name, Bishop John O'Brien was traditionally believed to have been a poet himself. He was also a great patron of other poets and scribes. One poem attributed to him is a lament on an affliction described as 'an chrith', the shakes / trembling.

Is tréith 's lag le tamall mé dhom chlaoi

Le taomaibh creatha 'om threascairt faon gan bhrí:

Níl géag im' chalainn, feacht ná féith im' chroí

Nár réab ar fad, 's do speal mo ghné 's mo ghnaoi

It is known from a letter of his that he suffered from a recurrent illness and that his final trip to the continent was partly occasioned by his doctor's instructions to him to change climate and visit a spa near Liège. He may have suffered from something akin to Parkinson's Disease. Another reason put forward for his rather hasty departure towards the end of his days was that he was confused with another O'Brien who was wanted by the authorities for Whiteboy activities. He did, however, leave quite openly and could easily have been arrested if anyone had sought to do so.

The famous Irish poet, Micheál (mac Peadair) Ó Longáin, was part of the cúirt filíochta in Carrignavar and had close ties with 'Filí na Máighe'. Ó Longáin was employed by O'Brien for periods between 1759 and 1762 as is testified by a number of manuscripts he wrote for him. He also had connections with the Ó Dálaigh family of Mitchelstown, who were said to have in their possession at the time of his death several manuscripts formerly belonging to the bishop.

Another interesting scribe / scholar who worked for O'Brien

during the last ten years or so of his life was the Rev. Seán Ó Conaire, parish priest of Cloyne, who is believed to have called himself 'Connery' in English. At least nine manuscripts written in whole or in part by Ó Conaire survive. One manuscript known to have belonged to O'Brien, and now in TCD, was at least partly written by Ó Conaire in France in the mid-1760s. Among the scribal work done by him for the bishop were annals, historical and genealogical matter, a duanaire of the 17th century poet Piaras Feiritéir, and work on his famous dictionary, *Focalóir Gaoidhilge-Sax-Bhéarla*, completed in 1762 but not published until 1768 because of scarcity of funds. A further two members of the Ó Conaire family, Seamus and Donncha, also did scribal work in Cloyne for the Bishop.

O'Brien perceived the practical use and necessity of the Irish language for priests in Ireland: this was an argument he used in his appeals to Rome for funding for the publication of his dictionary. He also stipulated that students who wished to avail themselves of bursaries he founded at Louvain and Paris should be able to speak Irish. It is clear from his writings that Bishop O'Brien had an exceptional knowledge of the literary tradition.

His wide general erudition and his vigour in controversy are manifest in a lengthy Mémoire which he wrote in 1764 in the prestigious *Journal des Sçavans*. This circumstance was brought about in the first place by one of the great literary hoaxes of modern times. The poems of 'Ossian' written and translated by a Scotsman, James Macpherson (1736-1796), caused a literary sensation all over Europe. Macpherson published them as coming from Scots Gaelic 'Ossianic' ballads collected in the Highlands of Scotland. They were retranslated into several European languages influencing and exciting people such as Goethe in Germany, and Cesarotti in Italy. Mendelssohn wrote his Fingal's Cave Overture, having been inspired by these tales, and a king of Sweden was named Oscar.

A great body of prose and poetry, fiannaíocht, dealing with the exploits of Fionn and the Fianna, had grown up in Ireland from the twelfth century onwards. This cycle of songs and tales was the material drawn on by Macpherson for Ossian. Sharing a common language, the fiannaíocht cycle was part of Macpherson's tradition, but all the tales were based in Ireland, not Scotland, and the poems he purported to have translated from the originals did not, in fact, exist. He took considerable liberties with Irish history and geography.

Different voices very quickly began to raise doubts about various aspects of Macpherson's work, the first being one Dr Terence Brady, an Irish doctor then living in Brussels. *Le Journal des Sçavans* decided to get to the root of the matter, and approached a person known to them as a scholar of distinction, namely, John O'Brien. In May 1764, they published the first instalment of a lengthy paper entitled 'Mémoire de M. de C. (Monsieur de Cloyne) à Messieurs les Auteurs Du Journal des Sçavans, au Sujet des Poèmes de M. Macpherson'. The full article extended over five issues of the *Journal*. M. de C. quotes over ninety different writers. He cites continental, English and Irish authorities, ancient, medieval and modern, Catholic and Protestant, secular and ecclesiastical, printed and manuscript. Parts of the Mémoire were subsequently translated into German and raised serious doubts about Macpherson, but in the short term did not succeed in shaking the credulous. The fashion was probably too strong to accept reasoned argument.

John O'Brien/Seán Ó Briain was clearly a man of broad attainments: well-travelled, well-read, well-versed in European culture and well-versed in his own. He worked hard in his diocese to bring his flock back to regular practice of their religion with the active help of their pastors.

On his last trip abroad, he went first to Dublin and thence to London, and ended up in Lyon in France. His departure was noted by many of the literati of the time e.g. Charles O'Conor of Belenagare and the Chevalier O'Gorman. Of his last months and years in France, we know very little. He died in Lyon on the 13th March 1769 and is buried in the church of St Martin d'Ainay. His epitaph was destroyed at the Revolution, but the wording of it had been copied into the flyleaf of a copy of his Focalóir/Dictionary:

Epitaphium Illustrissimi et Reverendissimi Johannis O'Brien, D.D., Episcopi Cloynensis et Rossensis.

Hoc in sacello, pio Canonicorum hujusce nobilis ecclesiae studio, sepultus

jacet Illustrissimus et Reverendissimus DD Joannes O'Brien, Epus Cloynensis

et Rossensis in Hibernia , ex regali et antiquissima O'Brienorum stirpe per

lineam rectam Conchubari O'Brien, cognomento na catharach vulgo

slaparsalach Regis Momoniae anno MCIV usque ad MCXLVII, de quo

Sanctus Bernardus in vita Malachiae. Exul e patria religionis tuendae causa,

hac in urbe supremum diem obiit XIII. mensis Martii, anno
salutis MDCCLXIX,

aetatis autem suae LXVIII., status Pontificatus XXI,
presbyteratus XXXV.

Requiescat in pace. Amen. [41]

Whether this is what was on his tomb or not, we will never know, but one Dr Green from Edmonton, Canada in April 1895 copied the following entry in the Archives of the city of Lyon for Frank Murphy:

Reverendissime et Illustrissime Jean O'Brien, Evêque des deux
Diocèses unis

de Cloyne et de Rosse, en Irlande, décédé le treize mars âgé
d'environ

soixante huit ans, a été inhumé le quinze du présent mois
mil sept cent

soixante neuf par moi Prévôt curé soussigné, dans le tombeau
près l'autel

de cette église, en présence de Mres Matthieu O'hea
et de Henry Schouler,

prêtres de la Congrégation de la Mission de Lyon
et des autres soussignés.

Schouler, ptre de la Cong. de la Mission.

O'hea ptre de la c.

Marquet ptre.

De Tocquet de Montgeffond, prévôt curé d'Ainay.

---

41   JCHAS 1895

Matthew McKenna (1706 – 1791)

Matthew McKenna was born on Great Island in Walterstown or Templerobin in 1706. (Eric Derr says Stream Hill, Doneraile). Of his early education we know nothing, probably a local hedge school. His later education was at the Irish College in Paris, an institution which remained dear to his heart, and to which he was later a benefactor. He received his Master of Arts degree in 1737, his Licentiate in 1742 and was described as a Doctor of the Sorbonne in 1743.[42] He was nominated Munster provisor of the Collège des Lombards in Paris in December 1737 with his certificate of approval granted by the archbishop of Paris in April 1738. Taking advantage of his position as Munster provisor, McKenna strongly supported John O'Brien in his bid for nomination as coadjutor to the bishop of Cork, Thaddeus McCarthy. He represented O'Brien's case to the exiled Stuart court. Ultimately, this close relationship resulted in McKenna's return to Ireland in 1750 to assist O'Brien in the governance of the diocese in the capacity of vicar general and parish priest of Great Island.[43]

In 1758, he published his 'Ancient and Modern Names of the Parishes of Cloyne'. As well as the names, he included the patron saints. This publication was probably necessary at the time as structures had become unclear due to the absence of church organisation during the height of the Penal Laws.

In Finn's Leinster Journal for Wednesday July 29th 1769, is the following item of news regarding Dr McKenna: 'Yesterday –

---

42 L.W.D. Brockliss and Patrick Ferte, 'Prosopography of Irish Clerics in the Universities of Paris and Toulouse 1573-1793' in *Archivium Hibernicum* LVIII, 2004.

43 Rev. William Holland, *History of West Cork*, p.39.

MCann (recte McKenna) of Cove, Popish Priest, was brought here from Youghall, guarded by a troop of light horse, and lodged in the county jail; but this day he was set at liberty again. The other priest, who was committed on Sunday last, remains in confinement'. 'The other priest' was the Rev. William Lonergan of Curriglass (Conna), who 'stands charged with officiating as a Popish Priest, and with being concerned in a most insolent and seditious correspondence, relating to the Whiteboys in 1762, and containing his contempt of the laws, and those appointed to execute them'. Matthew McKenna may have been arrested for the same reasons, or alternatively, for having aided Bishop O'Brien to escape out of the country.[44] He was appointed bishop of Cloyne and Ross in 1769. His episcopal promotion was strongly supported by his former colleagues at Paris and by the clergy of Cloyne and Ross. He had already been acting as de facto bishop during O'Brien's absence in the final year and a half of his episcopacy. Until the end he was a very proactive pastor. He was a great lover of the Irish language and spoke and preached in it as often as possible.

On October 5th 1777, Archbishop Butler presided at the Assembly of the Munster Prelates at Kilworth, which established a uniform system of discipline throughout the province:

(a)   Offerings for Masses in the tribunal of penance were forbidden.

(b)   Sunday patterns to be discouraged.

(c)   Night dances and balls also forbidden.

(d)   Likewise profanations at wakes.

---

44   Rev. William Carrigan, : 'The Old Priests of the County Cork, Part 1' in JCHAS 1895.

(e)   Action to be taken against riots and quarrels at fairs and markets.[45]

At the first outbreak of the Rightboys, their efforts were directed at the tithe system exclusively, and the exactions of the Protestant clergy. But by degrees a cry was raised against all ecclesiastical endowments, particularly in those districts where some pastors had been censured for exacting too high dues. At a general meeting of disaffected Catholics held in Cork, March 29th 1786, it was resolved to request that an inquiry be held into the conduct of the Catholic parish clergy. Four delegates were sent to wait on Dr McKenna, who paid little attention, initially, but when threatened with the defection of whole parishes, he appointed as commissioners, Dr Teahan (later Bishop of Kerry), and Frs O'Leary, Callanan and Lonergan (three distinguished Regulars), to inquire into the charges against the parochial clergy. Fr Lonergan declined. The others did their best to remove the causes of scandal and disunion. Dr McKenna by now was old, infirm and irresolute, and the priests who were most obnoxious to the people, and most averse to change, had greatest influence with him. Notwithstanding the repeated warnings of his best friends, no measures were taken immediately to allay the discontent which prevailed widely throughout the diocese.[46]

Another meeting of the bishops and the archbishop was held in Cork on June 26th 1786. Among the decisions taken there were –

(a)   Two clergymen, greatly disliked by the people, were requested to resign their parishes.

---

45 Dr Laurence Renehan, *Collections on Irish Church History*, p.345.
46 Dr Laurence Renehan, op. cit. p. 347.

(b)   The meeting promised to continue to make inquiries.

(c)   Once again condemned the rigorous exaction of dues under threat of withholding sacraments.

(d)   Marriage fees and dispensation money to be waived in certain circumstances.

(e)   Clergy again recommended to discourage costly entertainments provided by parishioners.

(f)   Priests cautioned to avoid altar denunciations.

(g)   Priests could reserve the right to condemn 'riotous illegal meetings', and 'oaths, rash and iniquitous'.

Finally, a notice to his clergy from Bishop McKenna was published in The Dublin Evening Post of 28th September 1786. '…we earnestly desire you to be as little burdensome to the people under your care as you possibly can …and we strictly enjoin that no clergyman under our care be so meanly mercenary as to demand anything for the administering of sacraments, but having performed the sacred functions of their ministry then gratefully accept the dues conformable to the regulations of the Prelates.'

Bishop McKenna was involved in a long-running dispute over Spike Island. Spike was in the Cork diocese from the seventh century, a fact confirmed by the Decretal of Pope Innocent III in 1199, where it was referred to as Inispich cum pertinentiis suis belonging to the diocese of Cork. It is not clear when or why the Rev. P. Donworth, PP Cove, began to minister on Spike, but Archbishop James Butler II of Cashel pronounced in favour of the diocese of Cork. Matthew McKenna did not accept this ruling and in July 1781 he requested that Spike and Carrigtwohill be 'a conjoint parish in the diocese of

Cloyne and Ross'. In 1784, he took his case all the way to Armagh. The immediate reason here was the marriage of Thomas Meade and Elizabeth Kelleher performed on the Island by 'Rev. Mr Coppinger's vicar' – William Coppinger was at that time parish priest of Passage. In 1790, McKenna restated Cloyne's claims to Spike. The matter was once again referred to Cashel. Both appellants, Bishops Moylan and McKenna, were ordered 'to appear in the North Chapel, Cork, on a certain day and date named and that evidence should then be adduced as to the validity of their respective titles ... After a long and searching investigation, it was ruled and decided that all land south of the Channel, down as far as low water mark, was within the jurisdiction of his Lordship of Cork; but that the Channel itself, together with the ships therein and the ships' crews, belonged of right to the Bishop of Cloyne and formed a portion of his Lordship's diocese'. The controversy died down, and Spike was run by Cork appointees until Bishop Keane in 1871.[47]

In 1785, Bishop McKenna made a visitation of his whole diocese. Fr Paul McKenna was at that time the parish priest of Cloyne. From his visitation notes we learn that Cloyne itself, dedicated to St Colman, had 643 habitations; Churchtown, dedicated to St Nicholas, had 135 habitations; and Kilteskin, dedicated to the Blessed Virgin Mary, had 143 habitations. In the parish were two chapels in good order and one silver chalice belonging to the parish, or rather to the Union. There were three schoolmasters 'who teach the Christian doctrine', and three midwives 'who know the form of baptism'. He mentions one man by name as 'an adulterer', and two others who 'do not cohabit with their wives', and one woman

---

47 Sr Angela Bolster, *History of the Diocese of Cork*, Vol. 3, p94.

as a 'mala fama'. He then goes on to report on the 'Union belonging to Cloyne'. In this Union were: –

(a)   Ahada dedicated to St Erasmus.

(b)   Rostellan – no saint mentioned.

(c)   Garrane dedicated to the Purification of the Blessed Virgin.

(d)   Inch dedicated to the Nativity of the Blessed Virgin.

(e)   Corcabeg dedicated to the Holy Cross.

In all, the Union contained 560 habitations, two Catholic schoolmasters who 'teach the Christian doctrine', one or two good chapels, and the other demolished. He suggests getting another one built in a more convenient place. There were five midwives, and six 'idle girls'… 'the district noted for such girls of pleasure', another lady 'kept publickly' and one described simply as 'bad'.

Towards the end of his days, Bishop McKenna was believed to be in urgent need of the help of a coadjutor. The first person appointed was Fr Simon Quin, parish priest of Castlelyons. Sadly, he died in 1783 and was buried in Ballynoe. Bishop McKenna wished for one of his own relatives as his successor, but, through the influence of Bishop Moylan of Cork, William Coppinger was appointed. Matthew McKenna was not happy as he claimed that he had not even been consulted. The relations between the two continued to be fraught right up to 1790. Complaints and counter claims continued to fly from both quarters.

Bishop McKenna died on the 4th June 1791 and is buried in Templerobin (Ballymore) graveyard in the tomb he himself had erected and where his cousin the Rev. Paul McKenna and

Dr Donworth were buried. The inscription on his tombstone reads –

IHS

Here lyeth the body of Matthew McKenna

In hopes of a happy resurrection

Doctor of the Sorbonne

Bishop of Cloyne and Ross twenty-two years

Born in the year six and died June 4, 1791 in peace with mankind.

He entreats the prayers of the faithful that God may be merciful to him.

Also buried in this graveyard is Fr Michael Harrington who ran the Reddington Academy.

Bishop McKenna's will included 16 points plus a codicil. He remembered most of his relatives to a greater or a lesser degree. For example, in point no.3 he says: 'As my niece X X, her son Richard X and her three daughters were of no small expenses to me during many years she lived with me and that she and her said son Richard X gave me many vexations and causes of dissatisfactions and giving her on leaving my house all she called for, which I judged to be sufficient for her during the rest of her days, I leave her only one shilling, and the like sum unto each of her children, to any brothers or sisters she may have at the hour of my death...' To some of his nephews he was more generous giving them one or two or even five guineas each. He left to 'the chaples(sic) of the Great Island (Cove and Ballymore) the suits of vestments kept in said chaples, my gilt chalice and the ornaments for the benediction of the Blessed Sacrament...' He left money and any income from his property to be distributed among the poor of the Island (Great Island) and Carrigtwohill. He asked that his books be auctioned to the clergy of Cloyne and Ross with half of the money therefrom going to charities. He also asked that monies given by him for the education of Irish students in Paris be repatriated should a seminary be established in Ireland. The will was witnessed by Revs Jno. Donworth, John Scanlan PP of Cloyne, and Danl O'Flinn. The codicil was also signed by John Scanlan and Daniel O'Flinn plus William O'Flinn M.D.

William Coppinger (1753 – 1831)

3.1 Bishop Coppinger

William Coppinger was born in the parish of St Finbarr in Cork city in 1753. His parents were Joseph Coppinger of the Barryscourt and Ballyvolane family and Mary Arthur of Limerick. Both families had strong links with the continent, especially France. Many members of both families lived there and Joseph traded constantly in both directions, exporting herrings and other Irish goods and importing wine. It is, therefore, no surprise that his son should choose to go to France to become an officer in the army. However, he quickly changed his mind and became a priest instead. It is believed he went to the Irish College in Paris but no record exists of his having lived there.

On his return from France, he became parish priest of Carrigaline and Passage West. It was during his tenure there that the argument arose regarding which diocese had jurisdiction over Spike Island (cf Matthew McKenna). Coming as he did from two wealthy and influential Catholic families, it is not surprising that William Coppinger rose very quickly through the ranks. 1788 saw him appointed as coadjutor to Bishop McKenna in the diocese of Cloyne and Ross, much to the displeasure of the latter, who wanted the position for his nephew. He also claimed not even to have been consulted beforehand, the appointment being due in large part to the influence of the kingmaker, Bishop Francis Moylan of Cork. He was not accepted by what Bishop Teahan of Kerry called 'the junta of Cloyne'. William Coppinger was philosophical even when things were slow to improve even after the demise of McKenna.[48]

Between 1780 and 1845, the Catholic Church in Ireland moved from being technically illegal to being an accepted part of the structure of power and influence within Irish society. In the early part of that period, William Coppinger was parish priest of Youghal, a town where the Orangemen were very powerful, a fact which was to cause him huge problems before many years had passed. However, he quickly set to

---

48   Sr Angela Bolster, op. cit. Vol. 3, p150.

and built the church which still serves the people of Youghal, largely out of his private means. He taught the children catechism himself twice a week. Never a man to avoid difficult decisions, he put the whole parish of Ballintotis under interdict in 1799 for their refusal to remove a notice near the chapel when requested to do so by the parish priest, the Rev. Michael Barry. The notice was 'against the paying of tithes and assisting the clergyman to draw them'. Having sorted the situation to the satisfaction of the authorities, he and the parish priest spoke to the congregation in Midleton, 'by myself in English and by the parish priest in Irish'. He told Fr Barry to convey the same message to the people of Ballintotis.[49]

In 1798, he was forced to leave Youghal and take refuge with his relatives in Cork for a time and then subsequently in Midleton. While living in Midleton in 1803, he wrote an account of his departure from Youghal, with a view to letting people know the truth, as many rumours and deliberate lies had been circulated. 'The United Irishman's oath having been pronounced a most criminal bond of iniquity by the Catholic bishops of Ireland brought a number of these delinquents every day to my house in Youghal... It was shrewdly surmised and whispered about that some dangerous intercourse must necessarily have subsisted between me and these questionable strangers'. One night 'a military man' knocked at his door to warn him of an imminent rising of Orangemen and to take care. He told his neighbour who told others, and the story got exaggerated, with the result that the bishop got a summons from the mayor. He was interviewed / threatened over a period of about three hours by the mayor and members of the military, and asked who his informant

49   Memoirs and Correspondence of Viscount Castlereagh, P.387.

was, but he refused to tell. A day or two after this meeting, a soldier came to his house and asked if he had given the name. He said 'No', and was then shown the man's sword, which he said he would have used had the answer been 'Yes'. The soldier also told him to make a declaration to that effect in the chapel before the regiment the following Sunday, which he did. His words were once again misrepresented. Even so, he did not perceive himself to be in any great danger.[50]

The Catholic Relief Acts of 1778, 1782 and 1793 had led to a general decline in religious prejudice and animosity.[51] Catholics could now buy, sell and lease land on the same terms as Protestants; they could hold commissions in the British Army and Navy; the profession of the Law was open to them, and they were permitted to take degrees at Trinity College Dublin.[52] All these developments probably led him to believe the threats were empty. Then one night, two priests were arrested. One was Fr John Maguire, the parish priest of Youghal, a very old man. His 'crime' was to have gone to give the last rites to someone who had received 'a most cruel flagellation'. He was thrown in the guardhouse and left there for twenty-four hours. The other was a young priest who had just been appointed curate in Cove. At that point he believed the authorities intended 'to lay hands on me'. He blamed the United Irishmen for the whole debacle!

He had previously addressed a remonstrance denouncing them 'to the lower orders' which he began 'My dear deluded people', and in which he told them they had been cruelly deceived, and the incentives employed to allure them were

---

50 Patrick Francis Moran, *Spicilegium Ossoriense*, p606-610.
51 S.J. Connolly, *Priests and People in Pre-famine Ireland 1780-1845*, p160.
52 Maureen Wall, 'The Decline of the Irish Language' in *A View of the Irish Language* ed. Brian Ó Cuív

'fallacious' e.g. 'that farmers would become estated men, that mechanics and labourers would be enriched'. He went on to wonder 'where shall you find tillers if all become gentlemen?' He told them that they had a 'duty to your God, to your country, and to your King; a King who has such claims upon our gratitude, our zeal, and attachment'.[53]

Even if he disagreed with the United Irishmen and their methods, he supported fully Fr Peter O'Neill, the 'priest who was flogged at Youghal'. Fr Peter was accused of aiding and abetting the United Irishmen in the parish of Ballymacoda and was sentenced to be transported. The verdict was overturned but the ship bearing Fr O'Neill to Australia was by then on the high seas. When word got through to Australia, he was released and made his way back to Ireland and was restored to his old parish of Ballymacoda, Lady's Bridge and Shanagarry by Bishop Coppinger. His restoration irked some of the ascendancy and gave rise to a public debate between the bishop and Lord Redesdale.[54]

Around the turn of the century, Thomas Newenham asked the clergy to furnish a report on the state of education in their respective dioceses, which he published in 1803 as 'A View of the National, Political and Commercial Circumstances of Ireland'. Included was William Coppinger's report for the Cloyne area – 6 schools and 377 scholars; payment per pupil per quarter as follows – reading 3/3d, writing 4/4d, arithmetic 3/91/2d. It has been suggested that the number of pupils was underrated because schoolmasters suspected a plot and did not trust the authorities with the true state of things.

53   Thomas Francis Moran, op. cit. p588-612.
54   Fr Anthony O'Brien, Father Peter O'Neill in *A History of Shanagarry*.

While in Midleton, Bishop Coppinger built a parish church on the site of the present St Mary's High School hall. He had hoped to build a cathedral at The Rock, but Lord Midleton would not agree to a Catholic church on such a prominent site. About 1800, he expended £600 in building a dwelling house for himself in Castleredmond on the Youghal Road. Around this time, Lord Midleton offered the job of estate agent to one Mr Haynes who was registrar to the Church of Ireland bishop of Cloyne, Bishop Bennett. Mr Haynes wished to hold on to his position as registrar in Cloyne and at the same time accept the Midleton offer. This would have necessitated a move to Midleton. In a letter to Lord Midleton, dated January 31st 1801, Mr Haynes says that *Dr Coppinger… wishes to reside in Cloyne and a few days back called on me under, as I conceive, a pretext of paying compliments, but in fact to see my house with which he seemed vastly pleased and on my returning his visit he showed me his. This brought on a conversation respecting an exchange … I since find that he is much bent on the business.*

Bishop Bennett refused Haynes's idea for double-jobbing; he did not become Lord Midleton's agent, so the exchange never went ahead. This is the only effort which has come to light to return the seat of the Bishop to Cloyne after the Reformation.

On November 1st 1809, Dr Coppinger asked for a lease of the property of six or seven acres which had been in his possession for some years. Lord Midleton was prepared to allow him to retain the property but only 'as a tenant at will'. The following advertisement appeared in The Cork Mercantile Chronicle on June 8th 1812: 'Dr Coppinger, being resolved to reside in Cove, will sell his dwelling house and out-offices in Midleton'.[55] Cove, at that point, was possibly the most thriving town in the diocese with huge naval and commercial activity. Mrs S.C. Hall in her *Hall's Ireland* published in 1841, says of Cove : 'So late as 1780, Cove had scarcely advanced beyond the dignity of a fishing hamlet. Soon afterwards however … Cove gradually rose in importance; houses were built, fortifications for defence constructed, government stores established and it became the naval station of an Admiral's flag. Bustle, activity and a thriving trade followed. It was no unusual sight to behold … three hundred sail of merchant vessels assembled, waiting for convoy.'

The aftermath of the Napoleonic Wars saw an immediate and dramatic economic slump. Prices fell dramatically, major industries collapsed, investment and growth stagnated, and unemployment and destitution became widespread. The Cork Mercantile Chronicle reported in January and February 1814: 'a great fall of snow, which far exceeds any similar calamity within the memory of the oldest inhabitants of the country'. Large scale emigration began. In 1816–1818, bad weather destroyed grain and potato crops, and smallpox and typhus killed over 50,000 people. The potato failed again in Munster in 1821, and people starved to death in Cork. There were further crop failures in 1825–1830, and in 1832 stark famine struck Munster and south Leinster. Throughout the early 1830s cholera repeatedly ravaged the poorer classes.

In Cove, Bishop Coppinger lived at Mount Crozier at the top of what was called Bishop Street after him. While in Cove, he oversaw the building of a church, the general hospital, the

---

55   Canon B. Troy, Midleton Parish Bulletin 12th April 1998, from the Midleton
     Papers in Guildford Muniment Room, Surrey.

church at Ballymore (1827) and the National School which bore the date 1831 making it one of the earliest national schools in the country. That Cove church was later demolished to make way for the present cathedral. Surprise has often been expressed that he did not reopen Reddington Academy, which was the school for boys run by one Fr Harrington and attended by such people as Daniel O'Connell, the Liberator, and his brother. Fr Harrington died in 1810 and the school died with him. Dr Coppinger intended opening a diocesan seminary possibly with Fr Crotty in charge, but the latter was made president of Maynooth which may have scuppered that plan.

Bishop Coppinger was never slow to express his opinion whatever the personal cost. His most famous battle was the one which became known as 'the Veto'. During 1799, the Board of Maynooth was meeting in Dublin, when Lord Castlereagh, then Secretary for Ireland, submitted two measures originating from the British Ministry: (1) A Crown veto to be allowed on the appointment of Catholic bishops; (2) Catholic clergy would receive a pension i.e. a salary from the Treasury. The bishops initially agreed, but the people and the clergy were not happy. Many in the Catholic aristocracy saw this as a stepping stone towards Catholic Emancipation which would open more doors for the ambitious. The argument rumbled on for many years. Communication with Rome was difficult as the pope was for a lot of the time in exile, sometimes protected by the English, and others were speaking for him. By 1815, the bishops were united in their condemnation of the Veto, having accepted the point made by William Coppinger at the very start, namely that it was difficult enough to find one suitable person for a bishopric and if the government could veto at will, very unsuitable and undesirable people could end up as bishops. A letter written by him to Rome in 1816 gave a fatal blow to the already detested spirit of Vetoism. The Veto was finally laid to rest in 1825 because of the unwavering opposition of the clergy of every rank, the attitude of the Catholic Board that civil liberty ought not to be obtained at the expense of religious liberty, the current attitude of Rome, and the convincing evidence in London of members of the Irish hierarchy including JKL, Bishop Doyle of Kildare and Leighlin.[56]

The work begun by Bishop John O'Brien in laying down guidelines for the running of parishes and dioceses continued during the episcopate of William Coppinger. Some of the regulations to be strictly observed by the RC clergy of Cloyne and Ross included (a) keeping regular registers (b) not drinking in public houses (c) not going to shows, horse races, goals, or fairs, and many more dealing with the conduct of religious services. At a further meeting of the prelates, it was agreed that no layman should be invited to dinner with the bishop when he was on visitation, and a sick priest must make his will before receiving the last rites. Some of these 'improvements' were not well received. In a letter from Bishop Moylan to William Coppinger in November 1808 they were said to have called forth 'publick animadversion'.[57]

Bishop Coppinger compiled a list of the clergy of the diocese who had died between 1770 and 1799 and sometimes gave a note on their character, often with brutal honesty. For example, *'a little excentric old man'*, *'a simple man and ignorant'*, *'an old ignorant drinking man aged 84'*, *'died old and had a bad character'*, *'a drunkard died in a hut near Muskery mountain'*, *'turned couple*

---

56 Rev. M.J. Brenan, *An Ecclesiastical History of Ireland, from the Introduction of Christianity into that Country, to the Year MDCCCXXIX*, p591-621.

57 CDA, Coppinger Papers, Box b, 1791.00/8/1808.

beggar and a drunkard', *'turned horse-jobber and died old'*, *'turned apostate, married and was a man of execrable behaviour'*, *'an old reprobate died by a hedge in Duhallow'*. Not all his comments were derogatory, however. Some he described as *'exemplary'*, *'a very regular man'*, *'a very intelligent man'*, *'a good missionary'*, *'a zealous and intelligent pastor'*. He also frequently gave the reasons for their demise: *'a fever'*, *'a compn of diseases'*, *'died of the gout'*, *'died of a scurvey'*, *'killed by some unknown persons'*, *'died by a fall from his horse'*, *'of a consumption young'*. Fever, gout and falls from horses claimed quite a few. In spite of his problems with Bishop McKenna during his early days in Cloyne, he says of him 'RR Dr McKenna a very sensible man died at the age of 90'.

There are three Visitations done by Bishop Coppinger of his diocese for which reports survive. He would appear to have visited Cloyne only during the first one in August 1818. He noted that the Rev. J. Scanlan was 'unable to attend'. He examined the vestments and noted that Churchtown had no vestments of its own but used ones belonging to the Rev. J. Scanlan. He lectured one midwife, but mentioned that there were two, Mary Broderick and Abigail Higgins. He met schoolmasters Jn Connor and Timothy Denahy but Thomas Fitzgibbons did not appear. 340 children attended school and he confirmed about 800. There were two chalices in the parish, one belonging to Cloyne and the other to Churchtown. He said that he slept two nights at Mr J. Fitzgerald's in Carrigacrump.[58]

In 1827, Bishop Coppinger asked his clergy to vote for the person they would like to succeed. It was a secret ballot and he did it to avoid the sort of divisiveness and rivalry

---

58 Eric Derr, op. cit.

which led to the unseemly incidents which occurred when he himself was made coadjutor.

The Limerick Chronicle reported on the day of his death, August 11ᵗʰ 1831: 'Ireland – Assassination, botheration, desolation, spoliation, starvation, transportation – the generation of agitation a curse to the nation'. Two days later they reported the bishop's death.

A Mournful Elegy
on the much–lamented death
of the Rev. Bishop Coppinger
of Cove Town
Come all ye Roman Catholics,
In mournful strains now with me join,
To lament in doleful anguish,
Our late Bishop of Cove Town,
A tender-hearted clergyman,
By cruel death now called away,
And taken off in his 87ᵗʰ year, [Should be 77ᵗʰ]
To the poor of Cove a distressing day.

Poor widows and distressed orphans,
In tears now lament and moan,
For their tender benefactor,
From them is forever gone;
Likewise the distressed sick poor,
Will feel his loss full sore
Since Bishop Coppinger is dead,
And ne'er can relieve them more.

On the 12ᵗʰ of August,
To them an awful day,
To behold their faithful bishop,
In grand procession brought away –
A sable cloud that mournful day,
Seemed to eclipse the sun,
And tears of sorrow fast did fall,
From thousands as it passed on.

Dáibhi do Barradh cct don Easbog Uill Copinéar. 1788
Fáilte et céad do dháilim go héag, don ardfhlath don chléir léagheanta
Fáilte tair aon na dháil uaim gan claon, anfhaig cheart na naomh thréithe
Fáilte gan ghruaim na ttáinte le fuaim, le gairdeachas nua bhréithre
Don gairim sollair chóir do thaisdiol chugainn ón Róimh chun teagasg
a mhór thréata.

Is subhac sultfar séimh an cughantas sa scéal, an prionsa sa Rex cléirdha
Do thurlint faoi réim sa dútha chun claon chughantais a thréad réighteach
Diadhre is teagasgóir gliadhre is searc na nord, riarus fleadh ag bhord Dé Ghil
Fear ionnaid mhic na hógh is crisdiol gille chlodh, is bille an chirt
gan ghó réimchur

Gan eochair acht a bhéal as socair is sis réig dosgalan don tréad daonna
Flaithas bhrog na naomh cathir chlog na ccaomh, absdal et saor aonta
Polla et túr colum et clúr, Solamh an gach pungc chéille
Borb flath is leoghan foirtil fhearis treón lonnabhir is beo sséimh-cruith

Abar? aoibhneas am dhuain is Taoiseach gan gruaim a cuoinfd soluaimh féin libh
Mín sgoith riug buadh na tíre gan duadh, air shaoithibh is air uaisle Eirionn
Ni gabhadh dhum an tréad o ttainne sé leagheadh, tá sár fhios gur géag aosda
Do threibh loingeas et stáit is imirt cluithe is clár cruitireacht is gáir éigse

Grásda an triúr atá an aon ceangal dluth, do shaothraig le rún daonnacht
A cclaonta na bpungc an tsaoghal nior chuir dúil acht seanbhirt
is fonn naomhthacht
Atchim et guidhig go mac ceannasach na Riogh do cheannaig sinn
is dhíol daorchruis
Go mairre an teasbog fionn chun gradaim et clúgh an prasbhille
de púlr Copinerach.

Michael Collins (1781 – 1832)

3.2 Bishop Collins

Michael Collins was born in Rossmore in West Cork in 1781. He joined the Physics class in Maynooth in 1798. Maynooth College had been founded only three years previously, and its board was still treading very softly, so as not to offend the authorities on whom they depended for funding. Robert Emmet's rebellion in 1803 caused unease nationwide. When a student revolt erupted in Maynooth, it was immediately assumed by some to be political. In truth, it probably had more to do with living conditions, but swift and decisive action was taken. A meeting of the trustees was held to investigate 'the general resistance to the legitimate authority of the immediate superiors which broke out … under pretence of grievances'. The inquiry lasted three and a half days, and the decision was to expel the five ringleaders, among them Michael Collins. They were 'convicted of formal disobedience'. The sentence of the board was executed in their own presence, and in the presence of all the professors and students, assembled for the purpose in the college chapel, on Thursday the 3rd of March 1803.[59]

One might have expected this to be the end of Michael Collins's ecclesiastical career, but, luckily for him, his potential had been spotted by the then bishop of Cloyne, William Coppinger, who arranged for him to finish his studies in Carlow. Being a very able and accomplished linguist, he was for a time professor of belles lettres in the college in Carlow. He subsequently became parish priest of Castletownroche and Ballyhooly, where he remained from 1811 to 1814. All through his career, he made a great contribution to the well-being of the people he served, but he could also be a controversial figure, and, from time to time, was involved in clashes with the local gentry. In 1811, in response to Horace Townsend's Survey, both Bishop Coppinger and Michael Collins refuted strongly the assertions made re. the Catholic population. Collins defended both the Catholic peasantry and the priesthood. Townsend had made an assertion that there were no books to be found in Catholic homes.[60] Collins's transfer from Castletownroche to Creagh and Tullagh (Skibbereen) in 1814 was because he fell foul of a Protestant branch of the Nagle family who were very powerful in the diocese.

However controversial he may have become, his extraordinary ability was still recognised by his bishop, who wrote him a glowing testimonial in 1819 to enable him to leave the diocese and accompany one Mr Byrne on a tour of the continent. He also enjoined him: 'Should your tour

59 John Healy, *Maynooth College: its Centenary History* (1895).
60 Cloyne Diocesan Archives (CDA); Collins Papers, Box a, 1792.04/2/1811.

on the Continent bring you to Lovain (sic), to Vienna and to Rome, I hereby commission you to make such enquiries concerning our foundations for education at these places as shall be suggested to you by our common friend, the Rev. David Walsh, VG of Ross'.[61]

He lived the rest of his life in Skibbereen, becoming coadjutor of the diocese of Cloyne and Ross in 1827 and bishop on the death of Dr Coppinger in 1831. In 1817, Bartholomew Crotty, then President of Maynooth, wrote to Collins to try and persuade him to take up the vacant Chair of Rhetoric, suggesting he could get an administrator to look after his parish for three or four years. The offer was not taken up.[62] He was also summoned before the House of Commons in London at one point to give evidence on the state of Ireland, which he is said to have done very well.[63]

In 1824, he began the construction of the Cathedral of St Patrick in Skibbereen. To fund this he levied 1/2d a week on each parishioner. The work was completed in 1826. In that same year he received a letter from Jephson-Norris seeking his support as a Liberal candidate for Mallow. He was very careful about coming out publicly in support of one candidate over another as shown in a letter written by him in 1832 to Thomas G. Coppinger regarding 'Mr Barry'. '… in my station I do not deem it prudent, nor, save on very rare and extraordinary occasions, in accordance with the character of a bishop, to mix my name with election contentions or jealousies.'

In 1827, he was shot and wounded at his residence by Fr

61   CDA; Collins Papers, Box b, 1792.02/9 and 11/1819.
62   CDA; Collins Papers, Box b, 1792.06/2/1817.
63   *Journal of the Cork Historical and Archaeological Society (JCHAS)*, 1935.

William O'Brien, a disaffected priest. The priest had come to plead with the bishop to use his influence to have him reinstated, but the bishop refused. A lynch mob gathered outside, but the bishop appealed from his window for the mob to disperse. He hoped that the sight of him, obviously not grievously wounded, would calm the feelings of the crowd.[64] The priest was subsequently tried and found guilty, but, while in Cork City Gaol, hanged himself in November 1829.

In 1828, Bishop Collins did parish visitations of the combined dioceses of Cloyne and Ross. Prior to his visitation, Bishop Coppinger reminded him that 'Ross is exclusively committed to your governance'. Almost everywhere he went Bishop Collins paid particular attention to church building and improving catechetical instruction.[65] He visited Cloyne on Wed 9th July, where he was received by the curates, Revds Kearns and Hogan. He noted 'the parish is one of the bishop's mensals. The chapel of Cloyne was built by the late Rev. John Scanlan who was for 34 years parish priest of Cloyne. It is one of the most respectable and commodious in the diocese, about 90 feet by 46. The altar is handsome and richly decorated. The population of the parish about 8000. The parish is one of the finest richest districts in the county. The acting clergymen seem to discharge their (duty) with zeal, diligence and effect. The vestments, altar linen are in good order. The registries which I inspected in Midleton, correct &c. No. confirmed 315 Males 305 Females total 620 – there are two Catholic free schools, one for males the other for females, in the town of Cloyne instituted to counteract the efforts of the proselytising fanatics who have established

---

64   Southern Star, Philip O'Regan.
65   Eric A. Derr, op. cit.

schools which are not resorted (to) by any Catholics. The Catholic schools are supported by subscription'.[66] This was a pretty glowing report at a time when want and famine were never very far away.

In June of 1822, Collins wrote to the Dublin Committee saying he didn't think it a good idea to make public works an indispensable condition for relief. In his opinion, better work would be done cleaning and white-washing the habitations of the poor 'with a view of obviating and restraining the progress of contagious disease'.[67] In 1824, a petition from the inhabitants of Skibbereen and adjoining districts of West Carbery to the authorities 'that the frequent recurrence of distress sometimes mounting as in the year 1822 to famine, to which the poor inhabitants of the south of Ireland, and particularly of these districts are liable on the slightest general failure of the potato crop, that is on an average every fourth or fifth year, is the admitted effect of a redundant population exclusively dependent on agricultural labour, and destitute of other means of profitable employment'.[68] Bishop Coppinger wrote to his coadjutor in March 1824 and again in 1826 to tell him that owing to the bad quality and scarcity of potatoes, and alarming sickness in several places he was 'compelled to allow the use of fleshmeat this Lent, as has been done by my confreres of Waterford, Limerick and Tipperary'.[69]

At this time also most bishops were reporting that the number of clergy was inadequate, but by 1830 Michael Collins is writing to Bishop Coppinger because he is puzzled how to dispose of the unemployed clergymen in the diocese

66 CDA; Collins Papers, Box e, 1792.06/7/1828. 1828 Visitation.
67 CDA; Collins Papers, Box c, 1792.05/7/1822.
68 CDA; Coppinger Papers, 1791/1/1824.
69 CDA; Coppinger Papers, Box d, 1792.02/3/1824.

and thinks, maybe, they should be spared to other dioceses.[70] As Bishop Coppinger's health declined, he came to rely more and more on his coadjutor, sharing his problems with him and sometimes getting him to translate letters. He knew French, Italian, Spanish and Portuguese. Even though a west Cork man, he only learned Irish as an adult and that with great difficulty.[71] When William Coppinger finally died in August 1831, Michael Collins became bishop of the combined dioceses of Cloyne and Ross. Life for him did not get easier. He risked his own health visiting cholera victims and endeavouring to the end to alleviate the suffering of the poor. He died on the 8th December 1832 in Skibbereen, some accounts say of cholera, others say of an apoplectic fit, that is, a stroke. He is buried in the cathedral he had built, and a monument by the famous Waterford sculptor, John Hogan, stands over his resting place. It is a seated allegorical personification of religion, with her attribute to the cross, gazing at an oval cameo relief of the deceased; she is seated on a cube, beside which are a mitre and an open book.

---

70 S.J. Connolly, op. cit:, CDA, Coppinger Papers, Box d, 1791.04/9/1830.
71 CDA, Collins Papers, Box h, 1792.00/1/1832.

Bartholomew Crotty (1769 – 1846)

3.3 Bishop Crotty

Bartholomew Crotty was born in Darrara, Clonakilty, son of a wealthy weaver, on the 1st September, 1769. Dr Murphy of Cork, speaking at the funeral mass for the bishop, said that he received his earliest education from a poor and aged female in Clonakilty, all the men having been either exiled or lurking in the mountains.[72] We are told that he then went to one of the four boys' schools established in Clonakilty by the then parish priest, Fr Paul McKenna, a relative of the bishop. On the advice of Fr McKenna, he was sent to a classical school in Glanworth. Such was his progress at his classical studies that, at the early age of sixteen, he was selected by Dr McKenna, and sent on to college to prepare for the priesthood. In giving a list of the students for Cloyne and Ross for the year 1785, Dr McKenna says: - 'I sent little Crotty, a promising youth to

---

72 Cork Examiner, 4th November, 1846.

Salamanca; but apprehend he was detained by the friars at Lisbon'. He was detained at Lisbon, not by the friars but by Dr Brady, who had succeeded in reopening the Irish College in that city after the confiscation of its revenues by the infamous Pombal.[73] Local West Cork lore has it that Crotty was smuggled out of Ireland in a potato barrel!

Before he had even reached the canonical age for ordination, he was appointed professor of philosophy in the Lisbon College in 1791, and in 1801 he became rector of the college on the death of Dr Brady. The Peninsular War made Dr Crotty's life very difficult. From 1806 to 1808 Lisbon was occupied by the French under General Junot, and the Irish students were little better than prisoners in the college. Before the war, General Junot had been French Ambassador at Lisbon and knew Dr Crotty quite well. Now, acting on a commission from Napoleon, he sought to entice him to accept the more lucrative post of Rector of the Irish College in Paris. Napoleon was anxious to attract Irish continental students to Paris, but it was believed his motives were more political than religious. His show of generosity to the Irish abroad would surely secure the sympathy of the Irish at home, thus embarrassing England. Dr Crotty refused the offer.

He returned from Lisbon in 1811, much to the delight of the then bishop, William Coppinger, who hoped that in the immediate future he would reopen the academy which had been run by the late Fr Harrington in Reddington near Cove. His ultimate plan for Dr Crotty was to head up the projected diocesan seminary, but this did not come to fruition at this time. In 1813, Dr Crotty was made parish priest of Clonakilty, but before the year was out he was sent to Maynooth as

---

73 John Healy, op. cit. p396-397.

president, where he distinguished himself over the next twenty years.

In 1826, a Royal Commission was set up to inquire into the nature and extent of the instruction given in the institutions in Ireland receiving public money. The examination of Dr Crotty lasted five days during which he astounded all by his knowledge and clear thinking. In 1830, while in Maynooth, he was visited by the famous French philosopher, Montalembert, who said of him: - 'le nom seul m'inspire une vénération solennelle'. Though, generally, he kept the world and its politics outside the college, he was opposed to the Veto on the appointment of bishops, was in full sympathy with the Repeal Movement, and in 1845 he, along with many other bishops, condemned the foundation of the Queen's Colleges.

In August 1827, he was examined in the court case of Fr William O'Brien regarding the shooting of Dr Michael Collins in Skibbereen. He said the prisoner, while a student in Maynooth, had 'evinced more than ordinary talent, but his state of mind at times was such as to make one apprehend that he would end one day or other in a mad house'.[74]

On the eleventh of June, 1833, he was consecrated Bishop of Cloyne in the College chapel in Maynooth. The Connaught Telegraph reported that, after the ceremony, the new bishop 'gave a splendid déjeuner to the bishops, clergy and respectable laity who attended the ceremony. A hundred gentlemen afterwards sat down to an excellent dinner'.

His early days in Cloyne were not easy as he was a stranger to many of the older clergy and not their choice; but his

74 Belfast newsletter, 31st August, 1827.

prudence and zeal, single-mindedness, and his inflexible justice soon gained their confidence and support.[75] On his visitations, he always inquired into the state of parochial property, the condition of the churches, altar requisites and the administration of the sacraments. He demanded high standards of his clergy, and made the teaching of religion a high priority. He loved to examine the children himself, as often as possible in the Irish language. He introduced the Presentation nuns to Fermoy, Youghal and Midleton, and the Mercy nuns to Charleville and Mallow.

In the newspapers of 1843 and 1844 we read of the bishop attending social/political occasions. The first was when the Right Rev. Dr Oliffe, the newly consecrated Bishop of Milene in partibus and coadjutor Vicar Apostolic of Bengal, entertained a large crowd at the Victoria Hotel in Cork. 'The tables were crowded with every delicacy of the season … Rare wines flowed in profusion.' Sitting next to Dr Oliffe were Bishops Murphy and Crotty. The new bishop proposed toasts to the Pope, Gregory XVI, and to the Queen, who he said 'was impartial between all her subjects'. He also proposed toasts to Counsellor (sic) Maguire and The Cork Examiner, and to Daniel and Nicholas Murphy and their family.[76]

A couple of months later, he attended a dinner in honour of Francis B. Beamish who was a member of the Repeal Association. The dinner was to celebrate his having been Mayor the previous year. Dr Crotty was seated on the left of the then Mayor and said Grace. There was a toast to Daniel O'Connell, and another to Dr Crotty and the Hierarchy and clergy of the people. Dr Crotty returned thanks, and said 'the

---

75 John Healy, op. cit. P. 401.
76 Freeman's Journal, 14th October, 1843.

Catholic clergy of Ireland … so far from advocating anything like disloyalty, if it had not been for their exertions we would have had Ireland a desolate country now, instead of being the abode of millions of peaceable, orderly, though impoverished people'.[77]

In August 1846, a conference of the Roman Catholic clergy of Cloyne and Ross was held in Fermoy for the election of a coadjutor, and three names were sent forward to Rome – the Rev. David Walsh PP Clonakilty, the Rev. Morgan O'Brien PP Mitchelstown, and the Rev. Timothy Murphy PP Fermoy.[78] By September 1846, his health was failing. He made his will, leaving his library (1200 volumes) to Maynooth as Cloyne still had no seminary. The rest of his possessions he left to the poor. He requested that he be buried in the Presentation Convent Chapel in Midleton and spent the last few days of his life composing his epitaph in Latin, which was to be inscribed on a stone in the Chapel.

> *Requiescant hic in pace et in die judicii gloriosi resurgant*
> *Exuviae mortales, Illustrissimi et Reverendissimi Patris*
> *Barthlomaei Crotty*
> *Per tredecim et amplios annos harumce dioceseon Episcopi Catholici*
> *Hanc autem in terris ultimam sedem corpusculo suo exoptat*
> *Ut in coelis, precibus devotarum sororum hujus Communitatis, et fidelium*
> *Huc religionis erga convenientum, ad aeternam beatitudinem*
> *Per merita salvatoris Jesu Christi, a quo solo, gratia et gloria, pervenire queat*
> *Natus est die primo Septembris, A.D. 1769. Mortuus est die quarto Octobris,*
> *A.D. 1846*
> *Requiescat in pace*

(May they rest in peace and rise on the day of glorious

---

77 Freeman's Journal, 4th January, 1844.
78 Freeman's Journal, 31st August, 1846.

judgement the mortal remains of the Most Esteemed and Most Reverend Father Bartholomew Crotty. For more than thirteen years Catholic bishop of this diocese. Moreover he has chosen this as the final resting place for his mortal remains so that in Heaven, by the prayers of the devoted sisters of this community and of the faithful gathered here in this place of religion, he may achieve eternal happiness through the merits of our Saviour Jesus Christ, from whom alone grace and glory comes. He was born on the 1st Sept 1769. He died on the 4th October 1846. May he rest in peace.)

He was remembered as gentle as a child, courteous and affable to all, kind to the deserving poor, and kind in a special way to ecclesiastical students and to sick or troubled priests. The grace of his manner, his extraordinary memory, and the charm of his conversation were often remarked on. However, those who were unfortunate enough to receive a reproof did not forget it in a hurry!

David Walsh (*c.*1797 – 1849)

Bishop Walsh was born about the year 1797. He did his matriculation in 1814 and was ordained in 1819. He was then appointed as curate in Midleton, next in Cloyne, then in Cove. While in Cove, he accompanied the then bishop, Dr Coppinger, as his interpreter. In 1826, he was sent as curate to Clonakilty and in 1830 he became the parish priest. On the 6th February 1847, while still based in Clonakilty, he was appointed bishop of the combined dioceses of Cloyne and Ross in succession to Bishop Crotty. He continued to live at Youghal's House, Island Road, Clonakilty, where he died at the young age of fifty-two on the 15th January 1849.

During his brief prelacy, the Diocesan Statutes were published in Latin. He paid little or no attention to Repeal, but was more occupied with the discussions regarding the Queen's Colleges and ecclesiastical tithes. He was always very concerned with the land question.

It was an extremely difficult time to have any sort of post of responsibility as people were becoming increasingly desperate. In order to protect their crops from thieves, many farmers were equipping themselves with guns. In November 1847, an armed watchman seriously wounded another at Rochemount near Whitegate. The labouring poor, whose demands for assistance were largely ignored, took matters into their own hands. Mobs from the country raged into the towns of Cloyne, Castlemartyr, Midleton and Cloheen, where they sacked bread shops and provision stores.[79] Pirate fishermen were plundering meal vessels and merchantmen around the coast. The Cork Examiner, reporting his death on the 22nd of January 1849, described him as 'grave, calm, modest, meek and withal dignified'. Every mention of him at this time refers to his quiet unassuming manner. It is all the more amazing, therefore, that he should have been 'the first Roman Catholic Bishop in Ireland who forwarded a memorial to the Throne in favour of self-government for Ireland' in early 1848. The Cork Examiner on the 21st April 1848 was loud in its praise of it. '… we hold it to be one of the most important that has been given to the public since the commencement of the agitation in favour of self-government….It is not in any way like the vehement outpouring of excited and reckless men…. (It is a) grave, dignified, unimpassioned declaration of opinion….he

---

79   James S. Donnelly, *The Land and the People of Nineteenth Century Cork.*

sees his people plunged in a state of woe and wretchedness beyond all parallel in civilized society … What has induced those non-political priests to join the national movement at this hour … ? They have seen their flocks mowed down by famine … They saw whole villages swept away … all these horrors convinced them that alien government is a curse'. Among the many priests of the diocese who put their names to the Address was John Russell, PP Cloyne.

Bishop Walsh is buried in Clonakilty in the same tomb as his uncle, also David and also previously parish priest of Clonakilty. Their remains were translated from the old parish church yard nearby to their present resting place.

Timothy Murphy (1789 – 1856)

3.4 Bishop Murphy

Timothy Murphy was born in Aghabullogue in 1789, the year of the French Revolution. Of his early schooling we have no official account. He matriculated in 1810, and was ordained in Maynooth in 1815. During his studies there he received many high academic awards. Immediately after ordination he was promoted to the Dunboyne establishment. He stayed on in Maynooth for a further four years, studying and lecturing in French.

On his return to the diocese he served initially as curate in Mallow, and was thence removed to Doneraile by Bishop Coppinger. While in Doneraile, he was responsible for getting the church in Shanballymore built. He was then sent as junior curate to Fermoy. The rest of his priestly life was to be spent in that town.

In 1834, he used his influence to prevent any organised protests against tithes in the parish, and in a letter to Bishop Crotty, spelled out his convictions: 'I have ever been hostile to large aggregations of the giddy populace … ' He went on to describe the local anti-tithe agitators as 'visionary disclaimers', 'village spouters', and 'eloquent nobodies'.[80]

In 1838, he brought the Presentation nuns to Fermoy, and, later in 1853, invited the Loreto order of nuns as well. His commitment to education was always in evidence. He founded St Colman's College as a seminary for the diocese, acquiring the plot of ground in 1856 and laying the foundation stone, but did not live to see its completion. He also saw the establishment of the first National school in Fermoy.

During his period as parish priest of Fermoy, the Great Famine raged across the country. He sacrificed all he possessed for the poor and hungry. Even though times were bad he managed to have the parish church in Fermoy enlarged.

---

80 Maura Murphy, 'Repeal, Popular Politics, and the Catholic Clergy of Cork 1840-1850. JCHAS 1977'.

Timothy Murphy was appointed Bishop of Cloyne and Ross on the 19th April 1849 and was consecrated on the 16th September of that same year. He petitioned the Pope to have Ross made a separate diocese, and his request was granted in 1850; William Keane becoming its first bishop in 1851.

When Cardinal Cullen returned to Ireland, he set about winning the allegiance of the bishops, and putting them in a position of indebtedness. One of those whom Cullen deliberately courted was Timothy Murphy. Cullen considered him important because he might be persuaded to oppose local Catholic support for the Queen's College in Cork, which was strongly defended by Bishop William Delany of Cork. His opportunity came to 'help' Murphy in September 1850 when his correspondent, Monsignor Tobias Kirby, Rector of the Irish College in Rome, let him know of a request made by Murphy:

> *I have at one period suffered much from colds in the head and whether it be in consequence I know not, but it has so happened that my hair has fallen off and therefore I have humbly and respectfully to solicit from the Holy See permission to avail myself of the very desired covering and protection of a wig.*[81]

Cullen, of course, was only too willing to help! All he got from Murphy regarding the Queen's Colleges, however, were letters expressing concern, but showing no inclination to oppose the popular local College.

Bishop Murphy did not confine all his efforts to Fermoy. In Queenstown, he purchased the range of buildings on Spy Hill which became the convent of the Sisters of Mercy. He never touched one farthing of his episcopal revenue from

---

81 Desmond Bowen, *Paul Cardinal Cullen and the Shaping of Modern Irish Catholicism*, p212-213.

Queenstown until the purchase money of the Mercy Convent had been fully paid.

He went to Rome in 1854 for the Papal Consistory on the definition of the Immaculate Conception. On his return, his health declined. On the 4th December 1856, he got a stroke from which he never recovered. He was buried by his own request in the Presentation Convent Chapel in Fermoy. He died not only poor but penniless, and was actually buried at the public expense. His house and property became the property of the Presentation Convent. His library was left to the developing St Colman's Seminary.

The Month's Mind for Bishop Murphy was celebrated in the Cathedral (sic) of Fermoy. Dr Croke, PP Midleton, the celebrant, mindful of Dr Murphy's dedication to education, quoted Aristotle: 'The poor man is deficient only in money, the ignorant man is deficient in everything that gives value to human life … they who give children a good education are much more their fathers than those who have begotten them, since the one party has only given them life, while the other has given them the means of passing it happily'.

Those who drive into the centre of Fermoy will be aware of the statue erected in front of the old Christian Brothers school. It was created by the famous Kilkenny sculptor, John Francis Davis, and carries the inscription:

Most Reverend Timothy Murphy D.D.
Curate and Parish Priest 1826 – 1849,
Bishop of Cloyne 1849 – 1856.
Zealous priest,
Dedicated Educationalist,
Wise Administrator
Compassionate Shepherd
Éarlamh Mór ar Oideachas

William Keane (1805 – 1874)

3.5 Bishop Keane

William Keane was born in the parish of Mogeely-Castlemartyr on the 7th April 1805. In a manuscript discovered in the Cloyne Diocesan Archives, we get the history of his family, the details of which were compiled by his nephew, Fr William Fitzgerald. The account begins as follows: 'Towards the middle of the eighteenth century there came to Castlemartyr a worthy Ulster Catholic named William Keane or O'Cahan, who held a post of trust under the Right Hon. Henry Boyle, then Speaker of the Irish House of Commons, and who continued in the service of the same gentleman after his elevation in 1756 to the Peerage as first Earl of Shannon. This William Keane was the father of Simon, whose eldest son, another William, was the father of the illustrious Prelate, of whose life, labours and virtues, we have undertaken to tell'. William married Mary Carey, but died after the birth of their eighth child. The young widow managed to raise her children, and gradually saw the older ones placed in business, but young William remained in education.

He attended a school run by Mr Maurice Leahy in Castlemartyr, then went to Mr Downing's classical school in Midleton. He also spent some time at school in Tallow. Besides his taste for the Classics, William had a great fondness for English reading, and was given access to the library of the Dowager Countess of Shannon where he read every good book available. Diligent in his intellectual pursuits, he also played handball with the force and skill of an expert.

In 1824, he presented himself at the *concursus* in Fermoy presided over by the venerable Dr Coppinger. The astonishingly large number of seventy candidates was examined. Then aged nineteen, William Keane took second place. He left soon after for the Irish College in Paris, where he entered the Logic class. He received minor orders - sub-deacon and deacon – at the Cathedral of Meaux near Paris. At Pentecost 1828, he was ordained in the church of St Sulpice in Paris.

Immediately after his ordination, he was appointed prefect of studies in the Irish College.[82] He was also for a time Vice-President of the College. We get an idea of his physical appearance, and of the esteem in which he was held, in a letter written by a former student, Fr Bernard Ivers, to the Nun of Kenmare, Sr Mary Frances Clare Cusack: 'In personal appearance he was of middle stature, compact and well-knit together, and though rather full in habit for one who was really youthful yet … he was agile and vigorous…. But his countenance was very striking. There was positive youthful

---

82   *The Nation,* 24th January 1874.

bloom upon his cheeks … a contradiction to the evidence of mature wisdom which sat so serenely upon his brow … I cannot remember an instance in which he was moved to anger … In the hours of recreation it was delightful to see with what a 'Gusto' he entered into the spirit of our games'.

In 1839, the See of Cloyne and Ross was held by the venerable Dr Crotty, who appointed the Rev. William Keane to the curacy of Fermoy. One of his fellow curates was the future bishop, Timothy Murphy. His stay in Fermoy was to be a short one, as in December 1841 he was made parish priest of Midleton.

While he was in Midleton the first State Census of Ireland was carried out, but the census forms were not preserved. However, Fr Keane himself made a census of most of Midleton in 1842, and another more complete one in 1848, this time including the surrounding area and Ballintotas. These censuses are still available. His first important move into the public arena on the Land Question was when he appeared to give evidence at the 'Devon Commission'. A hearing was held in Midleton in September 1844. He made a very strong case for tenant rights. To illustrate his point, he mentioned that on the Midleton estate the tenants had no tenant-right, whereas on Lord Shannon's estate the tenants had a kind of security. He went on to elaborate on the ripple effect of an underperforming farming industry. Tradesmen and labourers in the town of Midleton were unemployed, and had recently threatened that they and their families would soon have to resort to the Workhouse if the situation did not change.

Towards the end of his stay in Midleton, a very important event in the history of the Irish Church took place, i.e. the

Synod of Thurles 1850. This was the first National Synod to be held in Ireland since the Reformation. It had to deal with the questions of university and primary Level education. It also legislated for all the sacraments and tried to ensure that there was a standard practice in all of Ireland. With characteristic sagacity, the then bishop the Most Rev. Dr Murphy, chose William Keane as theologian to accompany him. It fell to him later in 1852, when he happened to be in Rome, to submit the decrees of the Synod to the Holy See for approval.

Another of the items discussed and agreed on at the Synod was the restoration of the diocese of Ross, and William Keane became its first bishop. His consecration took place in the parish chapel in Midleton. Here he expressed his regret to be leaving Midleton where he had many good friends and was loved by his parishioners. At that time, the towns and rural districts of West Cork were barely recovering from the devastation of the Great Famine.

Shortly after the Synod of Thurles, the great Tenant Right Conference was held in Dublin. Bishop Murphy was an ardent and outspoken advocate of popular rights, but his health prevented him from travelling. He chose as his representatives the Rev. Justin McCarthy, PP Mallow, and the Rev. William Keane, still PP Midleton at that point. Here again, Fr Keane dealt publicly with the issue with which his name was later to be closely identified. His contribution was remarked on by Lucas and Gavan Duffy. His commitment to the Land Question never wavered. He is credited with being the instigator of the Select Committee of the House of Lords on Land Tenure in 1865. He suggested that by giving longer leases and removing from the landlord the power of distress, agriculture could become more profitable to all concerned.

Later, as Bishop of Ross, he attended the Provincial Synod of Cashel in 1853. He preached the concluding sermon at this assembly of prelates. He shortly afterwards was sent to Rome with the statutes there decreed. He was detained in Rome from November to the following June. Two of the questions with which he had to deal in Rome were (1) the relation of Irish priests to the politics of the country, and (2) the holding of stations. His views were so clearly expressed that they were accepted without question.

Three years after William Keane's return to Ireland, his friend Bishop Murphy of Cloyne died. On the 3rd May 1857 Dr Keane was translated to Cloyne. In all the years he held this high office, he never lost sight of the needs of his people. In 1866, writing to Monsignor Kirby in Rome he said: 'The people are beginning to feel and to say, that the priests who were always their friends and their guides, no longer care for them, no longer sympathise with them, no longer take any trouble to redress their grievances'.

In the early 1860s an awareness was growing of the importance of rescuing from destruction Catholic and religious material in the Irish language which was still in manuscripts around the country. To that end it was decided to set up a body which was to be known as The Keating Society after the renowned priest and scholar, Geoffrey Keating/Seathrún Céitinn (1569 – 1644). Dr Keane was one of the vice-presidents of the Society along with the other Munster bishops. The Society would appear to have had a very short life as no more is heard of it after 1865.

Possibly because of his absolute fluency in the French language and his clear-thinking negotiating skills, he was chosen by his brother prelates to go and regulate the affairs of the Irish College in Paris, and to save from confiscation the funds of the Irish College in Louvain. In both cases he achieved a successful outcome.

Equal in importance to the Land Question to Bishop Keane was education. In 1856 he had overseen the establishment of St Colman's College, Fermoy, which opened in 1858 with Thomas William Croke as its first President. The church in Kanturk was built in his time as also were the convent and schools there. He also celebrated the opening of Christian Brothers schools in Doneraile, Charleville and Midleton. In 1868 he appeared along with the Archbishop and the Bishop of Down and Connor before a Select Committee of the House of Commons on the subject of primary education.

Among the ecclesiastical edifices which sprang up during his episcopacy, the greatest undertaking of all was the magnificent cathedral at Queenstown. He laid the foundation stone in 1868. Land had been leased in 1808 for the site of the old Catholic church in Queenstown. If not at that date, certainly in a few years after, this church was looked on as a precursor and a substitute for the cathedral. Fr Donworth had plans drawn up as far back as 1810/1812 but nothing happened until 1856 when Bishop Murphy called a meeting to commence operations. Sadly, he died before the meeting could take place and the project fell into abeyance for a while. When Bishop Keane was appointed to the see, he got to work almost immediately.[83]

In 1870 the Irish bishops were in Rome for the Vatican Council. Bishop Keane was the first Irish bishop to address that assembly. He attended every session to the point where his friends were pleading with him to take a break as he was

83   Cork Examiner 30th Sept 1868.

obviously fatigued, but he refused. On his return home he received an address from the clergy of his diocese welcoming him home but also congratulating him on his wonderful contribution to the proceedings. 'Cloyne may well feel proud that the name of her illustrious bishop shall descend to posterity, as that of one of the most eloquent defenders, and enthusiastic supporters of the doctrine of Papal Infallibility'.

Before the Council ended, Cardinal Cullen tried to organise his fellow Irish bishops to appeal to Pope Pius IX to condemn Fenianism. Archbishop McHale of Tuam spoke strongly against the motion, but the motion was carried nonetheless. The decree of condemnation was never promulgated in Tuam and Cloyne, and it is said that Fenians from other dioceses freely received absolution in Cloyne and Tuam. Bishop Keane also allowed collections to be made for the dependants of jailed Fenians in the churches of the diocese of Cloyne.

Bishop Keane made his will in February 1869 in which he stated that he had never had any personal property of any kind, except books, furniture, clothes and whatever was in the credit of his current account. The shares he had were only held in trust by him. He directed that his furniture be sold, half the proceeds to go to the poor, but promising, aspirants to the priesthood from St Colman's; the other half to go to the Presentation Convent, Fermoy and the Mercy Convent, Queenstown to be given to the poor. Monies left to him by one Michael Crean were to be divided between St Colman's, the Cathedral and the advancement of the Roman Catholic religion.[84]

After the Vatican Council he never regained his former vigour. During the last year of his life, his health and faculties

---

84   Cork Examiner, 27th April 1874.

were visibly failing. His death on the 15th January 1874 was universally mourned. All the ships in the harbour had their flags at half-mast, likewise the RCYC. The shops in the town had their windows shuttered. The consuls of every country stationed in Queenstown and Cork attended the obsequies. He lay in state from Friday to Monday in a temporary chapel as thousands of people came to pay their last respects. He was buried within the walls of the incomplete Cathedral as the wind howled through the unfinished arches raised not many feet from the ground. His remains were subsequently removed to the crypt, and the Cross which marked his resting place is now in front of the Cathedral. He was remembered for his courteous manners and dignified demeanour. He died in apostolic poverty.

John McCarthy (1815 – 1893)

3.6 Bishop McCarthy

John McCarthy was born in Fermoy, Co. Cork on the 15th June 1815, three days before the Battle of Waterloo. His parents, being reasonably well off, determined to give their children the best education the district could afford. At that time a school in Clonakilty was held in high regard, and the male members of the McCarthy family were sent there. The school was run by a Mr Goudy, a Palatine, who was assisted by a Mr Davis, father of the Rev. Charles Davis PP Baltimore. Here the future bishop studied until he was ready to enter Maynooth in 1835. As a student he won the highest honours in every class, and at the end of his course he was selected for the Dunboyne establishment.

He was ordained on the 20th June 1842, and his first mission was in his home town of Fermoy. His health had been weakened by the long and severe hours of study he had put in at Maynooth, and it was decided to transfer him to the comparatively easy and quiet mission of Kilmeen in the diocese of Ross. After one year in Kilmeen, he was removed to Mallow as curate to the Rev. Denis Collins, brother of the late Bishop Michael Collins. His fellow-curate in Mallow was his brother, Justin, who subsequently became parish priest of Mallow.

A few years after his appointment to Mallow came the Great Famine which devastated Mallow, as everywhere else in the country. Even though still not in great health, and ignoring the dangers of the fearful fever plague, he worked from dawn till dusk attending the sick and the dying. The inevitable happened. He and all the other priests of the parish were laid low with the dreaded fever. For weeks his life was hanging in the balance but he recovered. However, his health continued feeble, and, after the Famine, he was advised to go abroad for a short time.

He went to Rome and there made the acquaintance of the Most Rev. Dr Kirby, with whom he continued to correspond until the end of his life. During his stay in Rome, he attended lectures in the higher departments of ecclesiastical studies, and also acquired an accurate knowledge of the Italian language. On his return to Ireland, he resumed his work in Mallow and also continued to study. He was one of those selected by Dr Newman as special preacher for the Catholic University.

Shortly after, he was given a very different task by the Irish bishops. The Italian Revolution broke out and young Irishmen flocked to defend the Papal States. Dr McCarthy was appointed to superintend the work of recruiting at home and of arranging transport to Italy. He accompanied a large contingent of volunteers to Marseille, where he remained to meet succeeding groups arriving from Ireland and to see them transferred to Rome. This was no easy task but he later acknowledged the help he got from some former members of the Dublin Metropolitan Police who had joined the Papal Brigade.

After his duties were discharged at Marseille, he returned to Mallow. Not too long after he was to witness the death of his brother and fellow-priest, Justin. 'Father John', as he was fondly known to his parishioners, became the parish priest of Mallow. Anxious to continue the good work of his brother, he determined to introduce the Christian Brothers to Mallow for the education of the boys who had not been as well catered for as the girls.

On the death of Dr Keane in January 1874, a very large majority of the parish priests of Cloyne selected the pastor of Mallow as their candidate for the bishopric. His appointment was duly ratified by Rome to the great joy of the clergy and people of the diocese. He was consecrated in the parish church in Fermoy, and the sermon was preached by Dr Croke, Archbishop of Cashel, to whom both the new bishop and his brother were well known.

He set to work immediately to continue the work of his predecessors in rebuilding the diocese. During the half century preceding his consecration, many of the old chapels, basic structures built tentatively after the Penal Laws, were being replaced with more suitable edifices. Anywhere he found a building he did not consider adequate or in good enough order, he suggested the erection of something more fitting in its place. Churches, convents, schools, and parochial houses sprang up throughout the diocese under his watchful eye. He was frequently a liberal contributor to the building fund.

The great work of Dr McCarthy's life was the Cathedral in Cobh. The foundations had been laid and the designs agreed by his predecessor, Dr Keane, but most of the structural work was done under Bishop McCarthy. The roof was completed by 1879. He also adorned the outside with a number of statues of apostles and saints. He formally dedicated St Colman's Cathedral on the 15th June 1879, but work on it continued for the rest of his life, only to be finished by his successor, Bishop Browne. To these three bishops must go the credit for the beautiful building we have today.

Bishop McCarthy sent priests all over the world to collect money to finish the Cathedral, among them Fr James Sisk a native of Cloyne, who spent two years fundraising in America. During the nineteen years of his episcopate he collected £95,000 for the Cathedral and subscribed £25,000 himself. The high altar was erected at the expense of the priests of the diocese to celebrate the Golden Jubilee of the ordination of their bishop. He had resolved to say the first Mass on it, but this was not to be. The first Mass said on it was actually his funeral Mass.

In early 1880 Dr McCarthy addressed a letter to the people of his diocese regarding the approaching county election: 'Hitherto the people and priests of Cloyne have had some influence in the selection of candidates … It was so in latter times when the celebrated "Cloyne Resolutions" gave new life to the Home Rule cause. But now Mr Parnell has chosen a candidate without consulting the electors of Cloyne'. The bishop wanted only the sitting MPs nominated so that there would be no need for a time-wasting election, which would divide the electorate, and take up the time of farmers who ought to be 'devoted to the cultivation of the soil'.[85]

In October 1880, Bishop McCarthy called a meeting of the priests of the Cloyne diocese which was held in the sanctuary of Mallow church. The Bishop himself presided and the meeting was attended by over one hundred priests. The topic under discussion was the land question, in particular the peasant-proprietor scheme of the Land League. The Bishop said he could not subscribe to the sweeping and unqualified condemnation of landlordism as an institution because there were many good landlords. He only wished for the abuses to be swept away. He gave his reasons stressing they were his own personal views. The meeting came up with a number of fundamental principles on which legislation for the improvement of the land code for Ireland should be based.[86]

In early 1888 a letter from him to Canon Keller is reported in

85   Cork Examiner, 7th April 1880.
86   The Nation, 2nd October 1880.

The Cork Examiner. It is about the suppression of a meeting in Youghal. The bishop states that it looks as if the government is trying 'to drive the people to desperation' and force the tenants to do something illegal.

Two years later he gave £20 for the second time to the Tenants Defence Association to defend the tenants of the Smith-Barry syndicate. He suggested the aim of the syndicate was 'to depopulate and convert into a desert those estates where the tenants have had the manliness to assert their rights to a fair and equitable rent'. He says that if Mr Smith-Barry continues his struggle there will be no winners.[87]

In 1889, he was engaged in a battle of a different kind. He was libelled by the London New York Herald, which, according to The Cork Examiner of April 11th 1889, had written 'a gross perversion of the counsels addressed to his Lordship's flocks'. The bishop had said in his Lenten Pastoral that the difficulties of the time 'demanded from Catholics, with patience and devotion, great prudence, because that in the service of the National causes regard must be had not only to the efficacy of the means, but to their lawfulness'. The paper mutilated the passage so that it seemed as if Dr McCarthy was recommending his flock to consider the efficacy of the means rather than their lawfulness. When this came to the bishop's notice, he sent a copy of his Pastoral to the paper which did not publish a correction, just said that they had 'received a protest of the Bishop of Cloyne'. This the bishop considered disingenuous, so he complained again. The case went to court, but as the trial was about to begin, a settlement was reached, guilt admitted, 100 guineas in damages paid plus costs, and an apology for the hurt caused.

87   The Nation, 11th January 1890.

Up to late November 1893, the Bishop was in his usual good health and spirits, but on St Colman's Day he fell sick with influenza out of which he developed acute bronchitis. He never recovered and died two weeks later. He lay in state in the Cathedral for three days, after which the Solemn Requiem was celebrated. On the announcement of his death, signs of mourning were generally exhibited in the town. Shops were shuttered and blinds drawn in many private houses. Flags were at half-mast in all public buildings and shipping offices.

At a meeting of the County Cork Collection Committee for the Evicted Tenants Fund after his death, one of the secretaries, Mr J.C. Flynn MP, said that Bishop McCarthy was 'one of the most generous subscribers to the fund … The Church had lost a good prelate and the country a gallant, a fearless, and a far-seeing Irishman, and the evicted tenants a life-long and a staunch friend'.[88]

Many tributes were paid to him, all referring to his gentle manner and generosity. The Southern Star reported his death in the following words: 'The diocese of Cloyne has a sad loss to mourn, and for many a day to come that loss will continue to be felt by priests and people. Of his personal qualities little need here be said. What he was in character and disposition when he left Maynooth and began his priestly labours he continued to be to the end … Gentleness and consideration for others were, perhaps, the most conspicuous features in the outward bearing of the deceased Bishop … He was accessible to all who sought him, though an infirm sense of hearing compelled him to live of late years a retired life … He was a constant reader, and…retained most tenaciously all that he read. One must, however, weigh these tributes

88   Freeman's Journal, 15th December 1893.

against the courageous actions of the man who helped the tenants in their fight, and when misrepresented by no less a publication than The London New York Herald did not hesitate to publicly demand in the Courts that the wrong be put right.'

For his funeral Mass, the inside of the Cathedral was suitably draped and across the entrance door was a black cloth with the words 'For truly he built this house and decorated this temple'. After the Mass, his remains were carried in procession around the town and then deposited in the crypt of the Cathedral. His coffin bore the following inscription:

Reverendissimus D.D. Joannes McCarthy, Episcopus Cloynensis,

natus die 15a Junii, A.D. 1815,

obit 9a Decembris, A.D. 1893.

Anno Episcopotus Sui Vigesimo – RIP.

He was born in the year of Waterloo, and he died in 1893 when Conradh na Gaeilge was founded, the Irish Cultural Renaissance was about to start, and the Land Acts would change the face of Irish agriculture

Robert Browne (1844 – 1935)

3.7 Bishop Browne

Robert Browne was born on the 6th November 1844 in Charleville, Co. Cork. He was the third son of Robert Browne and Margaret Mullins. He first attended school in his native Charleville, and was then one of the first students of St Colman's College in Fermoy, where he spent two years. He matriculated in August 1860 and entered Maynooth at the age of sixteen, where he was received into the Rhetoric class.

In 1869, he was ordained deacon and received into the Dunboyne establishment, where he continued for a further three years. Later that same year, he was ordained priest. At the end of his Dunboyne period he was elected temporary Dean in the College. He then spent two years as a professor in St Colman's College, Fermoy before returning to Maynooth, where he was made Dean in 1875. He became Vice-President in 1883 and President two years later.

In the little more than a decade that he spent at the head of Maynooth, he accomplished an amazing amount of work against daunting odds. Shortage of money was always a problem. It was difficult to get some from dioceses and parishes which were already struggling, but he kept trying. He also worked very hard to get private benefactors to donate stained glass windows, altars, stations of the cross, for example.

His Presidency of Maynooth is remembered for his completion of the College Chapel, for adorning the cloisters with portraits of the various bishops who passed through Maynooth, and the building of the exhibition hall. He also oversaw the reclamation of part of the College grounds. On the academic front, he made important changes to the curriculum. The magazine, the Irish Ecclesiastical Record which had been founded by Cardinal Cullen in 1864, but had lapsed in 1876 was revived by Monsignor Browne, who remained as its editor until he moved to Cloyne. He was for a time professor of Liturgy in the College also.[89]

Dean Mulcahy, who was a student of Theology in the 1890s, while admitting that Browne was pompous, also wrote of him: We found him always kindly, affable, deeply interested in our welfare, engrossed in the improvement of the College. St Joseph's Square was redeemed by him from the condition of a wilderness'.[90]

An incident which occurred during the building of the Maynooth chapel might have given the people and clergy of Cloyne a warning of the power of the man who was about to come to lead them. William Hague was the architect for

---

89   John Healy, op. cit. p545-546.
90   Patrick J. Corish, *Maynooth College 1795-1995*. p445.

the project. Browne complained that he did not visit the site often enough. Hague replied that he was the architect and not the clerk of works. They had many fiery arguments over the different phases of the building, but they learned to work together in the end for the good of all.[91] The consecration of the College Chapel in June 1891 was a national event.

At a meeting of the Trustees of Maynooth on the 9th October 1894, the chairman, Cardinal Logue, praised Dr Browne for 'the indefatigable zeal and perfect taste by which he contributed… to the completion of the College Chapel: the important additions to the College buildings of the Aula Maxima, and the general embellishment of the College and grounds; … the standard of intellectual work, and much more of the traditional piety on the part of the students … '.[92]

Dr Browne was ordained Bishop of Cloyne on the 19th August 1894. His consecration took place in the new St Colman's Cathedral in Cobh. The chief celebrant was His Grace the Most Rev. Dr Croke, Archbishop of Cashel. Present also were the archbishops of Armagh and Tuam, most of the other Irish bishops and about one hundred and fifty priests from all over the country. All the clergy processed from the Mercy Convent to the Cathedral and back again at the end of the ceremony. Special trains and boats brought people from all over the county. The charge for the reserved seats in the Cathedral was two shillings and sixpence. On the façade of the church was a banner which read 'Gaudeamus omnes in Domino hodie'. His two brothers and three nephews were there to witness the great event, along with deputations from far and near, including one from Cloyne. The members of

---

91   Patrick J. Corish, op. cit. p195.
92   John Healy, op. cit.

the Cloyne delegation were Messrs D. Cronin, John Cotter, George Ryan (teacher), D. Leahy, W.J. Dunn, W. Crotty, M. Donovan, D. Walsh.[93]

The new Bishop was very quickly drawing on the building experience gained in Maynooth as he set to finish the work of his predecessors, Drs Keane and McCarthy. He concentrated on the outside of the edifice starting in 1899 and finishing in 1909. He also added the flooring, ceiling, side altars, and stained glass windows, sacristy and, finally, the spire. The Cathedral – free of debt – was solemnly consecrated on April 12th 1919.

In 1912, he and six of his priests successfully brought a case for libel against the Dundee Courier for 'having falsely and calumniously charged them with abusing their religious influence over the Catholic laity to procure the indiscriminate dismissal of all Protestant shop assistants in the employment of Catholics in Cobh'. The action was brought in the Court of Session in Edinburgh. An anonymous article in the paper had said that 'Religion makes all the difference in everything in Ireland. This incident will show what it can do and has done. Two years ago in Queenstown, Co. Cork, instructions were issued by the Roman Catholic religious authorities that all Protestant shop assistants were to be discharged. One shopkeeper – a Roman Catholic – refused to discharge an assistant he had for a number of years. The consequence was that his shop was proclaimed, and in three months he had to close and clear out, his stock being sold for next to nothing. He and his family left for Britain, where, as he said, he could employ an Atheist if he liked'.

---

93   Cork Examiner, 20th August 1894.

Bishop Browne was awarded £200, a sum of money which led to one of the great 'good luck' stories of the last century. The bishop had taken under his wing his nephew, Frank, after the death of both his parents. He bought him his first camera which led to a lifelong love affair with photography. The bishop, who did not need the libel money for himself, paid for a two day passage on the RMS Titanic and a brand new camera for his nephew, Fr Francis Browne, SJ. The photos which Fr Browne took during those two days between Southampton, Cherbourg and Queenstown are treasured today as some of them are the only photos in existence of certain parts of the ship. They could have been lost, as a rich American had offered to pay Fr Browne's passage the rest of the way to America, but his Jesuit superior refused him permission to travel in a telegram which read simply, *Get off the ship – Provincial*.

Very early in his episcopate, Bishop Browne started the Diocesan Inspectorship of Schools. He built boys' and girls' schools in Cobh. He started a central novitiate for the Sisters of Mercy at Bella Vista in Cobh in 1916. During his time, the College Chapel in St Colman's College was built, largely through the munificence of the late and famous Canon Sheehan. He saw new churches built in Charleville, Midleton, Milford, Ballycotton and Mogeely.

The architect for Ballycotton church was Mr George Coppinger Ashlin, and the contract was awarded to Mr J. J. Coffey of Midleton whose clerk of works was Mr Ned Shinnick. Preparation of the site began in August 1898 and Bishop Browne laid the foundation stone on Sunday 23rd April 1899. Just over two years later, on Sunday 11th August 1901, the dedication ceremony took place. The whole village was festooned for the occasion. Bishop Browne, attended by the clergy, blessed the walls externally and (with the doors closed) internally. High Mass was then celebrated with Bishop Browne presiding. The choir was under the guidance of Mrs George Ryan of Cloyne.[94]

In 1907, he is engaged in correspondence regarding the purchase of a site for Shanagarry National School. Always interested in education, he oversaw the erection of schools for the Christian Brothers in Fermoy. He brought the Bon Secours nuns to Cobh, and the Little Company of Mary to Fermoy in 1910 for the purpose of nursing the poor in their own homes. This latter convent was equipped with a dispensary. He was extremely active and retained all his mental faculties to the very end of his long reign. In 1930, he purchased, rebuilt and fitted out the Admiralty buildings in Fermoy as a Presentation Novitiate.[95]

Like his predecessors, he always took an interest in the politics of his time. The Irish Independent on February 6th, 1905 reported him sending £5 to Captain Donelan MP for the Irish Parliamentary Fund. He said he would be glad to see a collection in every parish in the county, and that 'all Nationalists are rejoiced to know that we have a thoroughly united Parliamentary Party'.

How times change! He once described dancing as a kind of mania and a 'great danger to modesty and decency'. He attacked the dance halls of the day in his diocese as 'promiscuous, ill-assorted dancing assemblies'.[96]

---

94   Canon B. Troy, Midleton Parish Newsletter, 21st October 2001.
95   The Irish Press, 23rd March 1935.
96   The Holly Bough 2014.

An event which will live forever in the memory of Cobh people was the sinking of the Lusitania on the 7th May 1915 during the First World War. Bishop Browne officiated at the mass in the Cathedral for the hundreds of victims who were brought ashore at Cobh, and prayed for them as they were interred in the local graveyard.

He died at the advanced age of 91 having been for forty-one years Bishop of Cloyne. *The Cork Examiner* of March 26, 1935 gave a long account of his funeral. It was attended by churchmen and lay dignitaries from far and near, including Mr W.T. Cosgrave former President of the Executive Council, the Lord Mayor of Cork, Alderman S. French, members of the Harbour Board and Cork Corporation, consuls and many more. Every shop in the town was closed from ten in the morning to three in the afternoon. Blinds were drawn and flags flew at half-mast. People wore rosettes of purple, yellow and black ribbon. The United Hunt Club meet which was to take place at the Paddocks was postponed. The Cathedral was draped in black and white.

The chief mourners included his nephews, the Rev. W.F. Browne PP Blarney, the Rev. M.F. Browne SJ Emo, and Dr J.M. Browne, Wolverhampton, and many cousins. He was buried in the new cemetery in Cobh which he had acquired and laid out, much to the surprise of many, who would have expected him to lie in the crypt of the Cathedral with his predecessors. He chose to stay with his people. Many of the tributes to him came from organisations dealing with the poor and with children, for both of which he always displayed great love.

For his eighty-sixth birthday a poem was published in The Cork Examiner by Marie Lynch.

To the Most Rev. Robert Browne,
of Cove, upon his Birthday.
Four score six rich years have circled
Lightly o'er our Bishop's head,
Four score golden years of labour,
Deeds of mercy; records read
In the great Throne Room of Heaven,
Mid the listening angel band,
Singing with triumphant paens(sic),
Welcome to the better land.

See he comes! So calm and tranquil,
Moving with a gentle grace,
Shedding peace and hope around him,
Lighting every worn face,
Speaking words of love and pity,
Moving hearts that long have slept,
Till, like Peter's words, contritely
Sinners prayed with him and wept.
Son of Peter! Great thy labours!
In the fields thy Master trod,
Meekly following the footsteps
Of thy Maker, Lord and God.
When thy work on earth is ended,
He shall call thee to thy rest,
And awaiting angels lay thee,
Radiant on his loving breast.

James J. Roche (1870 – 1956)

3.8 Bishop Roche

James Joseph Roche was presumed to have been born in Midleton on the 23rd October 1870 to William Roche and Mary Daly, who had been married the previous year in Midleton, and who continued to live there. However, according to Tomás Ó Riordáin in his book, *Lisgoold a Church History*, James Roche was born in Peafield in Lisgoold parish. His mother is said to have been visiting relatives there when the future bishop decided to make a premature entry into the world. William Roche was a native of Cloyne. He was born there in May 1840 to Henry Roche and Mary Cronin. Mary Daly was baptised in Castlelyons in the early 1830s, and her son, Bishop James J. Roche, donated a baptismal font to the church there in her memory in 1936. She would appear to have died soon after his birth, his father remarrying in November 1872. His second wife was Mary Parker of Curragrine, sister of Canon David Parker, PP Blarney, and mother of his second son, Henry J. born in 1874 and a daughter, Kate.

At the time of James's birth, William was the esteemed and respected Clerk of the Midleton Rural Council and Board of Guardians, a job he held for thirty-two years. The family lived at No.6, Brodrick Street. Young James received his early education from the Christian Brothers in Midleton where a classmate was William Barry, later Archbishop of Hobart. Both continued their education in St Colman's College in Fermoy. They then parted company as James entered Maynooth and William, All Hallows. James was ordained in 1893.

After ordination, he was sent immediately to teach philosophy in St Patrick's College in Carlow, where for six years he distinguished himself as a brilliant tutor and profound scholar. He subsequently taught in St Colman's College, Fermoy. After that he served as curate in the parishes of Whitechurch, Charleville, and, lastly, Mallow. While in Mallow he was appointed Bishop of Ross in 1926. He spent only five years in Ross, being then appointed coadjutor with right of succession to Bishop Browne in the diocese of Cloyne. On the death of Bishop Browne in 1935, he succeeded to the diocese of Cloyne. Bishop Cotter of Portsmouth was among the many bishops who attended his consecration.

While he was in Whitechurch, his ailing father, William, went to live with him, his step-mother having died in 1904. William died in 1907 and is buried in Dangan graveyard. At the time of his death, his other son, Henry J. was curate in Grenagh. Among those listed as present at his funeral were David Kearney, Ballycrenane, Michael Cronin, Ballyrussell and Maurice Donovan, Lady's Bridge. Later in his career, the bishop was a frequent visitor to the church in Whitechurch. On the occasion of his golden jubilee in 1943, he donated to it new altar rails and a stained-glass window. While he was bishop and living in Cobh, Dr Roche saw his people through good times and bad. In 1938, he witnessed the handing back of the ports to Irish jurisdiction. During World War II, life ebbed away from the formerly busy town of Cobh. By the end of the War the town looked sadly decayed and derelict. But a revival soon followed, in which the bishop's personal encouragement counted greatly. New shipping lines, with some of the largest liners afloat, began to call regularly at Cork Harbour. He also took a considerable interest in the proposed new oil refinery subsequently built at Whitegate.[97]

A statement issued from Bishop's House in Cobh on Friday, August 31st 1956 read as follows: 'His Lordship, Most Rev. Dr James Roche, Bishop of Cloyne, took suddenly ill tonight and died within a short time.' He was returning home from a visit to the house of the Very Rev. J. Cotter Adm. when he took ill crossing the Cathedral grounds.[98] Many tributes were paid to him, and representatives of Church and state attended the funeral. The Taoiseach, John A. Costello, was present and the President was represented by Col. Sean Collins-Powell, OC Southern Command. Also present were the Minister for External Affairs, Mr Liam Cosgrave TD and his father, William T. Cosgrave, former President of the Executive Council of the Irish Free State. UCC was represented by its president, Prof. H. St J. Atkins.

At a meeting of Cork County Council, Veronica Hartland of Cobh, seconding the vote of sympathy, said of him that he

97   Cork Examiner, 7th September 1956.
98   Irish Independent, 1st September 1956.

had given great attention to the orphaned children of Cobh and was a wonderful disciplinarian where Church matters were concerned. Tributes were also paid to him by the UDC of Skibbereen where he had lived while Bishop of Ross, also from Mallow and Cobh. A special mass was celebrated the day before the funeral to enable the children of the local schools to attend. He was buried beside the Cathedral after solemn requiem Mass, the first bishop to be interred in the grounds.

John J. Ahern (1917 – 1997)

3.9 Bishop Ahern

John Ahern was born and raised in Leamlara near Midleton where his parents, James and Ellen, were national teachers. Having completed his early education in his native parish, he went on to St Colman's College, Fermoy, where he distinguished himself, achieving first place in Ireland in Latin and Greek in both Intermediate and Leaving Certificates. From there he went to St Patrick's College, Maynooth, where he was ordained in 1936. In Maynooth, he continued his Classical studies, receiving a BA in 1932. He also studied for a Higher Diploma in Education and a Licentiate in Theology. He next went to the Irish College in Rome to do post-graduate studies.

From 1936 to 1940, he served as chaplain to the convent in Macroom. In 1940 he was appointed to the staff of St Colman's College, his old alma mater. In 1944, he began studies for a doctorate in Canon Law at the Dunboyne Establishment in Maynooth. In 1946, he was awarded the doctorate, and immediately took up a position as lecturer in Canon Law, becoming professor in 1948. During this period, he was a member of the Committee of the Catholic Record Society of Ireland. He contributed many articles to the Irish Theological Quarterly and to the Irish Ecclesiastical Record. He was also one of the editors of the Irish Theological Quarterly. He remained in Maynooth for almost ten years, and in 1957 he was nominated Bishop of Cloyne by Pope Pius XII. His consecration took place in St Colman's Cathedral in Cobh in June 1957 and was attended by the President, Sean T. O'Kelly and the Taoiseach, Eamon de Valera. The President was received at the urban boundary by an escort of the Army Motorcycle Squadron who accompanied him to the Cathedral where he inspected a guard of honour.

Over the years, Bishop Ahern served on numerous commissions of the Irish Episcopal Conference, most notably in the areas of doctrine and catechetics. As well as the academic side of his work, he was ever present in his diocese, for example, visiting Mallow Beet Factory where he said Mass for the workers. This visit was reported in The Cork Examiner of the 11th October 1957 alongside a report of Sean Lemass saying that the country was entering a new industrial phase, and that Irish companies now had to put more energy into producing for export.

One of the new bishop's early tasks was to perform the official opening of the International Carillon Festival of Ireland in Cobh in May 1958. The festival continued for a week and the final concert was attended by the President and Bean Ui Cheallaigh, where the President presented the awards and trophies won during the week. As well as ministering to his people at home, John Ahern never forgot the emigrants. In October 1966, he visited the Cork Association in London. In addressing them, he urged them to integrate and contribute to the communities where they lived. He empathised with their feelings of loneliness and insecurity, and assured them that people at home cared. Evidence of this, he said, was the number of priests lent from each diocese each year to look after Irish emigrants.

Probably helped by his background, he always expressed a great interest in education, especially in small schools and rural areas. In 1980, he was present at the opening of the new Midleton Vocational School, which was built to cater for 650 pupils and was the largest VEC school in the county. The new school opened less than thirty years after the opening of the first school, 'The Tech'. The new school was a sign of the phenomenal population growth in east Cork which followed the increasing industrialisation of the area. Bishop Ahern reminded the Minister for Education, John Wilson, that still further accommodation was needed in the immediate future in the primary sector. He spoke of the need for education to prepare people not only for their future careers, but also for them to be useful and unselfish members of society.[99]

Bishop Ahern retired in 1987 and went to live in Nazareth House near Mallow where he died suddenly in September 1997. He is buried in the Cathedral grounds in Cobh. He was the last surviving Irish bishop of those who attended Vatican II. He had worked hard to prepare priests and people for the changes which occurred after the Council, and frequently exhorted his flock to pray for the success of

the seismic changes that came about at that time. His reign was much different to that of his predecessors in previous centuries when involvement in national politics was a matter of survival for the role of the clergy. In the second half of the 20th century, politicians, for good or ill, took care of politics and, after John Charles McQuaid, bishops focused on the spiritual needs of their people. John J. Ahern was a man of extraordinary intellect who gave his whole being to his God and his people.

3.10
Bishop William Crean

Bishop Ahern was succeeded by Bishop John Magee, 1987-2010; Archbishop Dermot Clifford, 2009-2012; and the current Bishop, William Crean, in 2013.

---

99   Southern Star, 13th December 1980.

Bishops born in Cloyne
who served in the USA and UK

Bishop John Quinlan (1826 – 1883)

3.11 Bishop Quinlan
(Courtesy: John Quinlan)

Bishop John Quinlan was born in Ballycrenane, Cloyne on the 19th of October 1826. He was the son of Timothy Quinlan and his wife Mary Kenifeck. His father died in 1830 and was buried in the old graveyard in Killeagh where many generations of the family were interred.

John Quinlan left Ireland in 1844 and was accepted as a clerical student by Mallow born Archbishop John Baptist Purcell of Cincinnati, Ohio. The archbishop sent him to Mount St Mary's College in Emittsburg, Maryland to pursue his studies. He was ordained by Archbishop Purcell on the 30th of August 1852 and his first mission was in Piqua, Ohio, where he spent two years. He was then transferred to the parish of St Patrick in Cincinnati, and, subsequently became curate to Archbishop Wood of Philadelphia. His next move was to St Mary's Seminary of the West in Cincinnati where he taught theology and philosophy.

He was consecrated Bishop of Mobile on 4th December 1859, in the Cathedral of St Louis, New Orleans. In his diocese he found twelve churches and fourteen schools for which he had only eight secular priests. He visited Rome in May 1860, and, on his journey took the opportunity to visit Cork where he recruited eleven young candidates for the priesthood. On his visit to Cloyne he presented a chalice to the church where it is still kept today. The chalice is inscribed in Latin at the base.

During his tenure as bishop, he witnessed the horrors of the American Civil War. He saw many poor Irishmen act as substitutes for draftees. For this service they earned a sizeable amount of money. The most remarkable record that exists for Irish substitutes is that kept by Bishop Quinlan. He acted as a banker for many of them, looking after their fee while they served in the army, and also guaranteeing to the payers that their substitutes did not abscond. In Quinlan's ledger there is evidence of at least forty Mobile Irishmen between 1862 and 1863 receiving between $1000 and $3000 for replacing a draftee. On depositing their money with Bishop Quinlan they named the people to whom their money should go in the event of their death in service. After the battle of Shiloh, Bishop Quinlan is reported as having hastened on a special train to the blood-stained battle ground and ministered to the temporal and spiritual needs of North and South.

After the war diocesan activities were crippled. Nevertheless, besides repairing ruined churches, Bishop Quinlan built the portico of the Mobile cathedral, founded St Patrick's and St Mary's churches in that same city, and further churches in nine other towns in his diocese. In April 1876, he invited the Benedictines from St Vincent's Abbey, Pennsylvania to the diocese and they settled in Cullman, Alabama.

He visited Rome again in 1867 and was present at the canonisation of the martyrs of Japan and China. In 1869 he represented the American bishops at the First Vatican Council. His final visit to Rome was in 1882. While there he fell victim to a form of malaria known as Roman Fever from which he never recovered. On his return to America he went to stay with Fr Massardier in New Orleans. It was there that he passed away on the 9th of March 1883. He is buried under the portico of the Cathedral Basilica of the Immaculate Conception in Mobile.[100]

Quinlan Hall on the campus of Spring Hill College is named in his honour.

---

100 op. cit.

Bishop Richard Scannell (1845 - 1915)

3.12 Bishop Scannell
(Courtesy: Wikipedia)

Bishop Scannell, the first bishop of the Diocese of Concordia, was born May 12, 1845, in Cloyne to Patrick and Johanna (Collins) Scannell. After completing his classical studies in a private school in Midleton he entered All Hallows College in Dublin, Ireland, and was ordained in 1871. He was an assistant pastor at the cathedral (1871-78), then pastor of St Columba Parish in East Nashville (1878-79). He was named diocesan administrator in 1879 and served until 1883. He then took a two-year leave of absence for health reasons, and was subsequently assigned in 1885 to organise the new St Joseph Parish in West Nashville. He was appointed vicar general in 1886 and appointed bishop of Concordia on August 9, 1887, one week after the diocese was erected. He was consecrated at St Joseph Church in West Nashville on Nov. 30, 1887. He arrived in Concordia on December 6, 1887.

He ordained the first priests of the diocese - Father John Regan of Esbon on May 27, 1888, and Father August Heimann of Indiana on June 29, 1889. He also helped to establish the Sisters of St Joseph of Concordia.

He was named bishop of Omaha in late 1890 and installed there on January 30, 1891. Under his governance, the cornerstone of St Cecilia Cathedral was laid in 1907, and the diocese of Kerney was formed out of the western part of the diocese in 1912. He also oversaw the diocese's expansion to 95 parishes, serving more than 85,000 Catholics. Parochial schools and diocesan priests more than doubled in number. He erected the Creighton Memorial St Joseph's Hospital and St Catherine's Hospital, and a home of the Good Shepherd. He also introduced very many religious orders to the diocese. He died of pneumonia while still in office at the age of seventy. He was buried in Holy Sepulchre Cemetery in Omaha, but his remains were later moved to the bishops' burial plot in Calvary Cemetery in Omaha.[101]

Bishop William Cotter (1866 – 1940)

Bishop Cotter was born on 21st December 1866 at Cloyne, Co. Cork. As a young boy he was taken to Portsmouth to visit his father in the navy (on HMS Active). The English naval port certainly made an impression on the young William Cotter. After his education at St Colman's College, Fermoy, he studied for the priesthood at Maynooth and was ordained for the Portsmouth Diocese on 19th June 1892. His first appointment was at St Mary's, Ryde, on the Isle of Wight. Apart from a brief return to Cork for three months, where he served at Buttevant, he remained at St Mary's as curate until 1900 when he was appointed Rector in succession to Mgr.

---

101 Diocesan necrology, Diocese of Salina;
    http://en.m.wikipedia.org/wiki/Richard_Scannell

Cahill when he became Bishop of Portsmouth. In 1902 he was received in audience by Pope Leo XIII and promoted to canon. Despite the limitation of his parish work (he had only served at Ryde) he was nevertheless consecrated by Bishop Cahill as Titular Bishop of Clazomenae and appointed auxiliary to him at Portsmouth in 1905. An episcopal throne (carved from oak) was presented to him by parishioners of St Mary's, Ryde. (It is still used as the celebrant's chair in St. Mary's today).[102]

In 1905 Bishop Cotter was presented with two beautiful addresses: one by the priests and people of Cloyne; and the other by Cloyne G.A.A. Club and Cloyne Pipe Band. The presentation ceremony was held in the C.Y.M.S. Hall.[103]

On a visit to his mother in Cloyne in January 1906, he was presented in the Parochial House, in the presence of Bishop Browne and many of the priests of the diocese, with a handsome gold chalice studded with amethysts, garnets and other sparkling jewels. He was also given a costly set of vestments. The presentation was made by the Rev. John O'Riordan PP who had organised the occasion. Many priests were unable to attend because of the bad weather.

On the death of Bishop Cahill in 1910, it was, almost inevitably, William Cotter who succeeded him as Bishop of Portsmouth. He led the diocese of Portsmouth for thirty years. He took as his motto 'Non Recuso Laborem' (I will not refuse work). During this time he opened or inaugurated many churches, schools and convents.

Bishop Cotter is remembered for his lively sense of humour

---

102   Catholic Church of the Sorrowful and Immaculate Hearth of St Mary's , Ryde, Isle of Wight
103   Thomas Kelleher, op. cit. pp116-117.

and for fostering the good sense of fellowship that existed in the diocese between priests and laity. He had a powerful voice and used it to good effect both as a preacher and in the singing of the liturgy. He was certainly an Irish nationalist as exemplified by his coat of arms with the Celtic cross and shamrocks. Bishop Cotter died in 1940, having been in failing health for the previous two years, and is buried at Waterlooville Convent cemetery. The non-Catholic Lord Mayor of Portsmouth, Cllr D.L. Daly paid him a warm and generous tribute: He was the embodiment of all that Christianity stands for. *He always radiated kindness and that coupled with a sharp and genuine Irish wit made him a friend of all. To Catholics in his diocese he was a father in the true sense of the word.*

CHAPTER 4

Priests, Religious and Sacristans

Parish Priests

John Curtin (1656 – 1726)

A headstone in the cathedral graveyard in Cloyne bears the inscription –

Curtenius Jacet Hic Doctissimus Ille Joannes Cloneus Pastor
Myste/1812/oRumqe
Jubar Obiit An. D. 1726 Martii 25. Aetatis Suae 70.

(Here lies John Curtin Most Learned Pastor and
Light of the Sacred Mysteries
Died 25th March 1726. Aged 70.)

Seán Ó Conaire (John Connery) (1739 – 1773)

Bishop Coppinger mentions John Connery in his list of clergy of the diocese who died between 1770 and 1799. He says of him 'a very good missionary died young'. His work cannot have been easy in those troubled times. By 1764, the mass house in Cloyne appears to have been completed, and the Hearth Tax returns for that year give the following chapels in good order: Cloyne, Ballintemple, Kilmahon.[104] The 1766 Religious Census of Cloyne tells us that An t-Athair Ó Conaire had to look after 144 Popish families in the town and 113 in the country, and another 52 in Ballintemple (Churchtown).

---

104   Rev. M.J. Brenan: op. cit. p557.

Seán would appear to be the most important of the Ó Conaire family who engaged in extensive scribal work in the 18th century. Donncha, also a priest, and Séamus were probably his brothers. Séamus may also have been a priest, as a James Connery was parish priest of Buttevant from 1807 to 1835.[105] Much of Seán's scribal work was done for Bishop John O'Brien who was a renowned patron of poets and scribes. His work was mentioned admiringly in his own time and after his death by other renowned scribes. Sadly, they do not leave us much in the way of biographical detail.

4.1 Script of Seán Ó Conaire
(Courtesy: Margaret Hartnett)

---

105   Eric Derr: op. cit.

His work, which includes genealogies, poetry, the Annals of Inisfallen and much more, is to be found today in the archives of the Royal Irish Academy, Trinity College Dublin, the Jesuit Library, Leeson St, Dublin and NUI Maynooth. He also translated sermons from French for Bishop O'Brien. From notes in his writings we know that he was working in Cloyne 'Cluan Chollamaon' in the years 1757 and 1761. He also worked in Ballinterry and in France, presumably with the bishop.

His death notice appeared in the Cork Hibernian Chronicle of the 8th of July 1773: 'Died a few days ago at Cloyne, most deservedly lamented, the Rev. John Connery, a clergyman of the Church of Rome, and an honorary member of the Society of Antiquarians'. This was in fact a Committee of the Dublin Society set up at the urging of General Charles Vallancey in May 1772 and to which Ó Conaire had been appointed in the previous January. He was very quickly made corresponding member for the province of Munster, with Charles O'Conor of Belanagare for Connacht, to promote the work of the committee in their respective areas.

General Vallancey had come to Ireland some time before 1772 to assist in a military survey of the island, and made the country his adopted home. His attention was strongly drawn towards the history, philology and antiquities of Ireland. He published extensively on all aspects of Irish culture, but his efforts were subsequently roundly condemned as 'a fanciful compound of crude deductions from imperfect knowledge'. His work was not totally in vain, however, as it did awaken interest and stimulate others.

At a meeting of the committee on the 12th February 1774, Vallancey brought in some manuscripts done by Ó Conaire which he had got from the Bishop of Cloyne who was also a member of the committee (Bishop McKenna or the Church of Ireland Bishop Agar?). At a further meeting the following week, it was decided to pay four guineas for these manuscripts and a further four guineas when they received the rest. It would appear they received the remaining works pretty quickly as the accounts show: '3rd May 1774. Paid Mr Connery for Mss (By Rt Revd Bishop of Cloyne) £9-2-0'.

The committee did not survive past the end of 1774, and, at the back of the minute book, after the name of Seán Ó Conaire the word 'dead' appears. If the information in the manuscript RIA 23 K thirty-four is correct, it would seem he died at the young age of 34. He was in a long line of clerical scribes from St Colman and the Irish monks who rewrote the history of Europe for Charlemagne. His work alongside that of Bishop O'Brien and General Vallancey preserved much of Irish culture that might otherwise have been lost.[106]

Paul McKenna (1730 – 1786)

Paul McKenna was a cousin of Bishop Matthew McKenna. He served in the parish of Aghabullogue from 1766 to 1770. He was subsequently parish priest of Clonakilty, where he established four Catholic schools for boys and four for girls. While in that parish, he noted the potential of a young boy whom he recommended to the bishop for further education. This young boy was Bartholomew Crotty, who later became President of Maynooth and Bishop of Cloyne. McKenna became Archdeacon, parish priest of Cloyne and Vicar General of the diocese. While in Cloyne, he received Bishop McKenna on Visitation in 1785. The visitation notes show

---

106   Breandán Ó Conchúir, *Scríobhaithe Chorcaí 1700 -1850*

the parish to be in reasonably good order with vestments and plate well looked after. A notice appeared in the Dublin Evening Post of 16th December 1786: 'Died at Cloyne, the Rev. Paul McKenna, parish priest of that place'. He is buried in Templerobin (Ballymore) graveyard in a tomb which the bishop had ordered to be erected. In Dr Coppinger's list of deceased clergy, he is said to have died of consumption.

John Scanlon/Scanlan (? – 1820)

John Scanlon was appointed to Cloyne on the death of Paul McKenna. He had received his clerical education in Paris where he was conferred with a BD. Before coming to Cloyne, he served in the parish of Donoughmore. Neither religiously nor politically was it an easy time to take over responsibility for the Cloyne area. There were sporadic outbreaks of Whiteboy activity in the general area, which, it would seem, increased in number and ferocity the more the United Irish movement spread. In October 1797, Lord Longueville of Castle Mary, referring to a meeting held in Cloyne, complained that 'some United Irishmen have been sent down to alarm and disturb this (hitherto tranquil) country'. He also said that 'the damages of houghing (cutting the hamstrings) cows and cropping horses by persons, as yet unknown, are carried on in the parish of Cloyne'. The meeting at Cloyne was a precursor to many assassinations that took place in the following weeks, one at Cloyne, where Thomas Bourke, a soldier in the Royal County of Limerick Militia, was killed.

Despite the best efforts of the bishops in previous years, a lot of work remained to be done to provide buildings and structures for the observance of the liturgy. Partly because there was not always a chapel or a priest available, many people resorted to couple beggars (unauthorised clergymen) to perform their marriage. The poor, eloping couples and couples of mixed religion also sought the services of these gentlemen. The practice was outlawed by all churches, but it was still frequently used by Catholics up to 1827 when marriages not celebrated by a priest were declared void. It was also outlawed by the state to prevent mixed marriages and some convicted couple beggars were hanged while others were deported to America.

In 1791 baptismal and marriage registers for the parish of Cloyne were begun. It was reported in the Hibernian Journal of the 17th February 1794 that 'The Bishop of Cloyne (Church of Ireland) has granted the Roman Catholics of Cloyne ground to build a chapel on'. In 1796, there is a mention of the Cathedral Chapter giving the Roman Catholics ten guineas for the 'repair and maintenance' of their chapel. This mass house, presumably the one mentioned in the time of An t-Athair Ó Conaire, was on the site of the present church, but nearer to the road. We have the evidence of Fr Scanlon's memorial stone in the church to tell us that he organised the building of a new church, saw the laying of the foundation stone and some of the building work, but it would appear he died before the building was completed.

One of the rules which the bishops made in 1791 was 'whenever a new chapel is about to be built, it is strictly required that the pastor do give notice thereof to the ordinary, when assent to the site and to the terms and conditions of the lease, is to be first asked and obtained'.[107] No trace exists in the Coppinger Papers in the Cloyne Diocesan Archives

---

107   CDA: *1791.00/8 No 11.*

of any permission ever having been sought for the building of Cloyne church; neither have we found any report of a dedication ceremony.

In July 1818, Bishop Coppinger wrote to Michael Collins – later Bishop Collins – regarding a Mr Horrgan, who was being appointed curate in Cloyne: 'Is there anything like pedantick pomposity or assumption of self-importance about that gentleman? If there be, he ought and shall be lowered'. It has often been suggested that the said bishop was not the most tolerant! Coppinger's Visitation notes for the previous July state that during his visit to Cloyne 'Rev. J. Scanlan unable to attend'. Was his health failing at that point or was he one of those who did not welcome Bishop Coppinger when he succeeded Bishop McKenna? Many years before he had been one of the signatories to Bishop McKenna's will.

Fr Scanlon's remains must have been interred within the unfinished church as his stone reads :

Pray for the soul of
The Rev. John Scanlon
Whose remains are interred hereunder
Formerly Parish Priest of Cloyne
Which with exemplary virtue and notable zeal
He served for 34 years.
And this church whose foundation stone he laid,
And partly built.
Leaving all with a great feeling of loss
He departed this life
On the 20th day of May
1820.
R.I.P.

John Duane (1785 – 1834)

John Duane was born about the year 1785. He matriculated and entered Maynooth on the 1st September 1812, the year of Napoleon's inglorious retreat from Moscow, bad times for continental Europe, good times for Ireland as there was great demand for Irish produce to victual navy ships. He was ordained on the 13th May 1817. In his 1828 Visitation notes, Coadjutor Bishop Michael Collins mentions him as curate in Fermoy.

His work was cut short by his premature death in 1834 in his 40th year and the 18th of his ministry. The Cork Mercantile Chronicle of 30th April 1834 gives the following report: Died 22nd April at the residence of his brother-in-law T. Butler Esq. Fermoy … None but those who knew him intimately can properly appreciate his high and honourable mind, his varied information, his courtly and polished manners, his unaffected piety, modesty, and that sweetness of temper which accompanied him, even through a painful illness, to the grave. In him, it may be justly said, the Church lost a brilliant ornament, society one of its most accomplished members, the poor a liberal benefactor and his sorrowing relatives an affectionate and faithful friend'.

John Russell (17?? – 1867)

The name Russell does not appear very often in the records for the south of Ireland. On the evidence of 'Roots Ireland' the only families of that name at that time were in Ballinookera, Aghada. John Russell matriculated in September 1811, went to Maynooth, and was ordained in June 1816. He was curate in Youghal at the time of Coadjutor Bishop Michael Collins's Visitation in 1828. From the Tithe Applotment Books for

Youghal in 1833, we learn that the Rev. Mr Russell had a property of four acres and one perch. This would have been normal at the time as the priest would have needed a field in which to keep his horse.

4.2 Fr Russell's Palm Tree
(Courtesy: Patricia Lyons)

The following year, he was made parish priest of Cloyne. He did not live in the parochial house of that time but in Ballyrussell, which is not named after him as many people think. There he had a house and a small farm which he leased from the Earl of Shannon. A palm tree which he planted may still be seen on the land.

Even though times were hard, he managed to get churches built in Churchtown and Shanagarry. He set great store by education and was responsible for the construction of ten schools in the parish. According to Griffith's Valuation, as well as his own property in Ballyrussell, he held land from Thomas J. Keane of Shanagarry House in Town Parks (site of the old Girls' School), and in Spittal St from the Bishop of Cork, Cloyne and Ross (the church site).

As in most other parts of the country, the 1840s were very hard and troubled times in Cloyne. There were food riots by the starving poor in September 1846. A body of labouring men from the vicinity of Shanagarry came into the town and proceeded to rifle the flour and provision shops. The bakers, seeing it was useless to resist, just distributed their loaves to the hungry, thus protecting their property. Soldiers in Cloyne were 'billeted on the industrious but struggling householders'. While the poor starved and those who had a room to spare were obliged to give lodgings to the soldiers, there were reports of 'ill-conduct and continued drunkenness of the soldiery. Rows and disturbances [were] of frequent occurrence … '[108] The hard times continued for many years, well into the 1850s, as the potato blight attacked the crops year after year.

In June 1848, there was a court case involving Fr Russell and his curate, Fr Keppel. It was Thomas John Keane v. Major Stopford Keane/Cane regarding the will of one James Casey of Cloyne who died on the 12th August 1846. James Casey had lived all his life in Cloyne and was unmarried. From humble beginnings, he had become a gentleman of considerable property. He had a brother, Thomas, who had died in 1844. Major Stopford Keane of Sunville was his first cousin, and Thomas John was son of Captain Keane of Shanagarry House and Casey's nephew. The contention was that James Casey was not compos mentis when he made his will and that Thomas John among others had exerted undue influence. One lawyer contended that 'the Roman Catholic clergy of the parish became anxious that so notorious a sinner as Mr Casey was represented to have been, at least upon one subject as regarded his morality of life, should expiate his sins by consecrating his valuable property to the good of the Roman Catholic church.'[109]

---

108   Cork Examiner, *24th May 1847.*
109   Cork Examiner, *19th June 1848.*

Dr Russell apparently did not harbour any uncharitable feelings towards Major Stopford Keane as a result of the court case, as we find him in 1854 as celebrant at the mass for the month's mind of said gentleman, which was attended by many other clergy from near and far. He spoke of the major's army career, particularly, his being on the victorious side at Waterloo. He also mentioned his kindness and generosity to the poor especially during the famine years.

Towards the end of the Great Famine, Fr Russell accused the Church of Ireland curate in Ballycotton, the Rev. James Hingston, and a Captain Edwards, of proselytising. Mr Hingston retaliated by saying that Fr Russell had done little for famine relief in 1847.

In the following decade, the clergy continued to be highly involved in political matters. In November 1850, we read of John Russell PP, John Cullenane CC and Thomas Walsh CC signing a request to the Friends of the Tenant League to a public meeting in Mallow. March 1852 saw an increase in overt electioneering on behalf of Mr Vincent Scully, the Liberal candidate. A meeting of the Roman Catholic clergy and Liberal electors of the Barony of Imokilly and Barrymore was held in the parish chapel, Midleton with Dr Russell in the chair. A vote of thanks was proposed and seconded to the Right Rev. Dr Murphy, Roman Catholic bishop and to the clergy 'for their exertions on behalf of the tenantry of Ireland, to promote an equitable and satisfactory adjustment of the land question, to defend our Holy Religion … for their laudable zeal to procure for the Catholic youth of this country, a liberal and sound system of Education'. Fr Russell was a member of Scully's election committee as were most of the clergy of the county. In his election speech, Mr Scully urged protection for both landlord and tenant. He spoke against the tithe system which he said was 'a tax which oppresses the Catholic, harasses the Protestant, and disunites Ireland'.[110] John Russell was once again in 1865 on the General Election Committee, this time for Mr George R. Barry.

Towards the end of the decade, in October 1859, a more immediate human problem had to be dealt with. Daniel Moloney was murdered in Cloyne by having 'his throat cut across with a razor'. He was described as 'a very young, unmarried man, of rather quiet and inoffensive habits'. A local man was arrested and held in jail pending trial.[111] Cloyne was not long crime-free after that. In 1864, three farmers appeared in court on a charge of having 'unlawfully entered and taken possession of the lands of Commons West occupied by Mr F. Rowland of Kilboy'.

In 1862, an event took place in Cloyne which must have raised the spirits of all concerned. A statue of St Colman was erected on the front of the church. The Examiner reported that 'from being a plain country chapel it has, under the guidance of our Venerable Pastor, become a beautiful church. The designs of the Dean in beautifying and completing his church have been ably carried out by his curate, the Rev. Mr O'Farrell...' The statue was carried through the streets before being put in position on the church. It was believed to have been imported from Paris. Dean Russell seems to have been an indefatigable pastor. His name constantly appears attending meetings in Cobh. He was twice Vicar General of the diocese, and twice was nominated to be bishop but he declined both. Shortly after his arrival in Cloyne, the old parish of Kilmahon was removed from Ballymacoda/Lady's Bridge and added to

110   Cork Examiner, 15th March 1852.
111   Cork Examiner, 14th October 1859.

116

Cloyne.[112] Like Bishop Keane, he subscribed generously to the newly formed Keating Society. He also contributed to the fund for the diocesan seminary. In 1848, when the Famine was causing appalling suffering and misery, he and his curates, John Kepple and Thomas Walsh, were among the signatories of a letter from the Catholic clergy of Cloyne and Ross to the Queen. In his will, written a few years before his death, he left his house and land to 'my faithful and deserving servant, Patrick Kearney, together with my horse or horses … and the carts and other implements belonging to me, that are necessary or useful for farming purposes'. He left some money for charity, some for masses after his death, and a painting of Mary Magdalen and a relic of the true Cross to the 'Youghal Convent'.

A statement from Bishop Keane on hearing of his death was as follows: Died 7th October 1867 as supposed by the physicians of disease of the heart. He was at his station this morning, and appeared to be in his usual health and spirits. On arriving at home he was taken suddenly ill, and was dead in about an hour. A high-minded Irishman and a pure-hearted priest … '

John Eager (? – 1877)

John Eager was ordained in Maynooth in December 1823. When coadjutor bishop Michael Collins visited Charleville in 1828, he reported that the curate John Eager was 'recovering from the effects of a severe fever'. Fr Eager served as parish priest of Ballymacoda from 1839 to 1867 when he was transferred to Cloyne to replace the recently deceased Dean Russell. In 1869 he was appointed Vicar Forane.

---

112   Thomas Kelleher, op. cit.

In October 1868, a meeting of the parishioners of Cloyne, Shanagarry and Churchtown was held in the sacristy of Cloyne church with Fr Eager in the chair. It was unanimously resolved to support Messrs Downing and Smith Barry in the forthcoming county election.

In 1870, a lot of money was collected in Cloyne and sent to France 'for the relief of the sick and wounded French soldiers', victims of the Franco-Prussian War. In 1871, Fr Eager subscribed £3-0-0 to erect new national schools in Ballycroneen. A PS was added to the list of subscribers in The Cork Examiner of 4th October 1871 saying that there were already 150 pupils in attendance at the schools. (By 'schools' is meant two halves of one building, one half for the boys the other for the girls.)

In 1872, there was a National Testimonial to Mr Maguire MP on the twentieth year of his parliamentary services. The Cloyne Parochial Collection was forwarded by Canon Eager, who contributed £5 himself, the largest amount on the list.

In Canon Troy's lists of the clergy of Cloyne and Ross for 1876 -1877, he refers to Fr Eager as being 'superannuated'. At this time he left the parish and went to Belgium, presumably for health reasons. In his absence Fr Thomas O'Farrell was appointed administrator, but he died in June 1877. Fr Eager died in July 1877 in Bruges where he is buried.

Thomas O'Farrell (1821? – 1877)

Thomas O'Farrell was ordained in Maynooth in 1851. On his memorial tablet in the church in Cloyne, it says he ministered in Cloyne for a quarter of a century. The first six years of this period were spent in Ballycotton, after which he was transferred to Cloyne itself.

The ceremony of the laying of the foundation stone of the Cathedral in Queenstown (Cobh) took place on the 30th September 1868. There was a procession from Dunworth House to the site led by the Rev T. O'Farrell CC Cloyne bearing the cross, followed by acolytes and altar boys, Bishop Keane and members of the clergy.

In 1874, many pages of The Cork Examiner were given over to the saga of the Bennett children. Catherine Bennett stated that she had married her husband (who was in the coastguard service) in the year 1859 in the diocese of Cloyne, by a Roman Catholic clergyman, both of them at the time being Roman Catholic. Subsequently, her husband was stationed at Portlow in Cornwall, where he died. Mrs Bennett said he was attended by a Roman Catholic priest at the end, others said different. She said she was not entitled to any pension, and her own people were too poor to be able to help her and her four children, all of whom were under ten.

She sought help from a Protestant clergyman in Cork who put her in touch with a Rev. Mr Cotton of Naas, who kept an orphanage in that area. Mrs Bennett signed (with her mark) apprenticeship papers for the three older children so they could be looked after in this establishment, and the baby was put with a wet-nurse. Mrs Bennett later tried to get her children back, which led to a court case. The idea of their being 'apprenticed' was laughed out of court, as some of the clauses said that they could not marry during the period of their apprenticeship, could not gamble or play cards, dice or tables, haunt wine taverns and so on. Those present in court believed that the bottom line was that this orphanage was an underhand way of proselytising. The judgement was given in favour of the mother, which led to Fr O'Farrell setting up the 'Bennetts Minors Fund'. This led to the Rev. Mr Cotton asking in the papers why Mrs Bennett had not gone to Fr O'Farrell in the first place on her return from England. He replied that she had called on him several times, but that she did not take his advice at the time.

A 'Political Funeral' took place from Cloyne to Castlemartyr in August 1875. Mr John O'Brien, father of Michael O'Brien, the Manchester Martyr, died at the home of his sister, Mrs McCarthy, in Ballymacandrick, having some years previously been evicted from his farm in Ightermurragh. The funeral cortège left Ballymacandrick at two o'clock and went via Cloyne, Lady's Bridge and Castlemartyr to the graveyard in Ballyoughtera, which it reached about half past six. It was a dusty summer's day and local lore has it that the crowd 'drank Andy Connors's well dry'. People came from all corners, many coming by boat to Lower Aghada and walking the rest of the way.

The cortege was led by Fr O'Farrell who was accompanied by his two curates, Frs Twomey and McSwiney. Next came the coffin borne on men's shoulders. The body was enclosed in a shell, outside of which was a lead coffin enclosed in stout oak. Following the coffin came a hearse with four horses, followed in turn by about 800 men, all wearing on their left arm crepe with green ribbon. After them came country carts and butts, side-cars and private cars with a few horsemen at the rear, the whole extending over a mile. Some dropped off along the way but more constantly joined. There was no political display, but, as the cortège passed the spot where Daly, the blacksmith, was shot by the Castlemartyr police in 1867, every man raised his hat. The procession entered the demesne by the back gate, the front one having been locked, and made their way to the graveyard. Fr O'Farrell said the usual funeral prayers, and the assemblage dispersed quietly. The whole afternoon passed off without any interference on the part of the authorities.[113]

In August 1876, an advertisement appeared in The Cork Examiner for 'St Colman's Academy, St Colman's Square, Cloyne' saying that 'These new National Schools will be open on the 4th September next'. As well as the basic subjects, it was hoped to teach Latin, Greek and French, and there would be a 'Commercial, Mathematical and English Department'. There would be school fees, but it was hoped to keep them within the range of the not so well-off. Application to be made to the Rev. T. O'Farrell, Administrator and Pro-Manager.

As well as attending to educational matters in that year, Fr O'Farrell was fund raising for the new presbytery. Through the pages of the newspaper, he thanked the local Doctor Dwane and his wife for their donation of £100.

When Fr O'Farrell died in 1877, six weeks before the parish priest that he was standing in for, the Cloyne Petit Sessions adjourned as a mark of respect. A requiem mass was held for him in New York. The report from the New York Weekly Union said that he had many relatives and friends in America, among them Fr M.C. O'Farrell, Pastor of St Teresa's in New York. The service lasted one and a half hours. In 1880, a handsome monument was erected over his burial place inside the church in Cloyne, paid for out of funds raised 'for erecting memorials to the Cloyne priests, who died in the summer of 1877 of fever, contracted in the discharge of their sacred duties'. The other priest for whom a memorial was

---

113   The Nation, 28th August 1875.

planned out of this fund was Fr Edward Twohig CC who had died in Harrogate. Harrogate was a noted spa town at the time, and it is possible that Fr Twohig had gone there to recover from his illness. He died there on the 14th August 1877. That meant that three Cloyne priests had died within three months.

John M. Buckley (1823 – 1879)

4.3 Headstone – Canon Buckley
(Courtesy: Patricia Lyons)

John Buckley, who later became Canon John M. Buckley PP of Cloyne, was the son of Edmund Buckley of Lisgoold and Catherine Kent of Ballyhampshire, Castlelyons. He was born in the family home in Corbally South in the parish of Lisgoold on the 26th December 1823. His elder brother, Jeremiah, was also a priest and served in Scotland until he retired and came back to live in their old home in Lisgoold with another brother. Their sister, Johannah, married William Cogan of Midleton. It was she who erected the stained glass window to his memory over the Sacred Heart altar in Holy Rosary Church, Midleton.

John Buckley most probably attended the first national school in the parish of Lisgoold which was located in a tenant house on his father's land. Even though his name does not appear on the list of Cloyne students in Maynooth, he himself declared that he was ordained in Maynooth College in 1852. While at home in Lisgoold on the 22nd June 1847 he described the Famine in the district in a letter to his brother, Jeremiah, who was away on the continent at the time as a clerical student:

My Dear Brother,

Things are not so bad in this wretched country provided one enjoys the luxury of plenty of barley or Indian meal bread and even stirabout. What a change since you left home; many of our countrymen cut from the land of the living through want of the cheapest food in the world. Although our country has suffered much, this neighbourhood is not the worst off. I need not tell you of the many thousands who fell victim to starvation this year especially in Carbery.

Our parishes are divided into several localities where certain persons are appointed by committees to distribute meal or biskets(sic) or stirabout gratuitously to the poor. But who are the poor that come for assistance to those places? Alas they are not the beggers who in your day used live among the people taking breakfast here and dinner there. No I hardly saw one of them since I came home. The poor of these days are the strong and robust men of your day in Ireland. You can daily see men who a short time since would blush to be thought objects of charity frequent those relief places with their little bags for meal or vessels for stirabout. In every parish there are hospitals for the sick whether temporary or permanent. Fever is making its ravages in the country but not half so much in this part of the country. I need not speak of crowded poorhouses, sheds etc. Half the labouring men are idle for if they work they would receive no relief. Some families are entirely swept off the land, others are in America.

Your brothers and sisters are well and wish to be remembered to you. Poor Mama Kent is pretty well. Our father has a large family and is under great expense with you and me. He is also paying a very heavy rent at present and as you know he is a person easily troubled.

Your faithful and attached brother, John.[114]

His first appointment in Cloyne diocese was as curate in Fermoy where he spent fourteen years. In 1869, he became parish priest of Grenagh. He served in that parish until 1877 when he was transferred to Cloyne.

During his short time as parish priest in Cloyne, he built a school-house at little cost to the parishioners. He oversaw the building of the present parochial house. He bought an old glebe-house near the round tower as a curate's residence for the Cloyne curate whose previous accommodation was totally inadequate. He also bought a house in Ballycotton so that the priest with responsibility for that area could now live there permanently. Efforts had been ongoing for some time to provide the people of Ballycotton with their own church, thereby avoiding the weekly three mile walk to mass in Shanagarry, but without success. Canon Buckley opened a temporary church in a disused coal shed in the village. It was very inadequate as it could only accommodate about one third of the people wishing to attend mass, but it was a step in the right direction, and efforts were soon increased to build a proper church.

Very shortly after his arrival in Cloyne, a meeting was held in the court house to discuss an address to Mr John Litton. In November, Canon Buckley attended a luncheon where the address from the inhabitants of Cloyne was presented

---

114   Letter courtesy of James T. Quain.

to Mr Litton, in recognition of the benefit conferred on them by virtue of his supplying them with a supply of pure fresh water. Mr Litton had spent about £1000 on building a reservoir holding 7000 gallons, and bringing the water to the centre of the town. The water was supplied from a spring known as the 'Kerryman's Well'. Mr Litton said that the present fountain was only temporary and would be replaced with one 'more in character as to durability and ornament … as a tribute to [his] late wife'.[115] That fountain still stands in the Square.

Canon Buckley worked indefatigably for his people. In December 1878, he requested that a meeting be held for the purpose of inaugurating a fund for the relief of the poor of the parish. It was known as the Cloyne Charitable Coal Fund. Canon Buckley said that at no time since the Famine was relief so much needed in this locality. The population of the parish was about 7000 souls. There was no resident landed proprietor and very little employment. The meeting decided to supply coal, food and clothing to the poor of the district.

Less than two years after his arrival in Cloyne, Canon Buckley was struck down by a serious illness from which he died on the 6th March 1879. The funeral from Cloyne to Lisgoold church took place four days later, which came as a surprise as it was expected the burial would be in Cloyne. The reason for the change is not known. The Right Rev. Dr John McCarthy, Bishop of Cloyne, presided at the requiem high mass in Cloyne and led the long funeral procession to Lisgoold. Both Buckley priests were buried in the church grounds in Lisgoold with their parents buried next to them.

On the 4th April 1879, a month's mind mass was held in

---

115   Cork Examiner, 2nd November 1877.

Cloyne for Canon Buckley. An empty coffin surrounded by candelabra was placed in the centre of the choir, and the ceremonies were once again presided over by the bishop. There were thirty-six priests present. At a subsequent public meeting held in Cloyne, Mr E. F. Litton QC quoted from the father of English poetry, Geoffrey Chaucer –

> *Wide was his care, the houses far asunder,*
>
> *Yet never failed he or for rain or thunder,*
>
> *Whenever sickness or mischance might call,*
>
> *Tho' most remote, to visit great and small.*

William O'Brien (1816 – 1887)

William O'Brien succeeded Canon John Buckley in 1879. Even though Catholic Emancipation was now an established fact, and the Great Famine was over a generation away, times were still very hard in Cloyne. A meeting of the Cloyne Relief Fund was held on New Year's Day 1880 when large-scale famine threatened once again. There were two main reasons for convening the meeting so soon after Christmas. The first was for the purpose of giving assistance to those in great distress, and the second was to contradict some statements made in Midleton at the Board of Guardians meeting the previous Saturday, to the effect that the money distributed for Christmas had been consumed in drunkenness by the poor population of Cloyne. Fr O'Brien categorically denied this, saying that in the days leading up to Christmas he had been out and about, sometimes until quite late at night, and he had seen no evidence of excessive drinking.

Fr O'Brien went on to say that he believed that terrible

distress did exist. Twice during the past week about forty unemployed labourers came to him, saying that they could get no work, and that they and their families were starving. He said the town was steeped in poverty. He believed that in proportion to the population, there was more poverty in Cloyne than in any other city or town in the world. He demanded that the sewerage works approved about twelve years ago should be immediately carried out.[116] This had been mentioned at a previous meeting along with the building of tramways from Aghada to Ballycotton and from Cloyne to Midleton. As nothing seemed to be happening, a deputation including Fr O'Brien was appointed to go and put their case to the Midleton Board of Guardians.

It was during Fr O'Brien's tenure as parish priest that the Catholic Young Men's Society was set up in Cloyne. He gave the credit for this to Fr O'Riordan, his curate.

The economic state of affairs must have improved somewhat over the next decade as in 1886 the old Girls' National School was built. Fr O'Brien died the following April and is buried in the church. His will was proved on the 8th July by his curate Fr John O'Riordan and Fr James Rice of Charleville. His effects were valued at £4428-7-4.

Timothy Murphy (1826 – 1903)

Timothy Murphy was born on the 17th of January 1826 and baptised in the Youghal district. He was ordained in June 1852. Canon Murphy was parish priest of Cloyne from 1888 to 1903, having been parish priest in Ballindangan near Mitchelstown for the previous fourteen years. He was known locally as 'Canon Danger' as he was reputed to have

---

116   Cork Examiner, *3rd January 1880.*

once threatened a man who had taken possession of his uncle's property in Dungourney. During his time as parish priest of Cloyne, Star of the Sea Church in Ballycotton was completed. It was officially opened and blessed in 1901. He was a conscientious attender at meetings of the committee to oversee the building of the cathedral in Queenstown. He also religiously attended the meetings of the Conference of the Priests of the Midleton Deanery. Canon Murphy saw some traumatic times in Cloyne as he was in charge of the parish at the time of the Crotty murder. He was in failing health for the last two years of his tenure in Cloyne and died on the 1st of December 1903. He chose to be buried in the old Clonmult cemetery in the same grave as his parents and two other Murphy priests. His sister had an impressive Celtic cross erected over the grave.

John O'Riordan (1851 – 1916)

John O'Riordan was born in 1851, only a few years after the Great Famine when hunger still stalked the highways and byways of the countryside. Every year saw some appearance of the dreaded blight. In July of that year, Fr Richard Smiddy, who had just been transferred from Youghal to Charleville, said – 'A few days ago there were rumours of blight in the potatoes, but it is now stated that they have recovered and are doing well'. By early August things had changed for the worse, however. 'This mysterious disease has made its appearance in the country since the beginning of the month. The new species of potato are escaping best … while among the old seeds the disease has already committed very extensive injury'. He goes on to say that the disease in some places is even worse than it had been for the previous four or five years. He next refers to the 'emigration stream to America which has already drained this country of so many hundreds of thousands of its stalwart population'.[117] This was the Ireland that John O'Riordan was born into.

Fr O'Riordan had one brother and two sisters, one of whom became Mrs Denis Kelly of Ballyshane. The other sister, Hannah, became Sr M. Vincent in the Presentation Convent in Midleton, where she died suddenly on 8th March 1922. His brother, Michael, married in the home place and had eleven children.

4.4 Some priests, including Fr O'Riordan c. 1900
(Courtesy John C. Garde)

Fr O'Riordan came to Cloyne in 1885 as a young curate. He had previously served in Killeagh. A report in The Cork Examiner of 8th December 1888 says that John O'Riordan CC, Cloyne sent money to Alderman Madden. The money was collected all over the parish from priests and people for the

---

117   Diary of Fr Richard Smiddy PP Aghada (Internet).

Parnell Indemnity Fund. Fr O'Riordan is quoted as saying that if more is required he is sure the people will not be found wanting. By 1904, when he became parish priest, he was universally loved and respected by all. A meeting was held in January 1904 to decide on a presentation. The wish was to give him an illuminated address and a horse and covered car. The chairman, however, told the meeting that the secretary, Mr George Ryan, had ascertained from him that he would accept only the address, that he did not plan to keep a horse but to go on as he had been doing for the past twenty years.[118]

A large gathering of the citizens of Cloyne of all creeds sat down to dinner in the CYMS Hall on the 14th April 1904 to celebrate his appointment and present him with the address. The two curates, Frs Foley and Roche, were also present. There was great jubilation that their beloved priest was not to be moved to somewhere else, not least from the great man himself. On the address was a heart-felt message and pictures of places with particular significance for Fr O'Riordan. Various people spoke as the night went on. Mr T. Walsh said that Fr John was given no easy task as there were a great many difficulties still to be dealt with. Mr Charles Creed, on behalf of the non-Catholics, said that 'they all hoped that the unfailing good friendship which had existed between all classes in Cloyne would continue, and if the same good feeling existed in other places in Ireland, their country would be immensely the better of it'.

Fr O'Riordan, in his reply, thanked them all, and agreed that a good deal remained to be done for education and teaching the people sobriety and industry. He encouraged them to take an interest in their native place. He gave the example of

118   Cork Examiner, 20th January 1904.

Bishop Berkeley who had encouraged the people to become self-sufficient, and to produce what they needed as close to home as possible. He went on to say that this was the happiest moment of his life, to be made parish priest of a place and a people that he loved.[119]

Never a man to rest on his laurels, he saw the opening of the new Technical Hall in 1908. It was called the Technical Hall because it was envisaged that classes would be held there as well as other activities and lectures. It was later better known as the Parochial Hall. Among other things, a fundraising concert was held at Christmas 1904, and The Cork Examiner reported that, at the end, the national anthem, 'God Save Ireland', was sung!

4.5 Fr O'Riordan
(Courtesy Cloyne Literary &
Historical Society)

Fr O'Riordan became canon in 1914. He continued his work in the parish as before. He was founder and spiritual director of the Catholic Young Men's Society in the town.

He was transferred to Macroom in 1916. Another address was prepared for him by the people of Cloyne, but he died before it could be presented to him. It was hanging on the wall of the Young Men's Society Hall until that building saw a change of use during the

119   Cork Examiner, 20th January 1904 and 16th April 1904.

Celtic Tiger. It has since been looked after by Mrs Martha Wall, formerly owner of the premises.

Canon O'Riordan was one of the vice-presidents of the Cork Historical and Archaeological Society. His translation of the Pipe Roll of Cloyne from Richard Caulfield's annotated version of 1859, was published in the Society's Journals. Sadly, he did not live to see the last part in print. His obituary in the Society's Journal referred to him as 'a good Irish scholar and an ardent archaeologist, as was befitting his close relationship to Fr Matt Horgan PP of Blarney, a famous antiquary in his day'.[120] Canon O'Riordan was a grand-nephew of Fr Horgan, who was the priest who built the round towers in Waterloo and Whitechurch.

Canon O'Riordan died on the 28th June 1916 and is buried in Macroom. Bishop Browne presided at his funeral mass and again at his month's mind. His death was mourned in Cloyne and in Midleton, where he had served as a young priest as chaplain to the Presentation Convent. Even then he made a huge impression on all who knew him. At the Board of Guardians meeting he was described as 'a great scholar, and an ornament to the Church'. He was prayed for at all the Sunday masses in Midleton as soon as his death became known.

After his death, his library was auctioned by Woodwards of Cork on the instructions of the executors. The Cork Examiner of 30th November 1916 referred to some charitable bequests in his will. He bequeathed his 'stables, coach house, and barn, and the larger or southern garden plot used by the Catholic curate of Cloyne, and situate on the western side of Church St, Cloyne, to the Bishop, Dean and parish priest of Cloyne

120   JCHAS 1916.

on condition that they should pay £100 to his executors to be added to his Assets'. He left money to the Catholic Bishop of Cloyne for diocesan charities, and some to poor curates or parish priests of the diocese of Cloyne for masses for his intentions. In mentioning 'charities', he specified the poor of Cloyne.

Maurice O'Callaghan (1853/4? – 1920)

Canon O'Riordan was replaced by Maurice O'Callaghan in 1916. Fr O'Callaghan had previously been administrator in Fermoy.

4.6 8th Station of the Cross

The people of Fermoy seem to have felt about 'their' priest as the people of Cloyne felt about Canon O'Riordan. He had spent seventeen years in their parish when he was transferred to Cloyne. After his death many tributes were paid to him in Fermoy. The Fermoy correspondent for The Cork Examiner writing on the 28th August said that he was 'of an inherent, genial and optimistic temperament, full of good nature, big-heartedness and vivacity, and possessed of a generous share of the Irishman's proverbial wit and humour, the late Canon O'Callaghan's presence was sufficient to adorn and enliven any social circle. In the more serious side of his life as

Administrator of the affairs of a large and important parish, he exhibited to their fullest extent the characteristics of wise counsel, prudence and tact ... In all movements initiated for the material welfare of the people he took a leading and prominent part, and acted as Chairman of the Local Committees under the Old Age Pensions Act, School Attendance, Technical Instruction etc'.

It must have been a huge wrench to be transferred after such a long and successful stay in one place. However, Fr O'Callaghan did not stay idle in his new posting. He continued the work of his predecessors in leaving the church a better place. To him goes the credit for erecting the Stations of the Cross, still much prized by the people of Cloyne. He was made canon in 1919. Sadly, he died on the 25th August 1920 in the 41st year of his ministry and is buried in the churchyard in Cloyne.

An entry in the accounts for 1921 show a bequest by the late Canon O'Callaghan of £100 for Stations of the Cross for the church. An expenditure item in the following year of £168-5s-6p is shown for the Stations of the Cross, a gift of the late parish priest.[121]

---

121   Account Books of the Parish (unpublished).

Patrick M. Lynch (1850 – 1935)

Patrick Micheal Lynch was born at Clonmaine in the parish of Lady's Bridge/Ballymacoda in 1850. The family had moved there from Lisquinlan. Three of his sisters married in Cork. Some of his relatives are buried in the Hill Cemetery in Ballymacoda, others in Kilcredan. One of his nieces was Miss Motherway who owned the Corner Shop in Cloyne, and it was she who donated the statue over the Holy Well in Kilteskin.

4.7 Calvary monument
(Photo: Patricia Lyons)

He was for many years curate in Charleville. He was appointed parish priest of Cloyne in 1920 on the death of Canon O'Callaghan. Like his predecessors, he worked hard to improve the state of the church in Cloyne in all its aspects. One of his first tasks was to get the high walls around the church built. He later purchased more land for a graveyard from Curtins of Lisanley, and enclosed it in 1933. An amount of £96 and 6 shillings is shown in the account books in the year 1933 for the purchase of the cemetery field. Various other items of expenditure such as legal and works are shown in connection with the new cemetery.

He subsequently had an imposing Calvary erected in the centre of it. While doing all this, he did not neglect the spiritual side of his obligations. He organised frequent missions, bringing the famous Redemptorist preacher, Fr Collier, on a number of occasions.

Fr Lynch was an active member of the Cork Historical and Archaeological Society. He was interested in the history and archaeology of County Cork, especially of his native diocese of Cloyne. He was the author of *Life of an Irish Sagart*, an account of the life of Fr Bob Riordan, an early 19th century cleric, published by the Catholic Truth Society. He also published a prayer book, *My Manual*, which was very popular. He was considered to be a gifted writer and preacher. He was also a fluent Irish speaker, which is not surprising as the Ballymacoda area would have been a Gaeltacht in his time. In his younger days, he was well known as a hurler of some talent.

He was made a canon in 1924 and Prebendary of Aghulter in 1925. To the end of his days, he enjoyed a quiet, unannounced visit for a chat to his relatives in Lady's Bridge, Ballycotton and elsewhere. He died in a Dublin nursing home on the 2nd September 1935 aged 85 and is buried in the new cemetery in Cloyne, which he had purchased many years before.

Maurice O'Connell (1872 – 1958)

Maurice O'Connell was born about the year 1872. In the 1911 Census of Ireland, we find him in the parish of Cloghroe with responsibility for the church in Matehy.

In 1935, he was transferred to Cloyne as parish priest to replace Canon Lynch. In 1941 he was transferred to Doneraile. One of the projects which he embarked on in Doneraile was the construction of a new parochial house, which led to more trouble than he could ever have anticipated.

The English journalist and writer, Honor Tracy, happened to be doing articles on Ireland at the time. She thought that building such an expensive house for a clergyman when his people were living in extreme poverty was nothing short of scandalous. It was rumoured to be costing £9000. She wrote this in The Sunday Times saying that 'everyone is busy selling raffle tickets to everyone else. The winners will hand back the prizes as soon as received. The nuns are getting up a sale of work to which all will contribute and from which all will buy. The church dues are increased, the collections multiply and the Canon's voice so tired and confused at times, rises clear as the Shandon Bells from the steps of the altar as he pricks the faithful on to fresh endeavours'. The canon sued the paper. The paper surrendered without a fight and agreed to publish an apology and pay £750. He gave the money to the Society of St Vincent de Paul. Part of him must have been sorry he ever left Cloyne!

However, after all this publicity, he obviously did not hibernate, because an advertisement in The Cork Examiner of the 9th August 1958 finds him looking for a dance licence for the Crowley Memorial Hall in Doneraile – presumably for a fundraiser for his next project!

Later in the same month was a notice of the forthcoming auction of his household furniture etc because, it said, Canon O'Connell was retiring. He died in 1958 and is buried in the churchyard in Doneraile.

Canon Patrick Sheehan (1882 – 1967)
Patrick Sheehan was born in Ballymounteen near Ballynoe to James Sheehan and Ellen Mahony. He was baptised in the parish of Conna on the 3rd April 1882. Having received

his primary and secondary education locally, he entered Maynooth and was ordained there on 17th June 1906. He was first sent on the Scottish mission, serving in Glasgow until 1918 when he was recalled to the diocese of Cloyne. He was curate in Aghinagh, Coachford and Newmarket before being appointed parish priest of Ballyvourney in 1935. He served there until 1942 when he was translated to Cloyne.

While in Cloyne he acquired a site for Shanagarry School from Mr B. Brazier. Getting the deeds etc. for this took quite a bit of his time. He was very fastidious about the upkeep of existing church property. In June 1943 he reported to Dr Ronayne in Cobh that the painters and decorators were in Cloyne church for seven weeks. While strict and demanding high standards of behaviour from his flock, he was a popular pastor.

In 1948 he was transferred to Blarney where he spent nineteen happy years. In 1950 the bishop, Dr Roche, raised him to the dignity of Canon of the Cathedral Chapter. In Blarney he was known for his simplicity and generosity, his love for his parish, and the interest he took in the spiritual and social welfare of the district. He was very popular with everybody.

He died in 1967 a few days short of his 85th birthday. He was buried in the church grounds in Blarney after requiem mass presided over by the Bishop, Dr John J. Ahern. The factory of Messrs Martin Mahony & Bros closed to enable the employees to attend the mass. He was survived by three brothers and four sisters.

Canon Michael Fitzpatrick (1885 – 1968)

4.8 Canon Fitzpatrick
(Courtesy Betty Curtin)

Canon Michael Fitzpatrick was born in Ferryfort between Dromina and Liscarroll in north Cork to William Fitzpatrick and Ellen Connell. He was baptised in the parish of Milford on the 9th April 1885. He had three brothers, and one sister who died in infancy. His early education was in the local national school and then in the Christian Brothers Secondary School in Charleville from which he went to Maynooth. He was ordained in the chapel in Maynooth on the 20th June 1910 by the Most Rev. Dr Walsh, Archbishop of Dublin. There were seventy-five priests ordained that day. He was one of five new priests for the diocese of Cloyne. Like many before and after him, he was first sent to serve in Scotland.

On his return to Ireland he was appointed curate in Ballynoe. He subsequently served in Kildorrery, Grenagh and Aghada before coming to Cloyne as parish priest in 1948 in succession to Canon Sheehan. He acted as manager for all the national schools in the parish. In his early days he spent an amazing amount of time writing to Dr Richard Ronayne, bishop's secretary in Cobh, regularising the deeds of all the different properties in the hands of the parish. There is mention in papers in the Cloyne Diocesan Archives in Cobh of the graveyard which had been bought from David Curtin, the parochial house and the 'Technical School', also of Cloyne School and grounds which had previously been acquired from David and Daniel Curtin.

A request by Fr Fitzpatrick to the bishop in January 1948 is difficult to understand in 2015. He asked if he and the curate, Fr Fitzgerald, could attend a play in the Parochial Hall, directed by Fr Finn in aid of Castlemartyr Parochial Funds by Castlemartyr Dramatic Society. The request was granted. A similar request by the Ballycotton curate, but for an open-ended permission, was turned down. He was told in no uncertain terms that permission had to be sought each time there was an event.

On the 2nd July 1956 Fr Fitzpatrick wrote to Dr Ronayne wondering what to do with a bequest and £200 designated for the poor left to the parish by Col William O'Sullivan Murphy. Col Murphy was a relative of Fr Frank Murphy of Barnabrow.

During Canon Fitzpatrick's tenure, new schools were built in Ballycroneen, Churchtown, Shanagarry and Ballycotton. It also fell to him to oversee the changes in the four churches in the parish necessitated by the new liturgical recommendations of Vatican II.

He died on the 3rd December 1968 and is buried in front of the church in Cloyne.

Fr John Fitzgerald (1910 – 1977)

Fr Fitzgerald was born in Macroom in 1910. He had two brothers and four sisters. He received his early education in the local national school and from there went to St Colman's College in Fermoy. He studied for the priesthood in the Irish College in Rome where he was ordained in the Lateran Basilica on the 26th June 1934. He said his first Mass in his home town of Macroom shortly after. The first couple of years of his priesthood were spent in England. He then came home to be curate in the parish of Aghina. He subsequently served in Aghabullogue, Beeing, Carrigtwohill and Youghal. His next appointment was as parish priest of Meelin, from which he was transferred to Cloyne. In his youth he was quite a formidable sportsman. He won a county football medal with the Macroom team in 1931. During his time in Meelin he started a hurling team which was quite successful. In that enterprise he had the help of his curate, Fr Finbarr Kelleher, who also later became parish priest of Cloyne. It was during his tenure in Cloyne that the new national school was built to replace both the Girls' School and the Boys' School.

Everywhere Fr Fitzgerald went he was remarkable for his kindness to everyone and his inability to see anything but good in people. His sermons always had a positive message and usually came down to 'Love your neighbour'. He carried this through in his own life down to giving away his own cooker to a needy family in one of his parishes. He said they needed it more than he did. He died prematurely in Cloyne in 1977 having suffered for a while from health problems.

Canon Séamus Corkery (1916 – 2008)

4.9 Canon Corkery
(Courtesy: Denis Cronin)

Canon Corkery was born in Macroom, Co. Cork in 1916. He had one brother and one sister. Their father was a TD who had voted against the Treaty. Their mother and step-mother both died when the children were very young. Maybe it was for this reason that family was so important to him. All through his life nothing gave him greater pleasure than to have his immediate and extended family around him for a family celebration, a birthday, an anniversary or any other excuse he could come up with. Séamus Corkery received his early education in the local national school in Macroom and from there went to St Colman's College in Fermoy. He did his Leaving Certificate in 1934. That year the bishop decided to take ten students from the class for the home diocese. He chose six to go to Maynooth, three for Paris and one for Rome. Séamus Corkery, Joe Kenneally and Con Casey were the ones chosen to go to Paris. The Munster Arcade in Cork supplied the clothes for the young clerical students. There were subtle differences between the outfits worn in Ireland and those in France; for example, the French soutane was belted.

Their first journey to Paris probably took longer than

going to Australia today. They sailed from Dún Laoghaire to Holyhead, then train to London. Having spent the night in lodgings near Victoria Station, the following morning they got the train to Newhaven, from where they sailed to Dieppe. Newhaven to Dieppe was chosen because it was cheaper than Dover to Calais! Then another train journey to Paris. In his account of this journey written over sixty years later, he described his reactions to his new country as if it were yesterday – the French smells of Gauloise cigarettes and garlic, the fields with no ditches, the medieval hill-top churches and his arrival in Gare St Lazare. From St Lazare they got a taxi across Paris where he wondered at the tree-lined streets, the sidewalk cafés with people eating in the sunshine, Place de la Concorde, the Eiffel Tower, the Arc de Triomphe, the Champs Elysées, and, for him, the jewel in the crown, Notre Dame Cathedral, finally arriving at Le Collège des Irlandais. By that time they were too tired to be homesick.[122]

As there were very many other Cloyne students in the college before them, it did not take the new boys long to settle in. In the college they followed a pretty intense course of studies in the Institut Catholique in Philosophy, Theology, French, Sacred Scripture, Church History and Christian Art. One gets the distinct impression that in this last subject Séamus Corkery was in his element. Their professor did not confine his lectures to the lecture theatre but took his students out around the streets of Paris where they admired Roman remains, Romanesque Paris, the beautiful Gothic churches, the work of the Renaissance artists and that of Le Corbusier etc. Some of the churches he mentioned included St Médard which was

---

122   Canon Séamus Corkery. *Memories of 5 Rue des Irlandais and its Students.*

originally dedicated to the Irish Saint Fiacre (Fiachra). He later fell in love with the Impressionists in the Jeu de Paume and in the Musée d'Orsay. The students were allowed to go on walks around Paris, but only in groups. They discovered places like the beautiful gardens and parks for which Paris is famous. The college also had a villa in the suburbs of Paris at Arcueil. Here the young students had space to play hurling and football and generally get some much-needed exercise. At Arcueil there was a cemetery containing the graves of some Irish priests and students who had died in Paris.

There was no going home for Christmas and Easter in those days. At Christmas, the students put on their own entertainment. In 1935, the latest Irish contingent had among them John Finn and Dan O'Mahony. Fr Finn was a wonderful singer as all in Cloyne will remember, as he served here as curate for many years before being transferred to Conna. He must have been a great asset to the Christmas entertainment. Fr Dan O'Mahony was an uncle of the present Cloyne parish priest, Canon Donal O'Mahony. Fr Dan was for a period a very popular curate in nearby Midleton. In his day he was a very skilled hurler who played with his local team during the summer holidays. At Easter the students went on 'excursions'. The most popular venues for these outings were the Great War battlefield sites of the Somme, the Marne and as far afield as the Maginot Line. Most of the battlefields then were as the soldiers had left them: trenches, barbed wire and dugouts with rusting machine guns and other leftover weapons of war. They also went to Lisieux and Nevers.

Séamus Corkery was the last prefect to live in the Irish College which he had to leave in 1939 at the outbreak of World War Two. He and all the other students were brought back to

Maynooth which was quite a culture shock. Mgr Dalton was President of Maynooth at the time. One of his first activities with his new charges was to bring them on a tour of the gardens and encourage them to take up gardening. He said it would be good for their health and would keep them home among their people. Séamus Corkery was one who took that message very much to heart.

He was ordained on the 31st March 1940 and said his first Mass in his native Macroom. He got a week's holidays and was then appointed to Ballindangan. Here he lived in a fine two-storey house about a mile from the church, except that it had neither piped water nor electricity. The water came from a rainwater tank in the roof and a boy with a donkey brought a churn of drinking water three times a week. For light he had oil lamps and candles. Because of the War, soldiers were based in Kilworth Camp and he went to say Mass for them every Sunday. Having been raised in town, this was his first encounter with Stations in people's houses. The former government Minister, Ned O'Keeffe TD, was one of his altar boys!

In 1942, he was moved to Berrings in the parish of Inniscarra. By now his aunt had bought him a Ford 8. Here too his house was about a mile from his church, but he now had electricity and a water pump near the house.

In 1947, he was transferred to Castlelyons where his parish priest was Cloyne native, Fr Nathaniel Smyth. The two got on extremely well from the word go, mainly because they were both 'Paris men'. While he was in Castlelyons, Bridget McCarthy became his housekeeper and stayed with him in Mallow, Aghina and Cloyne. She died at Christmas 1983. Castlelyons Cooperative Creamery was founded in

1916. Watching the farmers bringing in their milk churns reminded him of his previous parish. He himself had a cow and a neighbour took his churn to the Creamery for him. He witnessed Castlelyons grow to become part of Waterford Co-op and then part of Glanbia. In the Holy Year of 1950, he and his brother took their father to Rome. After sixteen happy years in Castlelyons he was moved to Mallow.

There too he took an interest in the progress of the Ballyclough Co-operative Creamery and the Mallow Beet Factory. After a shaky start, he saw the establishment of the Mallow Credit Union of which he was the first chairman. Its first home was in the old garda station next door to Fr Corkery's own house, and which was by then parish property. Mgr Sheedy, the parish priest, gave it to the Credit Union. Fr Corkery's first task was to lodge the money with the local AIB every Monday morning. The new Church of the Resurrection was being built at that time and responsibility for fundraising was given to him. He was very happy in Mallow partly because his brother and family lived there and he was able to visit them often.

In 1974, he was made parish priest of Aghina. Here he was almost home as Aghina is quite near Macroom and many people there were related to him. Fr Anthony Cronin, who later became a curate in Cloyne, was his curate.

After a few years in Aghina he was transferred to Cloyne in 1977 where his curates were Fr P. Halliden and Fr Bertie Troy. As a man who had spent much of his time previously making order out of chaos in various gardens and graveyards, one of his first tasks was to tidy up the Cloyne graveyard and make it accessible for funerals and visitors. He enlisted the help of the late Jimmy Daly and his wife Babs. Jimmy drew up a plan for four concrete paths which would give easy access to all graves. Voluntary labour was organised by Bunty and Kitty Cahill, and a great job was done for which the people of Cloyne and elsewhere will be forever grateful. While in Cloyne he was made a Canon of the Cathedral Chapter. Canon Corkery was always interested in the education of the youth wherever he was stationed and Cloyne was no different. He had the highest praise for the two principal teachers of the schools in his charge, Margaret Hartnett in Ballycroneen and Michael O'Brien in Cloyne. While in Cloyne he had the opportunity to indulge two more of his great passions: namely, his love of the sea and his great interest in art. He exhibited his paintings most years with the Shanagarry Art Group. They were the work of a very talented artist and always had red stickers before the launch was over!

At the age of almost sixty-nine, Bishop Ahern asked him to transfer to Charleville, because he had a job there that needed doing i.e. the reordering of the church in line with Vatican II directives. Canon Corkery was both surprised and shocked, but, as he had always done – he went. He surrounded himself with the best talent he could muster and got to work. The job was tastefully done respecting the beauty of the original building.

He had always planned to retire back to Cloyne to be near the sea, but the presence of the nursing sisters in Charleville who provided an unparalleled service to the old led him to change his mind. When he reached the age of seventy five, he retired and built himself a house in Charleville near the convent. His successor, Fr Maurice Brew, gave him some ground for a garden. His friend, Charlie Wilkins, described him in his column in the Irish Examiner as a priest pushing on into his eighties, making his eighth garden. In his own words: *'Of all the gardens I set up, this is the crowning glory.'* He celebrated his Diamond Jubilee in Charleville in 2000, but did not enjoy great health after that. He was hospitalised in 2003 and diagnosed with osteoporosis. He died in 2008 and is buried in Charleville.

Canon Donal O'Driscoll (1918 – 2002)

4.10 Canon Donal O'Driscoll
(Courtesy: OnStream Publications Ltd)

Canon O'Driscoll was born in Berrings in the parish of Inniscarra where his parents were teachers and farmers. He had one brother and one sister.

Having received his education in St Colman's College Fermoy and St Patrick's College Maynooth, he was ordained in 1944, along with five others from Maynooth, in Holy Rosary Church, Midleton by Bishop Roche.

His first appointment in the diocese was as curate in Rusheen in the parish of Aghina. His parents bought him some furniture and a car. Many priests who came from large families had to take out bank loans to provide themselves with the basics. Many found it difficult enough to repay these loans. Wherever he went, the 'Doc', as he was affectionately known in Cloyne, hit the ground running. Rusheen was no different.

To help with his personal finances, he and his housekeeper raised broiler chickens which they sold at Macroom Market. His housekeeper got 'a small commission'! He admitted that one could live cheaply in those days. He had no electricity bills and no fuel bills. Turf was delivered to him free of charge. There was a constant supply of vegetables and pork when the pig was killed. His other 'enterprise' was geared to the Christmas market. As his neighbours and parishioners were exceedingly generous, his small household could never eat all the turkeys, chickens and geese which he was given for Christmas. His way around this was to catch all the unwanted birds after dark and sell them in the early morning to John Lane Egg & Poultry dealers in Cork. More commission for the housekeeper!

He worked tirelessly for the good of his parish. One of his first efforts was to set up a drama group. His next was a football club for those who preferred the outdoors. This led to the formation of the first GAA club in the parish. As a student in Maynooth he had heard Canon Hayes, the founder of Muintir na Tíre, speaks on several occasions and was very impressed. Canon Hayes's message of community development through self-help was made for the parish in which he found himself, where unemployment and emigration were denuding the countryside. He motivated a few like-minded individuals to set up a branch of Muintir na Tíre. One of their first projects was to build a hall which would cater to the social, cultural and educational needs of the community. Many nights of entertainment were held there in which Fr O'Driscoll played the accordion. His crusading spirit was not to everyone's liking and he was reported to the bishop for acting outside his brief. The bishop ignored the complaint.

His next appointment was as curate in Lisgoold. He immediately got involved in the local branch of Macra na Feirme. Together with the other members, a campaign was started to bring rural electrification to the parish. Some people were afraid of this new power and more were actually superstitious, blaming it for the subsequent bad harvest. In Lisgoold his personal enterprise was not broilers but a cow. At first she supplied him with milk, butter, cream and buttermilk, and even left some butter over to sell in the local shop. Then his housekeeper left to get married so he bought two calves at the mart and went into calf-rearing with the help of a local farmer. When this farmer developed a very serious kidney ailment requiring hospitalisation, Fr O'Driscoll saw the need for an up-to-date dialysis machine as extremely urgent. He approached a young genito-urinary surgeon, Mr Denis O'Sullivan, who had just commenced practice in the city. His friend's family bought the machine which had to be imported from the USA and later donated it to the Bon Secours Hospital in Cork.

After some years in Lisgoold he was transferred to Killavullen. Killavullen was well catered for as regards organisations, having the ICA, a guild of Muintir na Tire, a branch of Macra na Feirme and a GAA club. The new curate conceived the idea of forming a development association, an idea which was enthusiastically received. They did up the local hall in which they had dances, concerts and quizzes among other things. For the younger members of the community he established a branch of Macra na Tuaithe. He also went back to being a student himself, studying for a PhD in the field of Aesthetics which led him to an interest in Music Therapy.

In 1968 he was transferred to Newmarket where he worked

for two years. His project here was to establish a Credit Union. Newmarket at that time held an annual festival. He decided it needed a novel event and the one they/he came up with was Rat Racing! They were no ordinary rats but sophisticated university rats from TCD. The races took place through transparent tubes, bookies were present and betting was brisk! It was while in Newmarket that he developed his interest in poitín. Not all his activities were in the lay sphere. He also set up the Kanturk Deanery Priests Study Group and organised talks from people like Fr Eamonn Goold (now Mgr Goold PP Midleton), Dean Charles Grey-Stack of the Church of Ireland, Bishop Eamonn Casey, Dr Maire Mulcahy UCC, Louis McRedmond and Dr James Good. In these sessions they discussed topics such as Family Law, Children Before the Law and the Family Planning Bill.

In 1969 he was moved to Charleville where he spent thirteen years. There he was heavily involved in developing services for the handicapped. He also helped to promote a project for sheltered housing for the elderly and saw the first phase open in March 1984. Having from an early age worried about youth unemployment, he was an active member of the Charleville Industrial Committee. As Charleville was in the heart of the Golden Vale he felt it had the potential to hold a major annual agricultural and business show. He watched with great pride as the show grew in later years. He was also a very vocal member of the group set up to agitate for the retention of Mallow Hospital.

In 1984, he was appointed parish priest of Churchtown and Liscarroll. Here both villages were well-equipped with organisations which he attempted to amalgamate without success. In line with Vatican II and its emphasis on concepts like Church – the people of God, collegiality, community, and lay involvement – he considered the idea of a parish council. After just one year and four months he was transferred to Cloyne.

Like everything else about the Doc, his arrival in Cloyne was dramatic. He arrived in a sporty Opel, leading immediately to the nickname 'Nightrider' from the then popular television series. His first job in Cloyne was the renovation of the parish church. For the duration Mass was said in the local school. Around this time he retrieved the Costine Chalice from the parish church in Kilworth. He also introduced a healing ceremony at the end of each station mass. To tackle the many problems of dereliction etc. in the town he assisted the Muintir na Tire Community Council in the setting up of a specific Cloyne Development Association. Churchtown South church also needed extensive and expensive renovation which was funded generously by the local community. It was with great joy that he witnessed the rebirth of the Cloyne Races on St Patrick's Day 1993, seventy years after the last meeting was held. He supported generously every organisation in the parish from sport to history and art. In June 1994, he marked the golden jubilee of his ordination to the priesthood, a celebration which he shared with the Ballycotton curate, Fr Dan Coakley, who was celebrating his silver jubilee.

Over the years he was frequently re-elected a member of the diocesan Council of Priests. He served as diocesan representative for two terms on the National Council of Priests in Ireland, and he was honorary secretary for a number of years of the Cathedral Chapter of Cloyne. He was a member of two new committees which to him were very important: the Financial Committee which dealt with priestly incomes and the Retirement Committee. Another effort of which he was justly proud was the magazine Pobal Dé which he started in 1985 with Fr David O'Riordan as its first editor.

In October 1995 he bade farewell to the people of Cloyne when he retired from active ministry. As a parting gift to the parish, he commissioned an icon of St Colman, patron and founder of the parish and the diocese. The iconographer was Fr David O'Riordan, now parish priest of Ballymacoda and Ladysbridge.

Over the years he travelled to many wonderful and exotic places like Russia, the Philippines, India and China. Wherever he went he commented on how the people were working the land. His last project 'Poitín Aoibhinn Teo' did not see the light of day. The Doc who had so many plans for his retirement did not live long to enjoy it. He very soon began to experience serious health problems and died in 2002 and is buried in his native Berrings.

Canon Finbarr Kelleher (1932 – 2015)

Fr Kelleher was born in Clonmoyle, Aghabullogue in Mid-Cork. He received his early education in the local national school. He then went to St Colman's College, Fermoy before going on to St Patrick's College in Maynooth to study for the priesthood. He was ordained along with four other Cloyne students in June 1956. His mother and sister were pictured in The Cork Examiner receiving his first blessing. He was first sent to minister in the diocese of Southwark in England. On returning to Ireland he served as curate in the parishes of Youghal, Araglen, Meelin, Kilbrin, Inniscarra, Ladysbridge and, in 1995, in Cloyne as parish priest, where he succeeded

Dr Donal O'Driscoll. He retired in 2006 and went to live in Ballindangan where he continued to help out as curate until his death in 2015. He is buried in his native Aghabullogue.

4.11 Fr Fitzgerald & Canon Kelleher

(Parish Archives)

Canon Donal O'Mahony

4.12 Canon Donal O'Mahony, P.P.

V. Rev. Patrick Linehan

4.13 Fr Pat Linehan, P.P.

Fr Joe Rohan C.C.

4.14 Fr Joe Rohan, C.C.

Curates of Cloyne Parish

William Collins .... (c. 1824)

Patrick Kearns.. (1821 – 1830)

W. Hogan.. (1830 – 1831)

John Riordan .... (1830 – 1831)

Roger O'Flynn .... (1833)

Thomas Purcell .... (1836 – 1837)

Philip Burton... (1836 – 1845)

Charles McCarthy .... (1838)

Timothy Murphy .... (1839 – 1840)

John Kepple.. (1841 – 1849)

William Daly .... (1846 – 1847)

Thomas Walsh... (1848 – 1855)
(His first three years as curate for Ballycotton)

William Tuomey .... (1850)

John Cullinan.. (1851 – 1852)

Thomas O'Farrell .... (1853 – 1877)
(His first 7 years as curate for Ballycotton, then Cloyne and
briefly administrator in the absence of Canon Eager, PP)

Cornelius O'Connell .... (1856 – 1867)
(His first 4 years as curate in Cloyne, the rest in Ballycotton)

Jeremiah McSweeny .... (1868 – 1884)
(His first 10 years in Ballycotton, the rest in Cloyne)

Edward Tuohig....................................... (1877)

James Barry .... (1878)

Michael Walshe...................................... (1879 – 1882)

Michael Norris....................................... (1883 – 1892)

John O'Riordan... (1885 – 1903)
(He was then appointed PP until 1916)

Bartholomew O'Keeffe .... (1893 – 1894)

John Browne.. (1895 – 1903)

Thomas Roche .... (1904 – 1909)

Daniel Foley .... (1905 – 1925)

Michael Rea.. (1910 – 1915)

Nathaniel Smyth.................................... (1915 – 1916)

Cornelius Murphy.................................. (1916 – 1924)

M. Cusack... (c. 1921)

Michael Ahern .... (1924 – 1932)

Michael Curtin....................................... (1925 – 1930)

Jeremiah Russell .... (1929 – 1935)

Richard Thornhill................................... (1932 – 1937)

Timothy O'Brien..................................... (1935 – 1939)

Edward O'Riordan.................................. (1937 – 1941)

Edmond/Edward O'Callaghan .... (1939 – 1942)

John Cotter .... (1941 – 1945)

Philip Mortell... (1942 – 1945)

Martin Cusack .... (1945 – 1951)

Thomas Fitzgerald .... (1945 – 1957)

John Walshe.. (1951 – 1960)

Donal Ryan... (1957 – 1964)

Cornelius O'Flynn.................................. (1960 – 1967)

John Finn .... (1964 – 1973)

Michael O'Brien..................................... (1967 – 1976)

Bartholomew Troy .... (1976 – 1986)

Patrick Halliden .... (1973 – 1985)

Anthony Cronin .... (1985 – 1990)

Michael Madden .... (1986 – 1992)

David Herlihy .... (1990 – 1996)

Donal Coakley .... (1992 – 1994)

Joseph McGuane .... (1994 – 2003)

Michael Fitzgerald .... (1996 – 2007)

Peadar O'Callaghan .... (2003 – 2008)

Aidan Crowley .... (2008 – 2011)

Joseph Rohan .... (2011 – Present)[123]

123   Various sources including the Diocesan Office, Cobh.

Priests Born in Cloyne Parish who serve /served elsewhere

4.15 Priests of the Diocese- Bicentenary Mass

Fr William Ahern (1772 – 1811)
Fr Philip Mahony (1812/1818 – 1843/1849)
Fr Maurice Geary (1802 – 1850)
Rev. Thomas Ahern (1808 – ?)

Gravestone No 280 in the Cathedral graveyard in Cloyne reads as follows –

> *This tomb has been erected by Philip Ahern of Castlemary in memory of his lamented Brother The Revd William Ahern who departed this life July 20th 1811 Aged 39 years The goodness of his heart, his superior knowledge and the unrivalled manner in which he exhorted his Auditors were such as rendered him an Ornament to the Mission and to human Nature Here also repose the remains of his Nephew(s) The Rev Philip Mahony who died on the 24th of March [1843 or 1849] in the [31st year of his age and the 7th] of his Ministry Rev Maurice Geary who died on the [1-] day of [February 1850] in the [44th year of his age] and the [18th of his Ministry] May they rest in peace. Amen.*

Richard Henchion in his book on the gravestones of Cloyne Cathedral gives a statement taken down from Miss Bridget O'Mahony formerly of Castlemary. The statement is as follows: John Ahern and his son-in-law [Stephen] Myles from Ballymacandrick, Cloyne were executed in Cork. John's son, Father William, had ridden to Dublin seeking a reprieve from the Lord Lieutenant. He got the reprieve but arrived back in Cork too late to save his father and brother-in-law. Fr Ahern himself was executed in 1811 and subsequently buried in Cloyne, his relatives having recovered the body through bribes. They brought it back to Cloyne for burial in the middle of the night.

Fr William had six sisters all of whom are reputed to have had two sons each priests. Ellen married William Mahony of Lisanly and was mother of Philip who became CC Kilnamartyra and is buried in the family grave. Fr Maurice Geary also buried in the same grave was the son of another sister, probably Anstice. According to the late Canon Troy and taken from the Catholic Directory, Fr Geary served as curate in Skibbereen, Aghadown, Lisgoold, Ballymacoda and Macroom. Philip, who had the headstone erected, had a son Thomas born in April 1808, who later became parish priest of Kilnamartyra.

Canon Michael McAuliffe (1849 – 1934)

4.16 Canon McAuliffe
(Courtesy Anne McAuliffe)

Michael McAuliffe was born in Carrigatogher, Cloyne in 1849. He was educated in Mount Melleray and in St John's College, Waterford, where he was ordained in June 1882. His first appointment was as curate at St Patrick's in Huddersfield in the diocese of Leeds. In 1890, he was moved to Holbeck in Leeds to take charge of what was then a small mission dedicated to St Richard. He immediately set to work to build the church of St Francis of Assisi which was opened in 1894. He went on to build two other churches: St Anthony's in Beeston which opened in 1909; and a chapel-of-ease in Holbeck dedicated to Our Lady of Lourdes and St Clare, which opened in 1927. The latter he built and dedicated in gratitude for a cure vouchsafed at Lourdes to a pilgrim from his parish. As a church builder, he was said to have raised about £153,000 in the course of his work.

In 1911, he was made a canon of the Leeds chapter. In 1932, the parish of St Francis of Assisi devoted an entire week to rejoicings for Canon McAuliffe's fifty years of priesthood. One of the city's newspapers, the Yorkshire Evening News, wrote at that time of his achievements:

The task which was before the Canon when he arrived in Leeds from Huddersfield forty-one years ago and took charge of a small, poverty-stricken church in Manor Road, which had a debt of £3000, would have been too much for many a man more faint-hearted. But the Canon, a sturdy and genial Irishman, set to work to change the pitiful state of things, with the result that in twenty years' time he had raised £50,000, which he spent in replacing the meagre church and school, hemmed in by dirty piggeries and stables and a pond, by the fine new church of St Francis, a presbytery, boys' school and parish hall.

Canon McAuliffe died in 1934 and is buried in Killingbeck Cemetery in Leeds. The bishop of Leeds celebrated the Requiem Mass. The canon had continued to work up to six months before his death, and the Tablet Archive humorously stated that *With all his labours, Canon McAuliffe* [had] *found time to be a holidaymaker; for it is known that during a period of thirty-six years he once took three days off.*

Fr James Kearney (1872 – 1937)

Born in Ballycrenane to James Kearney and Catherine Russell, he was baptised in Cloyne on the 2nd October 1872. Ordained in Maynooth, he was appointed to Corpus Christi Parish, Maiden Lane, London (Westminster Diocese) on St Patrick's Day 1908, having already served in several other London parishes. There he remained for close on twenty-five years, celebrating his silver jubilee there in 1922. This was marked by a presentation in which very many prominent Irish Catholics in London took part. In late 1932, it was evident that Fr Kearney was suffering from a serious illness which quickly forced him to enter a nursing home. He died on the 2nd of February 1933. His Requiem Mass in London was attended by many prelates and clergy and by delegations from various

Irish societies. The Irish Free State was represented by the High Commissioner, Mr John W. Dulanty. His lifelong friend, Bishop Cotter, Bishop of Portsmouth who had celebrated the Mass accompanied the body back to Ireland for interment.

Canon Nathaniel Smyth (1879 – 1962)

Born in Tullough, Cloyne to John Smyth and Ellen Millerick, he was baptised in Cloyne parish on 12th January 1879. He was ordained in the Irish College in Paris in 1903. He spent his first ten years in the parish of Wigan in England. On his return to Ireland, he served first in his home parish as curate in Ballycotton 1915–16, then in Donoughmore, Buttevant, Charleville, Kanturk and Cobh. In 1941, he was appointed parish priest of Castlelyons where he ministered until a few months before his death. Church land had been given for the building of the creamery in Ballyarra, and so it was traditional that the parish priest was chairman of the committee. While in Castlelyons Fr Nat served in that capacity and was the last priest to do so. He died in St Paul's Home in Bushmount, Clonakilty on the 7th September 1962, aged eighty-three and in the fifty-ninth year of his ministry. He is buried in the church grounds in Castlelyons next to the famous priest and writer, an t-Athair Peadar Ó Laoghaire.

Canon Laurence Kenefick (1869 – 1947)

Born in Ballybranaugh to James Kenefick and Elizabeth Smith (sic) and baptised in Cloyne on 20th October 1869. He was appointed curate in Ballyhooly in 1920 and served there for a number of years. In 1934 he was made parish priest of Meelin, and was transferred to Blarney in 1937. There he was to spend the rest of his active ministry. In 1940, he was appointed Canon of the Cathedral Chapter. He died in Blarney on the 18th November 1947 aged seventy-eight. In his will he left money to the Maynooth Mission to China, the Medical Missionaries of Mary in Drogheda, the hospice in Harold's Cross, the Sisters of Charity in Blarney, the Youghal branch of St Vincent de Paul, the Brothers of Charity in Lota and many other groups who were involved in helping the poor. On the day of his funeral, Blarney Woollen Mills suspended work to enable its hundreds of employees to attend the Mass and convey their late parish priest out of the village on his last journey to his native Cloyne. The celebrant at the Mass was Fr Nathaniel Smyth PP Castlelyons and a relative of the late Canon Kenefick.

Fr Daniel Kenneally (1880 – 1957)

Born in Ballylanders in the 1880s he was ordained in St Patrick's College, Carlow in 1912. Parish priest of Danville, Wichita Diocese, USA for 40 years. Served under four different bishops. Retired in 1952 to Wilton in Cork. He died on the 7th December 1957 and is buried in Cloyne. His funeral mass was celebrated by Rev. A. Murphy-O'Connor CC Cork, deacon Rev. D. Ryan CC Cloyne, Master of Ceremonies Rev. J. Kenneally CC Cloghroe, nephew. The chief mourners were his brothers John and Martin and his sister Mrs E. McCarthy, Providence. Fr Kenneally was an uncle of the Kenneally and Curtin families of Churchtown South and Ballycroneen.

Fr Michael Kenneally (1879 – 1954)

Born in Ballyregan in 1879. Studied at Mount Melleray. Ordained in Genoa on the 1st July 1903. Spent five years in the diocese of Goulbourn in Western Australia. In 1908, he returned to Ireland and joined the Cistercian Order in Roscrea, where he took the name Ignatius. Having spent 30 years as confessor-priest in the Abbey, he died in 1954 and is buried there.

Fr Martin Kenneally (1850 – 1927)

Born in Ballylanders on the 17th October 1850. He studied in Blackrock College, Dublin where he won a Classics scholarship in 1867 and a prize for Greek verse at the Catholic University examination in 1870. He was junior house-master from 1869 to 1871. He was ordained in 1876 and went to Trinidad. He returned to Ireland in 1883 and joined the Cistercian Order at Mount Melleray, where he took the name Joseph. In 1888, he was sent to Rome as secretary to the procurator of the Order. He subsequently returned to Mount Melleray, but in 1894 he volunteered to go to the Mother House of the Order in Citeaux in France, where he became prior. He was Director of Retreats and Professor of Theology there until his death in 1927.

Canon James Sisk (1841 – 1910)

James Sisk was born in Cloyne to James Sisk and Catherine Ryan and baptised on the 14th September 1841. Two sisters and two brothers were born, one of whom, Mary Ann, married David Lawton of Cloyne. As with most young clerics of his time, he was ordained at the age of 24. He served in Midleton and in Queenstown, where for some years he was President of the Young Men's Society, and Spiritual Director of the Men's Confraternity. From 1872 to 1877, he was curate in Inniscarra. He subsequently served as curate in Fermoy and Cobh. He spent 1885 and 1886 in the United States, having been specially selected by the Bishop, Dr McCarthy, to collect money for the building of the Cathedral in Cobh. In 1896 he became Administrator of the parish of Fermoy, where he remained until 1899 when he was made parish priest of Ballymacoda and Ladysbridge. Here he worked tirelessly to the end of his days for the good of his flock. 'Many were the instances in which he negotiated between landlord and tenant with much success and considerable advantage to the tenant.'[124] While not actively political, his sympathies were known to be on the side of the Irish Parliamentary Party. The report in the Cork Examiner on his death described him as 'one of the oldest clergymen in the diocese of Cloyne'. He was, in fact, only 69. He died on the 3rd November 1910 after a prolonged illness. The solemn high Mass in Ladysbridge was presided over by Bishop Browne. His 'remains were borne through the village on the shoulders of four Cloyne friends'. The chief mourners were Mr Patrick Sisk, his brother, Mrs Lawton, his sister, Mary and Leonora Lawton, his nieces, and Mr David Lawton, his nephew. At the Queenstown Council meeting reported in the Cork Examiner of the 7th November a vote of sympathy was passed, and the Chairman recommended that as many members as possible should attend the funeral. There was also a vote of sympathy from Midleton Urban Council. In his will, he made charitable bequests to St Vincent de Paul, the Lady's Clothing Society of Fermoy, Queenstown and Midleton. He also left monies to be used for the benefit of the poor of Inniscarra and Cloyne. He is buried in the churchyard in Ladysbridge.

Fr James Joseph O'Brien MSC

Fr JJ, as he was always known locally, was born in Cloyne. He attended the Christian Brothers School in Midleton,

---

124   Cork Ex 7 Nov 1910.

a place in which he took a lively interest for the rest of his days. Having been a keen hurler in his day, he always took a particular interest in their Harty Cup failures and successes. He entered the Sacred Heart Order in Cork where he was ordained in 1951. He subsequently went to Rome for further studies in Canon Law. On his return, he taught in the Sacred Heart College in Moyne Park in Galway. He was, for a time, superior of the Community in St Alban's, Hertfordshire in the diocese of Westminster. He then returned to Cork to promote the work of the Missions. He died in Western Road and is buried in St Joseph's Cemetery in Cork City.

Father Thomas McGrath (1911 –   )

Born in Ballyandreen on the 4th April 1911. He first attended Churchtown National School and received his secondary education in St Colman's College, Fermoy. In 1929, he entered St Patrick's College, Maynooth, and was ordained in 1936 for the diocese of Ross. He was appointed to Clonakilty where his duties included the Hospital and Mercy Convent as well as parish work. From there he was sent as curate to Sherkin Island, and then to Glandore where he spent a number of years. He then returned to Clonakilty as senior curate and his final appointment was as Parish Priest of Rosscarbery. A man who loved to travel, he frequently went on holiday with Bishop Lucey of Cork and Ross and Monsignor Barrett to places like France, Spain and as far afield as India. Even though an East Cork man, he was much loved by the people of West Cork. At Glandore, he had his own boat and loved his trips down the harbour. He frequently visited his many relatives in the Ballycotton/Ballyandreen and Shanagarry areas. Three of his nephews also became priests, two Fathers O'Brien from Gortroe, and Father Tom McGrath of Portsmouth Diocese. Bishop Murphy Cork and Ross, Auxiliary Bishop Buckley and Bishop JJ Ahern Cloyne along with a large number of priests concelebrated his Requiem Mass in a church packed with his many friends from the parishes in which he had served.

Canon Francis (Frank) Murphy (1906 – 1990)

Francis Murphy was born in Barnabrow on the 9th May 1906 to Michael Murphy and Johanna Foley. After his education in St Colman's College, Fermoy, he began his priestly studies at St Patrick's College, Maynooth, where he gained his BA and was ordained for the diocese of Cloyne on 22nd June, 1930. Immediately after ordination, he accepted a temporary appointment with the Diocese of Shrewsbury and was sent to St Werbergh's Church, Chester. He returned briefly to Ireland where he worked as a convent chaplain for a short while before returning to Chester where he stayed until 1939.He was then appointed parish priest in Wythenshawe in the Manchester area (1940 – 1959). During his time there he oversaw the building of several schools, churches and presbyteries, as well as being involved in the foundation of a new parish at St Anthony's in Woodhouse Park. In 1959, he was sent back to St Werbergh's in Chester, this time as parish priest. Here he began to raise money for a new church. His experience in Wythenshawe had taught him that after a church, a presbytery and a hall would also be needed. With amazing foresight, he knew that a car park would also be a requirement in the not too distant future, so not every site was acceptable to him. The foundation stone was laid on the 6th September 1964 and reads as follows:

Ad majorem dei gloriam

Et in honorem sancti Columbae

Lapidem hunc primarium sacravit dediquavitque

Ad Rev Franciscum Can. Murphy

Die 6 September 1964

The interior of the church owes much to the vision of Canon Murphy, for everywhere the Celtic influence is evident. The main altar is in Kilkenny and white perlato marble. The tabernacle, high altar, candlesticks, sanctuary gates and sanctuary lamp, baptismal font cover, ciboria and chimes were all fashioned in bronze to designs by the famous Irish artist, Ray Carroll, the work being carried out by Messrs M. H. Gill of Dublin. The suspended cross over the altar was designed and made by Father Benedict Tutty of Glenstal Abbey. The baptismal font is of polished limestone and comes from the Earley Studios of Ecclesiastical Art in Dublin. The pews were made by Messrs F.H. Kenny of Dublin, and the wooden carving of St Columba on the side altar by Frank Haugh of Newry.

Here too he maintained his special interest in education. He served on many committees in the Chester area and in 1962 he became a member of the Cathedral Chapter. He retired in the summer of 1982, but continued to be extremely active in the pastoral life of the local parishes. On the 22nd June 1990 he celebrated his Diamond Jubilee with a Mass in St Werbergh's. In September of that year, at the age of 84, he suffered a heart attack while preparing to say a weekend Mass to help out a serving priest. He died within a few hours. His funeral service was attended by many prominent dignitaries and a huge crowd of his former parishioners. He was buried in the Franciscan Monastery at Pantasaph. He was described as a giant of a man in every way, six foot four in height, and possessed of a great intellect, being a scholar of Greek, Latin and Mathematics, having a vast store of knowledge and a great spirituality, shown in the care he extended to all his parishioners right to the end.

Fr William Daly (1907 – 1991)

Born in Cloyne in 1907, son of John and Mary Daly. He attended the local national school and St Colman's College, Fermoy. He then entered the Novitiate of the Redemptorist Order and was ordained in 1931. In 1936, he was sent to the Philippines where he was to spend the next forty years as a missionary. For the first six years everything was normal and he went about his daily business of holding missions, baptising etc. But then on December the 16th 1941 a violent earthquake shook Iloilo city. Worse was to come. Two days later, during the recreation hour, the priests heard a 'peculiar purring noise'. It was their first sight of Japanese warplanes, thirty of which had come to bomb an important bridge nearby. The first group failed but returned very soon after and bombed oil tanks and residential areas. Fr Willie and his colleagues went to the hospital to help out, but the following day good sense forced them to head for the hills one by one or two by two. They wandered around from barrio to barrio holding missions because that was their duty, but also to take the people's minds off the ever present danger of capture.

During the second week of July 1942, news reached them that Father Rector and the Brothers had been put into 'concentration' and that their church and monastery had been confiscated. They began to wonder seriously if the right thing for them to do would be to surrender to the Japanese lest others should suffer accused of hiding undesirables. They decided to wait another while but to be extremely cautious and stay on the run. On his 35th birthday, August 27th 1942, he heard that the Philippine offensive against the Japanese had begun. This made life even more dangerous.

In the account he wrote of the war years he described 'poor evacuees, forcing themselves on in rain and mud. The old were there, the blind also…. They roll their belongings into a coloured cloth. Any animals they can bring, they force along.' Later he tells of how they, the priests, are forced to travel around in the dark to avoid meeting the Japanese. His positive mental attitude, which probably kept him going during these awful years, is evident here. Instead of describing how frightened they must have been he says, 'There was a touch of the romantic, as beneath the silvery moon, we crossed rivers, standing two to three feet deep in water …. This is the most pleasant of all times for walks in the Philippine Islands – early morning before the sun rises. It means coolness – no perspiration. The most soothing of all walks is a walk at such an hour through the dewy grass.' With a certain amount of amusement and resignation he tells of his Philipino carriers who insist on stopping to take their morning bath in spite of the danger lurking at every bend in the road.

From January to May 1943, they stayed in a house which they referred to as Camp Ford, but then set off again about their business, by now barefoot. By the time they reached Barrio San Vicente, they were extremely hungry and were driven

to sit outside the school house and beg for food. As the
Philippines are made up of 7107 islands, about 2000 of which
are inhabited, it is not surprising that some of Fr Willie's
travels were in boats. One such journey to Barrio Caleso
is described as follows by him in his memoirs – 'Our wee
boat, two small canoes tied together, would have capsized
if we had to voyage another ten yards, losing thereby all
my portemanteaus, Mass-kit, everything – and perhaps my
life…. We were always within a foot of water, so when the
water rose (waves), women kept pumping it out with one tin
and their hands.'

At a certain point, they decided they had better give
themselves up to the Japanese, as by not doing so, other people
could suffer torture or death if accused of sheltering priests
on the run. They walked barefoot the five miles to where the
Japanese colonel was. They met the Japanese on November
9th 1943. Their initial encounters were pleasant enough, but
things changed very quickly. A preliminary investigation
lasted an hour. They were later accused of being connected
with the Philipino army and of only pretending to be priests.
This second 'procedure' took about three hours at the end of
which they were told they could lie down on the floor and
sleep. They were given nothing to eat. The following morning
they were given a very dirty house as a concentration camp
and told to sweep it. Some time later they were walked
about seven miles to another town. They were then taken
by boat to Iloilo, still without food except for a few bananas
they managed to find. When they must have thought things
couldn't get much worse, they were flung into a concrete jail
cell. Here they received two helpings of rice per day, one at
9am and the other at 5pm. 'A mysterious-looking vegetable

was added, if we wished'. The following morning they were separated and kept in solitary confinement for a further two weeks, at which time they were set free. Even though they made their way back to their base, things were not easy for quite some time. Fr Willie described the food they had to eat – rice, sugar and coffee, so they decide to plant their garden. They managed to grow sweet potatoes, squash and Indian corn. Meat was out of the question. Once, a 'find' of a tin of Japanese fish was made to last for three days.

Towards the end of the war, they were in more danger from the American bombers who were attacking the nearby Japanese posts. They decided to leave. They left by night, crossing the swamps in a canoe and then walking knee-deep in mud, all talk forbidden. After about three nights they met a bunch of Philipino guerrilla soldiers who looked hungry and in need of clothes. They begged the priests for vests and socks, which they gave them. The end of their journey was Alimodian where they met the bishop and the parish priest, and were fed royally. Here, he says, 'there is no more shortage of eggs, chickens and vegetables, as in Iloilo city'. So it was back to work!

Finally, the war ended and they were able to go back to their own house to find it was inhabited by United States Medicals whom they found very friendly and helpful. Shortly after the end of hostilities Fr Willie admitted to feeling worn out, and was very glad when word reached them that they could go home to Ireland. On the way home he visited a leper settlement and met many Irish-Americans among the troops with whom they travelled.

After a well-earned rest Fr Willie returned to the Philippines where he saw everyday life and religious practice evolve, not least those changes brought about by Vatican 11. In March 1990, he wrote his account of the War years from which most of the above is taken. In July of the following year, he died in Mount St Alphonsus in Limerick and is buried in the Community Cemetery.

Fr Joe Daly

Cousin of Fr Willie. He was also born and reared in Cloyne. His mother had a shop in Church St, Cloyne. As a young boy, he was known to be very 'wild'. One of his exploits was to walk around the top of the Round Tower. He was ordained to the priesthood in St Kieran's College in Kilkenny, and said his first Mass in the Young Men's Society Hall in Cloyne. His aunt-in-law, Fr Willie's mother, and her daughters organised the 'do' after the Mass. The young Fr Joe became a chaplain in the British Army. Having served for some years, he left the priesthood and married. He died suddenly in England while playing tennis.

Monsignor Thomas J. O'Shea (1911 – 1973)

Born in Cloyne on February 26th 1911, son of Michael O'Shea and Louise Godde, but resident in Port Chester, New York by the time he began studies for the priesthood. He attended Don Bosco College, Newton, New Jersey and St Francis Seminary in Loretto. He was ordained by Bishop Richard T. Guilfoyle in the Altoona Cathedral on May 18th 1939. Fr Tom spent half of his priestly life in Altoona, Pennsylvania serving as Assistant Pastor of the Cathedral of the Blessed Sacrament from the time of his ordination, until being named Pastor of St John the Evangelist Catholic Church, Bellefonte in May 1956.

Monsignor O'Shea served the Altoona-Johnstown Catholic diocese in many official capacities. He was vicar forane of the Centre-Clinton County Deanery, and appointed Chairman of the Diocesan Liturgical Commission in 1959, and diocesan consultant in 1964. He was also Diocesan Moderator of the Legion of Mary for many years and Master of Ceremonies for Bishop Guilfoyle while he was stationed in Altoona. On the Diocesan Marriage Tribunal, he served as notary from 1948, Pro Synodal Judge from 1959 and Pro Synodal Examiner from 1964. He was also the Bishop's representative at the Pennsylvania Catholic Conference. He was named a domestic prelate with the title of Right Reverend Monsignor on February 22nd 1955.

One of the highlights of his later years was his holidays in Cloyne where he stayed with the lady he called, Auntie Ciss (Ciss Molloy of River St). His godmother was recorded as Mary Ellen Molly (Molloy). He died aged only 62 after an extended illness in Centre Community Hospital, Bellefonte. At the moment of his death he was survived by one brother, Michael of Rye, N.J., his mother having died just two months before him.

Fr William Kearney (1916 – 1998)

Born in Ballycrenane on the 2nd July 1916. He was baptised on the 4th. He received his early education in Churchtown South NS and then went to St Colman's College, Fermoy. He was ordained in St Patrick's Seminary in Carlow in 1944, after which he was appointed to St Patrick's Church, Southampton. He later became an army chaplain, and on leaving the army he became parish priest of St John the Evangelist parish in Wallingford, Oxfordshire, where he oversaw the rebuilding of the church bought in 1924. He was also chaplain to the local hospital. He served in Wallingford from 1958 to 1970. He next became parish priest of St William of York parish in Reading, where he also looked after St Joseph's Boarding School. On his retirement he came home to Ireland and settled in Glanmire. He was a relative of Fr James Kearney and Fr Nathaniel Smyth. He died on the 6th November 1998 and is buried in Cloyne with his parents, David and Kate (née Smyth) and his sister, Margaret.

Fr Jeremiah Russell (1883 – 1938)

4.17 Fr Jeremiah Russell
(Courtesy: Patsy O'Mahony)

Born in Kilteskin to Edmund Russell and Mary Flynn of Leadington. He was baptised in Aghada on the 14th June 1883. Fr Jeremiah was the second youngest of a family of six. He received his early education in the local school and then went to St Colman's College, Fermoy. He served as curate in Castlelyons, Cloyne and Charleville. His sister, Hannah, who had trained as a nurse in England, was his housekeeper. His favourite pastimes were walking on the beach in Ballycroneen and fishing in the local haunts. He died on the 7th March 1938 at the young age of 53 while serving as a curate in Charleville. He is buried in the cemetery in Cloyne.

Fr Thomas McGrath

Born in Ballyandreen third of seven children, nephew of Fr Thomas McGrath of Rosscarbery, he attended Churchtown South National School and St Francis College, Rochestown. Many of the Rochestown priests spent their holidays in Ballycotton at that time. He then went to St John's Seminary in Waterford to study for the priesthood. In those days a young man would not be accepted for the diocese of Cloyne if he had not attended St Colman's College in Fermoy, so the young Tom McGrath opted for the diocese of Portsmouth. Portsmouth was quite familiar to him as he saw Frs Denis Walshe and William Kearney when they came home on their summer holidays. He would also have heard of Frs William O'Sullivan and Jack Moore from Midleton who also spent their lives in that diocese. He was ordained by Bishop Cornelius Lucey, Bishop of Cork and Ross, in the parish church of the Immaculate Conception in Clonakilty in June 1969, where his uncle was senior assistant curate.

He was first appointed to St Joseph's Parish in Aldershot in Surrey, which he soon discovered was the home of the British Army. It was a quick learning curve for him, getting used to doing priestly work in a totally new environment and living far from home. England at that time had a great mix of people from all parts of the world which was completely different to the Ireland of the 1970s. The soldiers he ministered to were at that time over and back from their tours of duty in Northern Ireland. Being a typical Irishman he enjoyed all the sporting opportunities that the south of England had and has to offer in the way of football, rugby and horse-racing.

Having spent some years there, he was moved to St James

Parish in Reading. His next move was his promotion as parish priest to the new parish at Bracknell. From there he was appointed parish priest of the parish of the Sacred Heart of Jesus and St Peter the Apostle. In 2011, he assisted in the concelebrated Mass for the dedication of the new church which he had worked hard to see built. Bishop Hollis appointed him Vicar General of the diocese in 2005 and with that came the title of 'Monsignor'. This was a task which covered the whole diocese and involved a lot of travelling from Jersey to Oxford. On the positive side it gave him the opportunity to meet many different and interesting people. He served as Vicar General for eight years and in all spent thirty five years as parish priest. When he reached the age of seventy he decided it was time to take a step backwards. He now works as curate in the historic city of Winchester.

Fr Philip Hegarty

Born in Ballinvoher, Cloyne, son of Peter Hegarty and Kate Hegarty. He attended Ballycroneen National School and St Colman's College, Fermoy. He then went to St Patrick's College, Maynooth where he was ordained on the 24th April, 1949. The Hegarty family had the distinction of having two brothers priests in the diocese and four sisters nuns in the Mercy Order, and another brother, Patrick, a TD who became Junior Minister for Agriculture. Fr Philip served as curate in Macroom, Aghinagh, Castletownroche, Killavullen and Ballyhooly. He then became parish priest of Castlelyons. He died on the 10th January 1997 in the 48th year of his ministry and is buried in Cloyne with his father and mother, his brother, Patrick, and sister-in-law, Eileen.

Fr Richard A. Hegarty

4.18 Priests of the Diocese - Fr Richard Hegarty, 3rd from left.

Brother of Fr Philip and also born in Ballinvoher. Like his brother, he went to school in Ballycroneen and then to St Colman's College, Fermoy. He studied for the priesthood in St Patrick's College, Carlow and was ordained on the 6th June 1963. He first served in Chepstow in Wales and in Crowthorne, Berkshire. On his return to Ireland, he served as curate in Youghal, Ballynoe, Kilcorney, Conna and Charleville. He then became parish priest of Killavullen where he is currently PE, CC.

Canon John Terry

**4.19 Priests of the Diocese –
Canon Terry 2nd from left front.**

Born in Ballylanders near Churchtown South. His early education was received in Churchtown NS and in St Colman's College, Fermoy, from where he went to St Patrick's College in Maynooth. He was ordained in Maynooth in 1958. His first appointment as curate was to the diocese of Cardiff where he spent two years. On his return to Ireland he spent the next two years as curate in the parish of Castlelyons, where his senior curate was Fr Séamus Corkery. It would seem Fr Corkery held him in very high regard even at that young age. He praised his dedication to the Liturgy. Fr Terry spent the next fifteen years away from the parish work which he enjoyed, because he was appointed Dean of St Colman's College in Fermoy. Famous all over the diocese for his interest in and love of music, he spent many years in charge of the Diocesan Choir. In 1977, he was appointed curate in Saleen in the parish of Aghada. Here he ministered to many relatives and friends, but after six years he was transferred again, this time to Mitchelstown. In 1992, he was made parish priest of Kanturk, where he remained until retirement in 2008.

During this period he was made a Canon of the Cathedral Chapter. Canon Corkery also praised his skills in carpentry, masonry and electricity, and retirement probably allows him more time to hone these. However, the present shortage of priests means he is called on very frequently to help out his confreres.

Fr Thomas O'Brien MSC
Born in Cloyne to Teresa (nee O'Brien) and Sonny, brother of Marina, Paul and Fergal. He is a nephew of Father JJ. He attended the local National School. He also entered the Sacred Heart Order and was ordained in 1983. He did parish work for a time in St Mary's Northwood, Kirby, Liverpool, and then spent a year in Spain. He served as Counsellor in Dundalk before heading to Venezuela on missionary work.

Fr Robert Anthony Morrissey
Born in Cloyne, son of local vintner, Edmund Morrissey. He received his early education in Cloyne National School and the Carmelite College in Castlemartyr. He then entered the Carmelite Novitiate in Loughrea, Co. Galway. He subsequently studied at St Patrick's Seminary in Carlow and did a one year course in All Hallows College in Dublin. He was ordained in St Colman's Parish Church in Cloyne in 1987. He was for five years a teacher in his Alma Mater, the Carmelite College in Castlemartyr, and then moved to Avila Carmelite Centre, Morehampton Road in Dublin. He then spent three years on the Missions in Edo State in Nigeria, after which he returned to Berkeley Rd parish in Dublin 7. He then transferred back to his native diocese of Cloyne and became curate in Glanworth where he served from 2002 -2007. His next move was to the Cathedral parish in Cobh for a further

six years. He is currently parish priest of Churchtown and Liscarroll.

Brother Gerard Canisius Brickley

Born in Cloyne he attended the local national schools. He received his secondary education from the Christian Brothers in Midleton and subsequently joined the Order. He was sent on the English mission where he taught at Prior Par School and at the CBS in Bristol. He later returned to Baldoyle in Dublin where he acted as bursar. He died in Baldoyle on the 26th February 1986 aged 64.

Sisters born in Cloyne from 1900 onwards

Sr Dympna McGrath, Ballyandreen. Mercy, Passage West.

Sr Assumpta Hegarty, Ballinvoher. Mercy, Passage West.

4.20 The Hegarty family, Ballinvoher
(Courtesy: Adrianna Hegarty)

Sr Peter Hegarty, Ballinvoher. Mercy, Passage West and Mallow (Superior).

Sr Finbar Kenneally, Ballyregan. Good Shepherd, Leaderville, Perth, Western Australia.

Sr Josephine Kenefick, Ballybrenaugh. Presentation, Midleton.

Sr Rosarii Walsh, Ballycroneen. Mercy, Kinsale.

Sr Immaculata Hegarty, Ballinvoher. Mercy, Staff CUH and Passage West.

Sr de Lourdes Hegarty, Ballinvoher. Mercy, Kinsale (Superior).

Sr May Terry, Ballylanders. Presentation, Midleton.

Sr Mary Ivers, Churchtown South. Presentation, Parish Worker Ecuador.

Sr Carmel Higgins, Ballinvoher. Mercy, Passage West.

Sr Eilis McGrath, Ballyandreen. Mercy, Clonakilty (School Principal).

Sr Peg Kenneally, Ballycatoo. Poor Servants of the Mother of God, Carrigtwohill and Bristol.

Sr Bella O'Shea, Cloyne. Poor Servants of the Mother of God, Portslade, East Sussex.

Sr Maura Ring, Cloyne. Mercy, Cobh.

In the photograph of the Hegarty family, Paddy (back row) was a T.D. for Cork North-East and a Minister of State in the FitzGerald government in the 1980s.

Sacristans

Some of the sacristans of the Church included,

Mary Ring (née Lawton) early 1930s-1942

**4.21 Unidentified, Mrs M. Ring, Mary Agnes Ring
Willie Ring, Mary Curtin, Kay Curtin,
Nicky Ring, (grandchildren of Mrs Ring)**
(Courtesy: Philomena Hurley)

Mary Agnes Ring 1942-1973

Hannah Ring 1972-1982

Hannah was followed by Betty and Denis Cronin. These were followed by Bridie McCarthy. When Bridie retired, Betty and Denis Cronin took over again.

4.22 Mary Agnes Ring
(Courtesy: Philomena Hurley)

4.23 Hannah Ring
(Courtesy: Paddy Ring)

4.24 Bridie McCarthy

**4.25 Cardinal Murphy O'Connor,
Betty and Denis Cronin, Bishop William Crean**

CHAPTER 5

Parishioners Past and Present

William Kenealy (1828 – 1876)

A plaque on the wall in River St marks the site of the birthplace of William Kenealy. He was born here on the 1st of July 1828. The plaque was unveiled on Sunday, the 29th of May 1988 by Mrs Maeve Kenealy King and Mrs Kathleen Kelly, granddaughters of William Kenealy.

5.1 Birth place of William Kenealy
(Courtesy: Patricia Lyons)

The son of a blacksmith and small farmer, he became a schoolmaster at the age of twenty and was appointed head teacher in Churchtown South. He was dismissed from his post for publishing an inflammatory proclamation addressed to St Colman's Club in 1848. Later he taught in the diocesan college in Derry, and, from there he went to Leeds, where he edited the Catholic newspaper *The Lamp*. He returned to Ireland to edit the *Tipperary Leader*, and, in 1856 he became editor of the *Kilkenny Journal*. Through his editorials he helped to create the climate which enabled Gladstone to introduce and pass the Land Act of 1881, which secured for the tenants of Ireland the means to obtain ownership of their lands.

William Kenealy was twice Mayor of Kilkenny in 1872 and 1873. He is best remembered for the famed song, *The Moon behind the Hill*.[125]. He died in 1876 at the early age of 48 and is buried in St Patrick's Cemetery in Kilkenny.

Nicholas Joseph Clayton (1840 – 1916)

5.2 Nicholas Joseph Clayton (Courtesy:http:// claytonproject.wordpress.

Nicholas Joseph Clayton, the Irish-born architect of Galveston, Texas, was the son of another Nicholas Joseph Clayton and his wife Margaret (nee O'Mahoney). He was born in Cloyne, Co. Cork, on 1 November 1840. His father died when he was still a child, while his mother appears as a confectioner in Cloyne in Slater's National Commercial Directory of Ireland for 1846. In 1848 his mother emigrated with him to Cincinatti, Ohio. After working in various cities as a plasterer, marble carver and architectural draughtsman and serving in the United States Navy during the Civil War, he settled in Galveston, Texas, where he established a flourishing architectural practice. He was one of the first professional architects in Texas. Clayton dominated

125 Nuala Roche, *William Kenealy,* in The Book of Cloyne (Editor: Pádraig Ó Loingsigh), p198.

Galveston architecture from 1873 to 1900, most prominently in the 1880s and 1890s. He designed Catholic churches and other buildings for Catholic religious orders, public and commercial buildings and private houses including St Mary's Cathedral, Austin, Texas and Gresham House, Galveston.

5.3 St Mary's Cathedral, Austin, Texas
(Courtesy: U.S. National Register of Historic Places)

5.4 Gresham House
(Photo: Rosa Morgan, Galveston)

He died in Galveston on 9 December 1916. Clayton married Mary Lorena Ducie of Galveston on July 6, 1891. They had five children. Clayton was a parishioner of St. Patrick's Church. He was a member of the Galveston Garten-Verein and the Catholic Knights of America, the Knights of Columbus, and the Ancient Order of Hibernians. He died in Galveston on December 9, 1916, and is buried there at Calvary Cemetery. A collection of his drawings and papers is in the Alexander Architectural Archive at the University of Texas at Austin.[126]

John Madden (1844 – 1918)

John Madden was baptised in St Peter's and St Paul's, Cork City, on 25th May, 1844. In January 1857, his family migrated to Melbourne, Australia, already having spent some time in London, where John Madden senior was admitted as a barrister to the Victorian Bar. The family lived in the suburb of Flemington. Madden was enrolled in St Patrick's College in East Melbourne. He later studied at the University of Melbourne.

In October 1875 he was made Minister for Justice in the McCulloch government. He lost his seat at the following election, but was temporarily retained as Minister for Justice until 1876, when he was elected to the Assembly for the seat of Sandridge. After McCulloch's resignation in May 1877, Madden left the ministry, but returned in March 1880 when he was made Minister for Justice in the Service government.

---

126   Irish Architectural Archive, Directory of Irish Architects 1720-1940, 2015; Alexander Architectural Archive, University of Texas, Austin; Robert A. Nesbitt and Stephen Fox, "CLAYTON, NICHOLAS JOSEPH," *Handbook of Texas Online*(http://www.tshaonline.org/handbook/online/articles/fcl22), accessed August 07, 2015. Uploaded on June 12, 2010. Published by the Texas State Historical Association.

Madden retired from politics in 1883 to concentrate on his successful legal practice, which flourished during the Victorian land boom of the 1880s. In 1887, he had a thirty-room mansion built for himself and his family in Chapel Street in St Kilda East. It was named 'Cloyne', after the town where he was reputedly born. He was appointed Chief Justice in 1893 and was knighted later that year.[127]

Denis Collins and Ellen Kirk

Denis Collins was for many years, in the mid 19th century, engaged as a navigator, and was prominently identified with the marine interests of Cork city. He commanded numerous vessels and had made many trips to foreign lands. He was known as a skilful and competent navigator and at his death in 1868 it was justly stated that the port of Cork had lost a good and useful man.[128] A son of Denis and Ellen, named Denis, was baptised in the Church in Cloyne in 1868.[129] A number of years after her husband's death, Ellen emigrated to the U.S. with her family. They settled in the Elizabeth port section of the city of Elizabeth, Union County, New Jersey, where she was a faithful communicant of St Patrick's Catholic Church. The son, Denis, rose to the rank of Major-General of the Second Brigade in the State of New Jersey.

---

127 Wikipedia contributors. "John Madden (judge)." *Wikipedia, The Free Encyclopaedia*. Wikipedia, The Free Encyclopaedia, 12 Apr. 2015. Web. 7 Aug. 2015.

128 Carl Schlegel, Schlegel's *American Families of German Ancestry*, Genealogical Publishing Co.,2003, pp141-142

129 04986/08, Cloyne- Catholic Parish Registers at the NLI

John McCarthy (1837 – 1926)

John McCarthy was born in Ballymacandrick in February 1837. His parents were Daniel and Mary (nee Rumley). He was one of nine children. As a young boy he suffered from impaired health and was unable to do manual labour, so his family felt that he should receive a better education than the rest of his siblings. His first school appears to have been in a private house not far from his home. In later years he tells of being *very homesick though only a hundred feet from my doorstep….* He goes on to say: *When old enough to find my way across country farms I was sent to a private school conducted for many years by a very kind old gentleman in one of the rooms of his residence. This schoolroom was furnished with long, solid, unpainted oak tables, having for seats long, backless benches.* According to McCarthy, this school was still operating nearly thirty years later and run by the same teacher. Here he studied reading, spelling, writing and arithmetic, and, as he got older, English grammar. His next move was to a National School.

Tough days were to come for the young scholar. His mother died on St Patrick's Day 1850, and his father, hoping to better the life of his young family, took them all to America. They arrived in New York in 1853 and all the members of the family became scattered for years. John went to work on a farm in New York State where he earned $4 a month. He mentioned his blistered hands, sore muscles and chronic homesickness. However, he was lucky in that his employers were very kind and 'provided the best literature of the time'. From there he went to work for a banker, and after three years he had enough saved to allow him to attend Fort Edward Collegiate Institute on the Hudson River where he matriculated. While he was attending school he worked for his board and taught part-time. On finishing his studies, he taught for a while in

Fort Edward. His father meanwhile returned to Ireland but all the children stayed in America.

He went on to teach in several other institutions in the New York area. In 1871 he married another teacher, and in 1872, in order to better his financial position got a job as Superintendent of the City Schools at Vinton, Iowa. Here he met with success both as a teacher and because of his administrative ability. Four years later he was prevailed upon to revive the nearby Blairstown Academy which had closed because of lack of funds. It was here that John McCarthy really came into his own as a teacher and where his work was most highly appreciated.

In 1874, the state of Iowa passed a law establishing Normal Institutes to give specialised training to young persons intending to teach in the public schools of the state. For many years John McCarthy was one of the leading teachers in these Institutes. He was also prominent in his community. He fostered the idea of library associations and reading circles. He was familiar with the Temperance Movement of Father Mathew, and, under the influence of Wendell Phillips's stand against slavery, was a confirmed abolitionist.

His philosophy of life was simple. He would go out into the cornfields and persuade the young people to come to school and develop the gifts they had. Service for the betterment of mankind was one of his basic principles. His earthy common sense was evident in some of his favourite sayings: *Don't demand the sweet-flavoured wealthy apple from the crab-apple tree; and you are the master of your fortune, but more so the maker of your own mind.*

Sadly, at a certain point he was obliged to give up teaching because of defective hearing. He continued for a while in the field of education as custodian of Morningside College where he was always on hand to help and advise students. The unnamed author of a pamphlet on his life was of the opinion that the words of Edmund Burke regarding his former teacher, Abraham Shackleton, might equally well be applied to John McCarthy: *He was indeed a man of singular piety and rectitude of heart, and he had along with these qualities a native elegance of manners which nothing but genuine good nature and unaffected simplicity of heart can give.* John McCarthy died in Sioux City, Iowa on the 10th of October, 1926. [130]

Michael Vincent McCarthy (1918 – 1975)

Michael McCarthy, MCC, was born in Cloyne to James McCarthy and Catherine Meade on the 14th February 1918. He was baptised three days later, his sponsors being James Cuddigan and Lizzie Terry. He ran the family business in Church St, Cloyne and in June 1950 was first elected to Cork County Council. He was re-elected in 1955, 1960, 1967 and 1974. He was the only East Corkman on the Wilton Hospital Regional Board. He was also a member of the Southern Housing and Sanitary Committee. In August 1974 he was taken ill suddenly. He continued to do his Council work but never recovered fully from his illness. He died on the 5th February 1975. The next meeting of the Council was adjourned as a mark of respect after a vote of sympathy was moved by Mr Denis J. O'Sullivan. In his tribute Mr O'Sullivan said that in twenty five years on the Council Mr McCarthy had made no enemies. The County manager praised his 'quiet diplomacy'.

---

130   John McCarthy, Pioneer Schoolmaster, presented to U.C.C. Library, 1929.

Christy Ring (1920 – 1979)

Christy Ring is perhaps Cloyne's most famous son: a hurler who played for the Cork senior team.

5.5 Christy Ring
(Courtesy: Mrs Philomena Hurley)

Christy was born in 1920 and first excelled at hurling during his school days. He arrived on the inter-county scene at the age of sixteen when he first linked up with the Cork minor team, before later lining out with the junior side. He made his senior debut in the 1939–40 National Hurling League. Ring went on to play a key part for Cork over the following twenty-four years, and won eight All-Ireland medals, nine Munster medals and three National Hurling League medals. An All-Ireland runner-up on two occasions, Ring also captained the team to three All-Ireland victories.

In a game as mythologised as hurling, Ring's universally accepted pre-eminence is remarkable. Throughout his lengthy career, Ring made 65 championship appearances for Cork, more than any other player in the county's history. His retirement came prior to the start of the 1964 championship.

Ring is widely regarded as one of the greatest hurlers in the history of the game, with many former players, commentators and fans rating him as the number one player of all-time. He has been repeatedly voted onto teams made up of the sport's greats, including the Hurling Team of the Century in 1984 and the Hurling Team of the Millennium.[131]

In addition to Christy Ring, Cloyne has produced some other notable Cork hurlers and camogie players including Donal Clifford, the Cusacks, the O'Sullivans and the Costines.

131   Wikipedia contributors. "Christy Ring." *Wikipedia, The Free Encyclopaedia.* Wikipedia, The Free Encyclopaedia, 10 Jul. 2015. Web. 8 Aug. 2015.

5.6 Pioneer Group, Cloyne
(Courtesy: Bunty Cahill)

5.7 De Valera Rally, Cloyne Cross
(Courtesy: Nora Brett)

5.8 Cloyne & Shanagarry Macra
(Courtesy: Mary Ellen Maguire)

**5.9 Going to Mass: Mary O'Neill, Ballydavid;
Ellen Hoare, Tullogh; Ellen O'Flynn, Ballydavid**
(Courtesy: Kathleen Walsh)

5.10 Boy Scouts Cloyne, 1983
(Courtesy: Kitty Cahill)

Pageants 1980s

For a few years in the 1980s the Church staged passion pageants during the Holy Week period. This was a major spectacle, with a large cast and choirs' participation. A number of performances were held with large attendances.[132]

The 1986 pageant was titled 'Choose Christ'.

The cast comprised:

THE CHRISTUS: Patrick O'Keeffe

The Baptist: Derry Keogh

Tax Beggar: Tony Barry

Levi: Dick Coffey-Walsh

Levi's wife: Betty Dorgan

Rich man: William Scannell

---

132   Donal O'Driscoll, Canon, *Parish to Parish*, OnStream Publications Ltd, 2002,

Sick boy: Mark Kenneally

Pilate: The Very Rev Dr O'Driscoll, P.P.

Pilate's wife: C. Flynn

Barabbas: Wm Scannell

Simon of Cyréne: Donal Higgins

Mary: Mary Dorgan

Selomé: Betty Cahill

Veronica: Catherine Greaney

Mary Magdalene: Nuala Whyte

Angel of the Agony: Jo McCarthy

Soloists: Ber Higgins, Ml P. Cahill

Holy Women: M. Harty, M. Coffey-Walsh

The Apostles: Jerry O'Sullivan, Stephen Beausang, Bob McCarthy, Niall Fleming, Dick Coffey-Walsh, Tom Canavan, Con Lehane, Tony Barry, Liam Walsh, Batt Murphy, Billy Walsh, Peter Hegarty.

Sanhedrin: John O'Lomasney, Diarmuid Savage, Donie Cahill, Ted Motherway, Domnic Neville, Johnny Murray, Jerry Cronin

The Roman Army: Derry Falvey, Oliver Beausang, Pat McCarthy, Bill O'Brien, Jim Murphy, Tony Walsh, Phillip Cahill, John Scanlon.

The Choir:

Basses: Richard O'Brien, Liam Cusack, Danny Cahill, Maurice Griffin, Liam Murray, Patrick McCarthy, John Motherway, Paddy Hegarty.

Tenors: Ml P. Cahill, Declan Hyland, Philip Cahill, Patrick Walsh, Brian Ahern, Michael O'Brien.

Sopranos: Geraldine Hyland, Eileen Sherlock, Catherine Walsh, Mgt O'Driscoll, Annette O'Driscoll, Nora McCarthy, Siobhán O'Driscoll, Mgt Forbes, Hannah Ring, Peggy Cronin, Ann O'Brien, Mary O'Brien.

Altos: Ber Higgins, Ann Whyte, Kay Ahern, Helen Shinnick, Noreen Deane, Evelyn Hyland, Helen Lynch, Frances Kelly, Theresa O'Brien, Claire Kenneally, Elsie O'Sullivan, Rosaria McCarthy, Pauline McCarthy, Nora Neville, Mgt McCarthy, Eileen Cashman, Josie Reaney, Brid Daly, Geraldine O' Brien, Kay McGrath, Linda Cusack, Margaret Cahill, Marie Walsh, Kathleen Costine, Josie Power.

Organist: Brid Walsh

Instrumentalists: Edmond Walsh, Norma Barry, Patricia Barry, Rory Allen

Credits: Austin Brosnan, Brian Daly, Fr B. Troy, C.C., Ann Cronin, Mona Geaney, Ann O'Callaghan, Kitty Cahill, Mgt Hartnett, Manuel Fashions.

5.11 Passion Play, 1989
(Courtesy Maria Walsh)

5.12 Passion Play, 1989
(Courtesy Maria Walsh)

The 1989 pageant was titled, 'Fisher of Men'.
The cast comprised:

CHRISTUS: Patrick O'Keeffe
Mother of the Apostles: Mary Dorgan
James & John: J. O'Sullivan/F. McCarthy
Women in the Courtyard: K. O'Flynn/M. Barter
Mary Magdalen: Marie Walsh
Ruth: Catherine Greaney
Pilate: John Cronin
Barabbas: John Kenefick
Angel of the Agony: Teresa Horgan
Mary: Bina Leahy
Nicodemus: Jimmy Murphy
Simon of Cyrene: Donie Higgins
Pilate's wife: Mary O'Mahony

The Apostles: Derry Keogh, Dick Coffey-Walsh, Jerry O'Sullivan, Finbarr McCarthy, Tony Barry, Dan Oosthuizen, Seamus Crowley, Liam Higgins, Niall Fleming, Philip O'Neill, Donie O'Connell, Denis O'Shea.

Sanhedrin: The Very Rev Dr O'Driscoll, P.P., John O' Lomasney,

Ted Motherway, Terry Birch, Eamonn Dorgan, Donie Cahill, Gerry Cronin, Con Lehane, Jim Murphy.

The Roman Army: Billy Dunne, Oliver Beausang, Philip Cahill, Billy Scannell, Ned O'Donovan, Pat McCarthy, R. Cusack, Tomas O'Brien, M Cahill, B. O'Brien.

Children: Linda Archer, Sinead O'Donoghue, Nessa O'Shea, Bernadette Stack, Catherina Fitzgerald, Angela Erangey, Sinead Casey, Karen Kearney, Michael O'Sullivan, Colm Crowley, Kevin Crowley, Mark Crowley, Gerard Ring, Eanna Falvey, Eoin McCarthy, Carl McAuliffe.

The Choir: Soloists: Patrica Connery, Margaret Forbes, Michael O'Brien, Michael P. Cahill.

Tenors: B. Aherne, M. P. Cahill, P. Cahill, G. Costine, Ml Deady, Ml Kenneally, D. Hyland, M. O'Brien, P. Walsh, E. Purcell.

Basses: J. Ahern, D. Cahill, Dd Cahill, J. Motherway, L. Cusack, P. Hegarty, P. McCarthy.

Sopranos: P. Cronin, N. Neville, H. Ring, C. Walsh, M. Forbes, E. Sherlock, M. O' Brien, M. O'Driscoll, A. O'Driscoll, A. O'Brien, G. Hyland, M. McGrath.

Altos: N. Deane, F. Kelly, E. Cashman, J. Reaney, B. Higgins, L. Aherne, A. M. Ring, K. Cahill, C. Kenneally, H. Lynch, E. O' Sullivan, P. McCarthy, R. McCarthy, M. McCarthy, L. Cusack, M. Ring, A. Naughton, S. Morrissey, M. Ahern, G. O'Brien, M. Cusack, B. Cronin, B. Daly, N. Fitzgerald, A. Smyth, R. Shinnick, E. Cashman, J. Cahill.

Organist: Bríd Walsh
Instrumentalists: Rory Allen, Norma Barry

Stage Manager: Billy Walsh
Assistant Stage Manager: Js Rigney

Credits: Margaret Hartnett, Kitty Cahill, Margaret Barry, Ann O'Callaghan, Ann McAuliffe, Austin Brosnan, Tallow Community, Brian Daly, R. Murphy, Eddy Fitzgerald, Ml McGrath, McCarthy Bros, Mr. O'Riordan, Bunty Cahill, Jn Savage, Billy Scanlon, Sean Dineen, Mona Geaney, Donal Clifford.

Shanagarry Guild of the ICA

The Shanagarry Guild of the ICA (Irish Country Women's Association) was set up in 1987.[133] Its members are from all parts of the parish and beyond.

5.13 First Committee Meeting Shanagarry ICA
(Courtesy: Mary Cullinane)

Within the ICA all members are very active and have won many accolades in all types of competition. The talents within the group are singing, dancing, talking and listening - which

133   Information provided by Mary Cullinane.

guarantees a great night. Excursions are very popular and over the years we have gone as far as Rome and Scotland. Each year we have an evening's outing and day trips. We have had a walking tour of some of our beautiful local towns: some that stick out were a visit to Barry's Court Castle and a tour of our own Cathedral here in Cloyne. All these events are always well-attended by both members and friends and, of course; we have tea and a chat afterwards. We also have a very active walking group during the summer months in both Churchtown and Cloyne. Our monthly meeting always has a speaker or demonstration and is always very enjoyable.

As well as various activities such as participation in competitions, talks, excursions etc, much needed funds are raised for various charities. Since 2007 an annual remembrance mass is held in November.

Mrs Mary O'Connell, Coolbay

One of a number of people that lived to be over 100 years of age in recent times was Mrs O'Connell (Mame) of Coolbay. Born in 1906 she was baptised in St Colman's Church. Her maiden name was Glavin and she married William O'Connell in 1938. Her cottage was a great place to get all the local news.

5.14 Mrs O' Connell, Coolbay

5.15 Inspecting the Costin Chalice
(Courtesy: Terry Costin)

Canon O'Mahony and Terry Costin from Chicago inspecting the Costin chalice in 2009. Terry's Costin ancestors lived in Co. Waterford in the 19th century.[134]

5.16 Patrick (Sonny) and Catherine Crowley, Ballybrannigan
(Courtesy: Pat Fitzgerald)

---

134 Private correspondence with Terry Costin.

The photograph shows the Crowleys on the day of Patrick's 100th birthday and Catherine's 96th birthday. Patrick received the President's cheque and letter from President Mary McAleese that year in 2011 and went on to enjoy three more years, receiving a medal each year from the President. Patrick and Catherine were married in Churchtown South Church in October, 1941 and celebrated 72 years of married life.[135]

5.17 Billy Walsh,
Chairman of Cloyne Parish Pastoral Council

5.18 At the Reception after the Opening Mass
Martha Wall, Brian Wall & Bridie McCarthy

135   Information supplied by Pat Fitzgerald.

5.19 Rev. Kevin Scallon, Donie Cahill, David Cahill

**5.20 Eileen Eaton, Betty Dorgan,
Rev. Kevin Scallon, Betty Cronin**

**5.21 Members of the Cloyne Literary and Historical
Society with Cardinal Murphy O'Connor**

(Photo: Billy Walsh)

5.22 Parishioners with Cardinal Murphy O'Connor

CHAPTER 6

Church Plate, Vestments and Records

Church Plate

In the bishop's visitation of 1785, the bishop records that Cloyne has one silver chalice belonging to the parish or 'rather the Union'.[136] He also notes a second silver chalice associated with the chapel. There are two extant chalices from the early 17th century associated with the parish church. The details of the first are given in the Journal of the Cork Historical and Archaeological Society which records,

The chalice is of silver gilt, hexagonal stand, alternate panels, plain and engraved; one panel has an antique crucifix engraved and a very large spear and (presumably) a sponge on a reed, and a large skull underneath.[137] The inscription records the name Maurici Costin and the year 1604. Maurice Costin is recorded as a priest in Cloyne in 1617.[138]

6.1 The Costin Chalice

---

136   Eric A. Derr, *op. cit.*

137   Memoirs of the Redmon family, Journal of the Cork Historical and Archaeological Society.

138   Ibid.

6.2 Inscription on the Costin Chalice

6.3 The Miagh Chalice

Stephen Meagh FitzGarrett, a Cork merchant, with extensive land holdings including some in East Cork is mentioned in the Court of Claims, 1663.[139] He died in 1637. James Miagh, who was Vicar Apostolic of Cork and Cloyne, had a brother Garrett, in the early 17th century.[140] Another Miagh, Robert, was also Apostolic Vicar in Cork and Cloyne around the same time. One Sir Robert Miagh is recorded as having reconciled to Catholic worship the cathedral of Cork and Cloyne in the early 17th century.[141] Meade families are recorded living in the parish of Cloyne in the Tithe Applotment Books.

139 Geraldine Tallon, Court of Claims Submission and Evidence, 1663, Irish Manuscripts Commission, 2006, p 356.

140 *Calendar of the State Papers relating to Ireland in the reign of James I, 1603-1625,* p 22.

141 Memoirs of the Redmon family, Journal of the Cork Historical and Archaeological Society.

6.4 Inscription on the Miagh Chalice

6.5 Family crest on the Miagh chalice

The Bishop John Quinlan chalice donated to the church on the occasion of Bishop Quinlan's visit to Cloyne.

6.6 Bishop John Quinlan chalice
(Photo: Betty Curtin)

Vestments

In 1785 there were two sets of vestments belonging to the parish, one set for the chapel in Cloyne.[142] The importance of the vestments can be gleaned from the bishop's visitation of 1818 in which he specifically records examining them and stating that they belong to the parish. In 1728 the vestments and altar linen are recorded as in good order. Some mid 20th century linen is shown in the photographs. Also shown is table linen and detail, the crochet work of the late Mrs Daly of Cloyne.

---

142   Eric A. Derr, op. cit.

6.7 Mid 20ᵗʰ century vestment

6.8 Mid 20ᵗʰ century vestment

6.9 Detail mid 20th century vestment

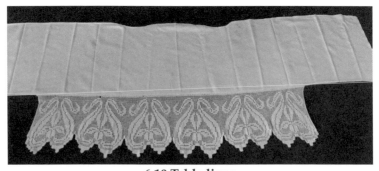

6.10 Table linen

6.11 Celebration of Mass

6.12 The Tabernacle

Registers

Year	Number of Baptisms Recorded	Comments
1791	77	See footnote. a
1792	186	See footnote. b
1793	149	Many pages missing
1793-1803		Re records c
1803:1804	58: 243	
1805	260	
1815	274	
1820:1821	184: 241	
1829	238	
1836	313	Including triplets
1839	291	
1840	283	
1842	297	
1845	324	
1847	219	
1849	203	
1855	134	
1861	167	
1865	156	
1870	174	See footnote. d
1875	154	
1880	112	Gaps in page
1885: 1890	108 : 80	
1895: 1900	82 : 78	
1905 : 1910	77 : 86	
1915 : 1920	42 : 68	

6.13 Baptisms in Cloyne Parish

The requirement to keep baptismal registers was addressed at a diocesan synod conducted by Archbishop Butler in Thurles, 1782.[143] It is noteworthy then that the first records from Cloyne parish are from a few years after this. The following are details of some early baptism records for Cloyne.[144]

(Footnotes)

a   Commencing August 2nd. Many pages missing from the original records
b   Commencing February 19th. Many pages missing
c   All records and baptisms from Dec. 1st 1793 to October 10th. 1803 have been lost or destroyed. Next book commences October 1803
d   Cf page 359 year 1870

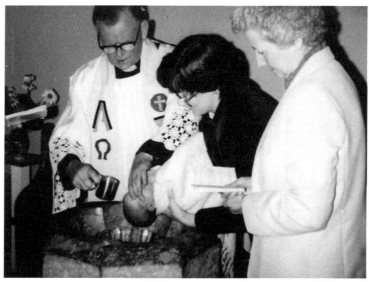

6.14 Baptism of Fiona Cahill in 1981
(Courtesy: Anne McAuliffe)

143   Michael A. Mullett, *op. cit.,* p 187.
144   Compiled by Margaret Hartnett

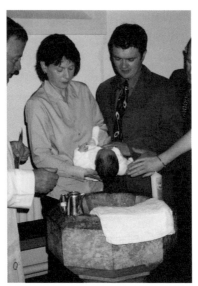
6.15 Baptism of Aidan McGrath in 2000
(Courtesy: Mary McGrath)

6.16 Baptism of Clare Cusack
(Courtesy: Bunny Cusack)

In the bishop's visitation of 1828 he records that the Registers for Cloyne which he inspected in Midleton were correct.[145] There is no mention in earlier visitations of inspecting the Registers.

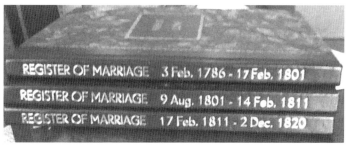

6.17 Registers

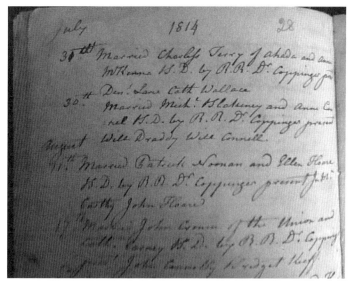

6.18 Page from Register

145   Eric A. Derr, *op. cit.*

6.19 Marriage Ceremony in 1962
(Courtesy: Anne McAuliffe)

The photo 6.19 is of the marriage in 1962 of John McAuliffe and Anne Harney. The chief celebrant is Canon Fitzpatrick.

Informal Records

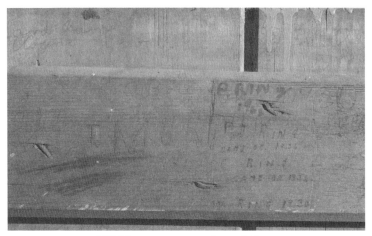

6.20 Names on a cupboard door

6.21 Names on a cupboard door

CHAPTER 7

Timeline

1815

It was *circa* 1815 that construction work commenced on St Colman's Church. Land had been provided some years earlier and the Church was not completed at the time of the then parish priest's – Fr Scanlon – death in 1820. Records are available of some early visitations by the bishops to the Church. In these visitations, confirmation of children was a big event in the life of the parish.[146]

1823

In January 1823, the ship, *Weare*, from Bristol was shipwrecked southward of Ballycotton with the loss of 23 lives. There were thirteen survivors. Local people provided every assistance they could.[147]

Kilmahon added to parish

In 1835, Kilmahon or Shanagarry was added to the parish of Cloyne. It formerly belonged to the parish of Ladysbridge and Ballymacoda. Kilteskin would appear to have been handed over to the parish of Aghada at the same time. Prior to this in the old parish registers, the parish is referred to as the United Parishes of Cloyne, Churchtown and Kilteskin.[148]

---

146   Eric A. Derr, *op. cit.*
147   Irish Shipwrecks database
148   Liber Chronicus Cloyne (unpublished)

Processional Cross

The antiquary, John Windele visited the church in 1838. He recorded on his visit,

> *In the Vestry Room we saw an old brazen Crucifix, one evidently of the old time; the priest said he understood it had crowned the apex of the Old Market Cross which formerly stood in the Square of Cloyne. I do not believe it. The little figure of the Redeemer on it, the Socket etc show that [it] was once used in processions.*

He also saw in the vestry a chalice, dated 1636, and deduced that it was coeval with the crucifix.[149]

7.1 Processional Cross, Cloyne,
drawn by John Windele in 1838
(Courtesy: Royal Irish Academy)

---

149   Cormac Bourke, *A Bell and Staff from the Day collection and related medieval metalwork,* in the Journal of the Cork Historical and Archaeological Society, 2014, pp130-131.

The Famine Period

With the failure of the potato crop in Ireland in 1845, a great famine ensued. By the time of the harvest in 1846 conditions had deteriorated to a significant extent. People became more vocal in their demands for relief. In September about 110 men entered the town of Cloyne. They demanded bread from all the baker shops 'which demand they were compelled to give'. They left peacefully again but threatened that they would return in greater numbers on the following Friday.[150] By 1847, the living conditions of the majority of the poor labouring/cottier class in East Cork deteriorated to an extent never witnessed before or since.[151] The Church in Ireland was concerned about the famine, the failure of the potato crop, the export of corn and the totally inadequate response of the London government.[152] In January 1847, the rector of Cloyne/Aghada wrote to the editor of the *Cork Constitution* detailing the extent of deprivation and death which was so common in the area. Fever and starvation were rampant throughout the Midleton Union, which includes Cloyne, in the spring of 1847.[153] In 1847 one M O'Sullivan writes from Cork, telling the rector in Rome, that the Americans are pouring in a great supply of breadstuffs. In the same year the bishop of Cloyne acknowledges receipt of money from Cardinal Fransoni for the poor. [154]

In 1848 the famine caused appalling suffering and misery. Fr Russell, parish priest of Cloyne, along with his curates, John

---

150 Sean Horgan, *Famine and Politics in Midleton Poor Law Union 1845-1851*, Litho Press 2012, pp67-69.

151 Ibid p16.

152 The Kirby Collection Catalogue, Irish College Rome, Part 2 Years 1836-1860.

153 Sean Horgan, *op. cit.* p17.

154 Cullen Collection – Master Collection, Irish College Rome.

Kepple and Thomas Walsh, were among the signatories of a letter of Catholic clergy of Cloyne and Ross to the Queen, in which they stressed their loyalty, obedience and sense of responsibility, but felt that in view of the widespread discontent among all classes, English legislation was totally inadequate to improve the social conditions of the people. They therefore requested the Queen to summons the Irish parliament of Lords and Commons in Dublin. It need hardly be said that their request was not complied with.[155] In the same year, a poster circulated in Cloyne calling for the formation of a repeal club in the town. According to the protestant rector of the town, this was posted "within the walls of the Roman Catholic chapel". There were fears among the protestants of a rebellion and additional Constables were sanctioned to be set up for the protection of protestants in the Cloyne/Ballycotton area.[156] In 1849, a request by the Rev W. Rodgers, from Shanagarry, a protestant clergyman and trustee of the Irish Reproductive Loan Fund for Cloyne, to have repayment of £400 deferred until after the harvest was refused by central authorities. This refusal letter is in Appendix A.

While Midleton Union suffered a 20% drop in population between 1841 and 1851, the rural part of Cloyne fared worse with a 30% drop in population. In the 20 year period between 1841 and 1861 the population of Cloyne Electoral Division fell by close to 60%. The Famine had a devastating effect on Cloyne and its hinterland. The immediate impact of the Famine and emigration was more pronounced for Cloyne than Ballycotton or Churchtown South. Over time the coastal areas of the parish suffered very large population declines. Inch Electoral Area, part of which is in Cloyne parish, had a

---

155   op. cit.
156   Sean Horgan, op. cit. pp80-82.

population of around 3,000 in 1841. In 2002, this figure was about 400, that is over an 80% decline in population.[157]

In the 1860s it is recorded that on Sundays the church was overflowing with worshippers.[158] Mass attendance increased after the famine.

John, the father of one of the Manchester Martyrs – Michael O'Brien - was living with his sister Mrs John McCarthy, in Ballymacandrick, Cloyne, in 1867. The family had been ejected from their farm in Ballymacoda some years earlier.[159]

1847

In January, 1847, the ship, *Sirius*, was shipwrecked close to Wear's Cove, Ballycotton. From a crew and passengers of ninety-one, nineteen lives were lost. [160]

Emigration

Since the early 18th century around eight million people have emigrated from Ireland. Of this number, perhaps five million left in the first seven decades of the 19th century. In the mid 19th century young Irish men and women had a one in three chance of emigrating. In fact the scale of departure was so large that by 1890 some 40 per cent of all Irish-born people were living outside their country of birth.[161] In 1844, the bishop of Cork in a letter to the rector of the Irish College in Rome, states that families are leaving for

---

157 AIRO, All-Island Research Observatory/ Maynooth University.
158 The Cork Examiner, 1st October, 1862.
159 The Cork Examiner, 27th November, 1867.
160 Irish Shipwrecks database.
161 Donald M. MacRaild, *Irish Migrants in Modern Britain, 1750-1922,* Macmillan Press Ltd., 1999, p9.

British North America and New South Wales.[162] In 1864, T.W. Croke of St. Colman's College, wrote to the rector of the Irish College in Rome of the deplorable state and the alarming extent of emigration. 64,000 left by 'one line of boats' from Queenstown between January 1st 1863 and January 1st 1864. Two years later Bishop Keane in a letter from Cobh to the rector states that emigration is taking 1,000 per week from this part of Ireland and they are happy to go.[163] Many people from Cloyne emigrated to Great Britain the United States and elsewhere in the world. The majority of these would have been familiar with Cloyne Church as children. They may have been baptised, received their First Communion, or have been confirmed in the Church.

Two young orphan girls from Cloyne were sent to Australia between October, 1848 and August, 1850.[164] They were Bridget Donovan, aged 19, daughter of Denis and Mary Donovan married in Cloyne and Ellen White, aged 18, daughter of John and Ellen White, also married in Cloyne.

Bridget Colbert (1848-1913), daughter of William and Margaret Kenealy, Cloyne, went to Australia in 1866 with her brothers Edmund and William. [165]

A list of those whose birthplace was Cloyne, from the 1881 U.K. Census is provided in the following table.[166] Thirty years earlier, in 1851, 25 people are recorded as having being born in Cloyne.

---

162 Cullen Collection – Master Collection, Irish College Rome.
163 The Kirby Collection Catalogue, Irish College Rome, Part 3 Years 1861-1866.
164 Valda Strauss, *Irish Famine Orphans in Australia*, in the Mallow Field Club Journal, 1993, Vol II.
165 Brian Trainor, *Researching Irish Australians: Directory of Research*, p10.
166 Ancestry.co.uk

Name	Birth Year	Name	Birth Year
Robert Bourke	1866	Anne Browne	1845
Edward Clayton	1811	Ann Clymore	1823
Francis Cotter	1809	Kate Cotter	1821
Maria Cotter	1830	Patrick Creamer	1843
Frederick Daly	1842	Cora De Vries	1872
Thomas Doran	1864	Jane Drewitt	1817
Gerald Fitzgerald	1859	William Fogarty	1827
Patrick Haley	1850	Patrick Hanley	1864
William Lloyd	1857	Michael Manning	1855
John Murphy	1824	Johannah Murphy	1826
John Murphy	1846	William Murphy	1853
Eliz Reeves	1811	Edmund Scanlon	1820
Margaret Somers	1849	Thomas Sullivan	1853
Michael Sullivan	1860	Mary Wigmore	1808
E.J. Wilkinson	1823	Richard Higgins	1838
Margaret Regan	1833	William Livomey	1861
Jessie Muir	1834		

7.2 People of Cloyne birth, U.K. Census 1881

The names of Irish immigrants being sought by their relatives as published in the Boston Pilot between the years 1843 and 1869 for the parish of Cloyne:[167]

Patrick Ahern, Thomas Ahern,
Michael Barry, Ballyduff,
Timothy Brennan, Denis Buckley,
Bartholomew, Honora and Catherine Carroll,
Michael Cashman, William Cashman,
James Cotter, Ballyfinn,
John Cotter, Ballybane,
John Cuddigan,
Mary Cuddigan, Tullough,
Thomas Cuddigan, Tullough,
Margaret Cullinane, Commons,
Patrick Curtis,
William Daley, Shanagarry,
John Delaney, Patrick Desmond,
John Dorgan, Kilmacahill,
Michael Dwyer, Ballyrobin,
Ellen Egan,

John Harnet,
William Harty, James Healy, Maurice Healy,
Ann Higgins, John Higgins,
John Hannen, Sleveen,
Michael Keefe, Thomas Keefe,
Denis Keeffe, Ballybraher,
Edmond Keeffe,
Jeremiah Keeffe, Ballybraher,
John Keeffe, Ballybraher,

---

167   From the Cloyne Literary and Historical Society Facebook page.

Mary Keeffe, Ballybraher,
Catherine Kenely, Kilmahill,
James Kenely, John Kenely,
Martin Kenely, Kilmachill
Mary Kenely, Kilmachill,
Mrs. Kenely, Kilmachill,
James Kenneally, Martin Kenneally, Maurice Kenneally,
Julia Magrath,
John Maher, Clough,
Martin Mahony, Kilteskin,

John McCarthy,
Charles McCarthy, Kilmachill,
Patrick McCarthy, Ballymacandrick,
Bridget Millerick, Ballymaloe,
David Millerick,
James Murphy, Ballycotton,
Thomas Murphy, Ballycotton,
Catherine Murray,
Margaret Norris,
Margaret O'Connell, Shanagarry,
Mary O'Connell, Shanagarry,
Michael O'Connell, Glanaurtine,
John Prendergast,
Michael Prendergast,
John Power,
Mary Power, Mary Regan,
Mary Regan, Ballybraher,
Mary Roche,
John Scanlon,
Hanora Scannell, Ballybraher,
John Scannell, Ballybraher,

Mary Scannell, Michael Scannell, Patrick Scannell,
James Sheehan,
John Sheehan,
James Sliney, Maytown,
Patrick Sullivan,
Catherine Walsh,
Margaret Walsh,
Patrick Walsh,
William Walsh

James Cotter, Ballyfinn,
Thomas Drinan, Ballyfin.

Advertisements in the New York Irish American Weekly included the following with Cloyne connections.[168]

9th August 1862

INFORMATION WANTED If Miss Mary McGrath, a school teacher by profession, and formerly of Cloyne, County Cork, Ireland, will make known her address, through the Irish American, or the 'personals' of the New York Herald, she will hear from a friend whom she met about two years ago on board a Hudson River Passenger boat, while in company with another young lady named Maggy.

---

168 'The Midleton Archaeology & Heritage Project', posted by Damien Shiels, May 23th, 2015, taken from *Irish Relatives and Friends* by Laura Murphy DeGrazia and Diana Fitzpatrick Haberstroh.

12th May 1866

David Wallace of Connecticut, uncle of Ellen Fitzgerald, Kilbree, Cloyne, was looking for her whereabouts.

15th February 1868

INFORMATION WANTED of John and Thomas Lewis, who left Ballintrim, Cloyne 27 years ago. When last heard of, they were in New York City. Their brother Maurice was looking for information about them.

7th November 1868

William Finn was looking for information on his brother Thomas, from Cloyne, who was in Massachusetts.

6th March 1869

John Hogan, Ballywilliam, Cloyne, who moved to Chicago from New York 13 years earlier was being sought by his cousin Catherin Battersbee (nee Higgins). He would hear something to his advantage.

4th September 1869

Hanora Cullinane who was in the U.S. four years was seeking her sister Margaret, from the Commons, Cloyne, who went to the U.S. 15 years earlier.

From the U.S. passport applications, 1795-1925, the following from Cloyne are recorded.[169]

Name	Year of Birth	Name	Year of Birth
Timothy Cahill	1890	Patrick Hyde	1873
John Crotty	1855	Daniel Kenneally	1883
Daniel Fitzgerald	1899	Francis Power	1895
Timothy Hartnett	1862	Frederick Sheehan	1904

**7.3 Some people from Cloyne who made
U.S. passport applications**

One of those who emigrated to America, in 1844, was Bishop John Quinlan.

Another who left Ireland was Bishop John Cotter. Another was Paul McKenna Terry. He was born at Kilva, received his early education at Ballycroneen N.S. and then St Colman's, Fermoy. He emigrated to the U.K. and became a medical doctor. He was a devout Catholic. Of his children, Bernard, who was in the Australian Royal Air Force, was killed in Libya in 1942; John, captain of the Hampshire Regiment was killed at Caen by a German sniper in 1944; and Philip, who was in the Staffordshire Regiment in India, died during a voyage in the Indian Ocean at the end of World War II.[170] Paul McKenna Terry was an uncle of Edmund Terry who was wounded in the Clonmult Ambush.

169   Ancestry.com
170   Kevin Terry, *Terrys of Cork 1600-2000*, pp193-209.

Education

In 1807, there were six schools in the parish with 377 pupils.[171] At this time, hedge schools also played an important part in educating children. A state system of primary education was introduced in 1831. In 1876, the then administrator of the parish, had a notice in The Cork Examiner, 24th August, that a new national school, St. Colman's Academy, St Colman's Square would provide teaching in Latin, Greek and French as well as Commerce, Mathematics and English. The objective was to ensure that children of 'humble' parents would have the opportunity to enter various colleges and the civil service. A concern of the parish priest in 1898 was the enforcement of the rule requiring children of the local school in the town, to stay in school until 4p.m. without a warm meal at 1.30p.m. He indicated that it was affecting school attendance and that it would impact on the health of the children, especially in cold weather: *It is too much to expect poor parents who take their own dinner at 1 or 1.30 p.m. to leave their occupation to prepare another meal for children at 4p.m.*[172]

1865

In 1865 the ship, *Eugenie*, was shipwrecked near Ballycroneen, with a loss of 13 lives, from a total crew of about 25. This was close to other shipwrecks in the area, including the *Ibis*. The impact some of the shipwrecks off the coast of Cloyne can be gleaned from the following passage:

---

171 Padraig O'Loingsigh, *Education*, in The Book of Cloyne, edited by Padraig O'Loingsigh, p275.
172 Parish Records, (unpublished).

Patrick Cronin who lives in Ballylanders graphically recounts details of the wreck, because on that night his father was christened and the story has been passed down from father to son. Some survivors were in fact brought to the Cronin family house during the christening celebrations and were given hospitality and comfort for their distress.[173]

1867

In March, 1867, the ship, *Florida,* was lost off Ballycotton with 37 crew drowned.[174]

UK Parliamentary Election 1868

Cork County returned two M.P.s to the U.K. parliament for much of the 19th century. There is evidence of church involvement in the 1868 election with respect to Cloyne. *The Cork Examiner* on 13th October of that year, reported as follows:

Pursuant to the Bishop's instructions a meeting of the parishioners of Cloyne, Shanagarry and Churchtown, took place in the sacristy of the Roman Catholic Church, Cloyne, on Sunday, the 11th instant; the chair was taken by the venerated parish priest the Very Rev. John Eager, V.G., it was proposed, seconded, and unanimously resolved:

That Messrs Downing and Smith Barry be supported at the ensuing County Election. Delegates to the County Meeting were then chosen.

It would appear that there was a preference by some of the electors of the parish in favour of Downing, as a notice

---

173   Margaret Hartnett, *Sea Lore,* in The Book of Cloyne, (ed. Pádraig Ó Loingsigh).
174   Ibid.

appeared in *The Cork Examiner* the following day that they intended to hold a meeting on the following Sunday in support of the candidature of Downing. There was also strong support from local clergy for Downing.

1894

The wrecking of the barque *Cooleen* was the saddest of all, according to Jim Murray of Ballyandreen. It was wrecked in Ballytrasna in 1894 with the loss of 10 lives.[175]

1904

When Fr O'Riordan was appointed parish priest in 1904 a large gathering of the citizens of Cloyne presented him with an address. There are some 88 signatures to this address. The townland or street where each of these people resided is recorded. The five pages of signatures are shown in Appendix B.

The First World War

The Irish Volunteers was a military organisation established in 1913 by Irish nationalists. It was ostensibly formed in response to the formation of the Ulster Volunteers in 1912, and its declared primary aim was "to secure and maintain the rights and liberties common to the whole people of Ireland.[176] Following John Redmond's appeal for recruits for the British Army in September 1914 the Volunteer movement split into The Irish Volunteers and The National Volunteers. Over 90% joined the National Volunteers and enlisted in the 10th and 16th (Irish) Divisions of the British

---

175   Ibid.
176   Mark Cronin, *To the Blackpool Front,* The Collins Press, 2014, p38.

Army, the rest remaining with the Irish Volunteers. In August 1914 there were 30,000 Irishmen in the British army.

The reception given to the Irish Volunteers at this time can be gleaned from the statement of Thomas De La Rue, of Mitchelstown, in 1955.[177]

> On returning to Mitchelstown after the St. Patrick's Day parade in Cork city in 1915 the Mitchelstown Company received a hostile reception from the local "separation women" (wives of soldiers serving with the British Army) and their followers.

> The Mitchelstown Company participated in a parade in Limerick city in May 1915. Amongst those who marched that day were Padraig Pearse, Toni Clarke, Ned Daly, Thomas McCurtain, Terry MacSwiney, Sean MacDiarmada and Eamon de Valera. Other units from the counties of Cork, Tipperary, Limerick and Dublin were represented. The march through parts of the city was through a barrage of abuse from thousands of excited women - British soldiers' wives and their supporters. Bottles, stones and missiles of all kinds were hurled at the parade as it passed through Irishtown district. This area was inhabited mainly by the relatives of those serving or who had served in the British Army. Pro German Sinn Fêiners we were called by this crowd as they showered abuse on us. When returning after the parade, the members of the Cork, Dublin and Galtee contingents had to fight their way to the railway station.

So at the beginning of the First World War there was general support for Irishmen to join the British army. The Irish

177   http://www.bureauofmilitaryhistory.ie/reels/bmh/BMH.WS1224.pdf

Catholic Church, by and large, supported John Redmond and the Irish Parliamentary Party's position in relation to the war.[178] Many people from Cloyne enlisted. At least twenty one Cloyne people lost their lives in the war and many more were wounded.[179] The Royal Naval Reserve Service Records Index includes the following persons born in Cloyne:

William Driscoll, born 1881

John Lawton, born 1885

Robert O'Neill, born 1885

John Joseph Power, born 1893

Paul Walsh, born 1876

Campaign medals awarded to merchant seamen born in Cloyne include:

Michael Rourke, born 1876

Pension records for people born in Cloyne include:

Michael Ahern, Michael Daly, Nathaniel Dawkins, Daniel Driscoll, John Grady, Owen Kelly, William Stanton and Robert Walsh.

The service record includes the following Cloyne people:

James Brien, Daniel Cahill, John Collins, David Costine, Maurice Cotter, William Foley, Richard Harrison, Richard Heaphy, John Higgins, John Kirby, William Kirk, John Lawton.

---

178 Mark Cronin, op.cit. p71.
179 www.ancestry.co.uk; Gerry White and Brendan O'Shea, editors, *A Great Sacrifice Cork Servicemen who died in the Great War,* Echo Publications (Cork) Ltd, 2010.

People of Cloyne birth who died in World War I

William Barry, Sec. Batt. Royal Irish Rifles. Killed in action, October 1914 in Flanders. Buried in Pont-du-Hem Military Cemetery, La Gorgue.

Daniel Cahill killed in action, in November 1914 in Flanders. He was the son of Thomas and Mary Cahill of Church St.

George Cahill, Machine Gun Corps. Killed in action, May 1918, in Flanders aged 24. He was husband of Hannah Cahill of Main St. Name on Soissons Memorial.

Timothy Cahill, Royal Garrison Artillery. Died October 1918, in Flanders aged 25. He was the son of John and Hannah Cahill of Spittal St. Buried Cantaing British Cemetery near Cambrai.

John Condon, died August 1917, aged 17, in Flanders. He was from Chapel St.

7.4 John Condon Memorial plaque
(Courtesy: Betty Cronin)

George Dawkins, died May 1915, France and Flanders. He was the son of Susan and Henry Dawkins of Barnabrow.

Michael Fitzgerald, Royal Munster Fusiliers. Died March 1918, in Flanders aged 29. He was son of John and Mary and husband of Ellen all from Spittal St. Name on Pozieres Memorial.

John Hannan, died in Britain, April 1918, son of Kate Hannan and Michael Hannan of River St.

Thomas Hartnett, died of wounds, December 1917, Western Front, son of Martin and Ellen Hartnett, River St.

7.5 Memorial stone to William Horgan
(Photo: Patricia Lyons)

William Horgan, Irish Guards. Died November 1915, in Flanders aged 24. He was the son of Michael and Norah Horgan of Castlemary and was married to Bridget Horgan of Rostellan. Buried in Aubers Ridge Cemetery.

Redmond Maguire, Irish Guards. Died October 1917 in Flanders aged 24. Buried Mont Huon Military Cemetery, Le Tréport.

Richard Walsh, Royal Garrison Artillery. Son of John and Johanna Walsh and husband of Julia of Midleton. Died January 1919 aged 46. Buried Cloyne Cathedral Cemetery.

Michael Horrigan, died July 1917, France and Flanders,

Thomas Kirk, died July 1916, France and Flanders,

William McCroddan, died May 1915, Gallipoli,

John Myles, died March 1916, France and Flanders. He was the son of George and Mary Myles.

Denis O'Driscoll, died March 1915, in Flanders. Buried in Chocques Military Cemetery, Pas de Calais.

David Quinn, died October 1917, France and Flanders. He was the son of Tobias and Ellen Quinn.

John Rainey, Machine Gun Corps. Died June 1917 in Flanders aged 22. He was the son of John and Hannah Rainey of Scariff. Buried Gorre British and Indian Cemetery near Bethune.

John Ryan, died September 1917, France and Flanders. He was from Spital Cottages.

John Sisk, Royal Munster Fusiliers. Died September 1916 in Flanders aged 19. He was from River St. Name on Thiepval Memorial.

Edward Stafford, died August 1915, Egypt. He was the son of Maurice and Kate Stafford of Rock St.

Maurice Stanton, Royal Irish Lancers. Died August 1918 aged 26 in Flanders. He was son of Kate Stanton from Saleen. Buried Fouquescourt British Cemetery.

1916 and the subsequent War of Independence

By 1915, public opposition to support for the First World War began to emerge in the country, first by the bishop of Limerick.[180] Support for the Irish Volunteers increased. The Easter Rising, 1916, and the subsequent execution of its leaders had a profound effect on public opinion. The Rising put an end to recruitment meetings to join the British Army in Ireland.[181] There was widespread, and successful, opposition to the introduction of conscription in 1918.

After the Rising of 1916, Volunteer units were established throughout East Cork. It was in 1920 that some of the major operational activities commenced. Following successful attacks on the R.I.C. barracks in Carrigtwohill and Castlemartyr, Cloyne was next.[182] On the night of May 8th the peace of the town was disturbed by an attack on the R.I.C. barracks. The barracks was burned down.[183] There were also other incidents in the parish. The following is part of the statements of Joseph Aherne and John Kelleher given in 1956 relating to the attack on Cloyne barracks.[184]

---

180   Mark Cronin, *op. cit.* p114.

181   Ibid p169.

182   Rebel Cork's Fighting Story, Anvil Books, pp179-183.

183   John McAuliffe, *The Troubled Times in Cloyne*, in The Book of Cloyne, Edited by Padraig O' Loingsigh, p269.

184   http://www.bureauofmilitaryhistory.ie/reels/bmh/BMH.WS1456.pdf

STATEMENT OF JOSEPH AHERNE of Glasheen Road, Cork in 1956.[185]

The 4th Battalion area, of which I write, corresponded roughly to the old Parliamentary area of East Cork. The extreme western tip was at Dunkettle Bridge. The western boundary ran north through Glanmire village to Knockraha. The northern boundary ran through Leamlara to Ballincurrig, to Clonmult, Inch, Killeagh, Youghal and the Blackwater. The eastern and southern boundaries took in the coastline to Ballymacoda, Ballycotton, Cobh and the estuary of the River Lee to Dunkettle Bridge. The first Volunteer Company was formed in Cobh in 1913, and many of its members were interned in Frongoch after the 1916 rebellion. After 1916 the area was thoroughly organised and companies were formed in all parishes. Midleton was the first company organised, under the leadership of Mr. Seán Brady, and Youghal, under M. Kelleher, some time later. Knockraha was organised in 1917 under M. Corry, now representing Fianna Fáil interests in An Dáil. Other companies in the area were as follows: Little Island, under M. Cahill; Carrigtwohill, under Tom Cotter; Lisgoold, under - ; Ballincurrig, under Jack Smart; Clonmult, under J. Lawton: Dungourney, under Con Ahern, Ladysbridge, under William O'Connell, Killeagh, under D. O'Leary; Inch, under T. Mulcahy; Ballymacoda, under T. Gumbleton; Ballycotton, W. Walsh; Cloyne, B. Walsh; Aghada, P. O'Keeffe ...

---

185   http://www.bureauofmilitaryhistory.ie/reels/bmh/BMH.WS1367.
pdf#page=3

The attack was timed for the 8th May, 1920, and as we had daylight up to a late hour a concert under the auspices of the Gaelic League was arranged to facilitate transport of arms and ammunition. Everything went smoothly; revolvers, carbines and ammunition were taken with traps for the concert to the local hall just outside the town of Cloyne. Cobh and Midleton Companies were detailed to make the actual attack, while other companies were instructed to block all the main roads. Reporting to the hall at Cloyne at about 8 p.m., the Volunteers collected their arms and instructions issued about the plan of attack. Volunteers were instructed to occupy buildings in the front and rear of the barracks for the purpose of keeping the police engaged. Two other parties, one under Comdt. Hurley and the other under Comdt. Leahy, were detailed to break into houses on either side of the barracks and were to carry out the main assault. Going up the Street it was necessary to pass the barracks, so that great caution was necessary as we did not wish to draw suspicion of the R.I.C. before the attack commenced. However, on arriving at the building my party were detailed to occupy, we found that after repeated knockings we were unable to gain an entrance. The opposite party had by this time safely negotiated their entry. As we were standing on the footpath under the windows of the barracks and fearing that our knocking had aroused the R.I.C., I decided to take no further risks. Seizing a pickaxe, I burst in the panel of the door on the ground floor and released the bar on the inside. The only occupants were an old woman and a girl. We got them to a place of safety a few houses up the street and returned to continue our task of rooting out the R.I.C. Leahy, Manly and the other parties had by this time opened the attack and Manly had climbed to the roof of an adjoining building and was dropping bombs down the chimney of the barracks. Hurley, to facilitate our return, was engaged in firing through the loopholes of the steel shutters on the ground floor. This mode of attack was quite effective while it lasted, as it compelled the R.I.C. to remain under cover and prevented them from using the loopholes to fire through. Fire had been also opened on the building from the parties occupying positions in front and rear of the building - Jack Aherne and P. Whelan. Our task was to breach a hole in the gable end and, if possible, to enter and capture the garrison. As we had no explosives at our disposal, we attacked the wall with a crowbar and sledge. The wall was sounder than we anticipated but after an hour's strenuous work we succeeded in making a small breach. The police were waiting and they now began to fire at and through the hole, which we returned. Hurley was slightly wounded at this time. In an endeavour to clear out the police I threw in a hand grenade. This had the desired effect and we continued the good work of widening the breach, but all our efforts were unavailing to widen the breach sufficiently to permit the passage of a man's body. The police, after an interval, had found a safe place to return our fire through the breach and additional hand grenades failed to show any appreciable effect. As the hours of daylight were limited, Hurley decided to set fire to the building. A tin of petrol was procured. I poured some through the hole and Hurley procured some rags, which he wrapped around an old brush soaked in petrol. This made an ideal torch. The building was soon ablaze and in a few seconds we had to quit the building. As I reached the front door leading on to the Street I had a quick look round to see that all the party were safe, when, to my amazement, I saw a white pillow being thrown from the top storey of the barracks. It was the signal of surrender by the R.I.C. The police were met at the door of the barracks by the Volunteers who quickly disarmed them. One of the R.I.C. handed his carbine to me. He was smiling as he handed it over and it was only afterwards I discovered the reason. He had removed the bolt from the carbine and thrown it into the burning building. As the ground floor was still intact we searched it rapidly but discovered nothing except empty ammunition cases. The police apparently, when they found the building was untenable, had thrown all the spare ammunition into the portion of the barracks that was on fire, as it was exploding fiercely in the upper portion of the building. However, Leahy decided to try and salvage some of it. Ordering the sergeant of the R.I.C. up the stairs, he told him to point out the spot where the spare ammunition was dumped. I accompanied Leahy and the sergeant but we only succeeded in getting halfway up before being driven back by the intense heat and exploding ammunition. The companies were now ordered to disperse and the police were marched a short distance outside the town and released. I succeeded in procuring a motor car, and together with Hurley and Manly drove to O'Shea's, Tubbernamine. O'Shea was Manly's brother-in-law and an extensive farmer in the district. Dog tired, our faces covered with grime from the smoke of the fire, we must have looked a disreputable lot. The following night, Sunday, the 7th May, was concert night in the town of Cloyne. Most of the Volunteers who had taken part in the attack on the previous night attended. Mr. Dan H (?), well known Cork comedian, was the principal guest artist. Everyone was in high good humour and songs were chorused with great gusto, winding up with "The Soldier's Song"', which, I am sure, was heard echoing through the town.

STATEMENT BY JOHN KELLEHER, The Rock, Midleton

Attack on Cloyne R.I.C. Barracks.

It was on the night of 10th May, 1920[186], that another success fell to the 4th Battalion, when the R.I.C. Barracks at Cloyne was attacked, the garrison (a sergeant and ten constables) forced to surrender and the barrack building almost destroyed by fire. The whole battalion took a part in the general plan of attack but, once again, as at Carrigtwohill, the assault party consisted of men from the Midleton and Cobh Companies. The Officer Commanding the operation was Commandant Michael Leahy of Cobh. His second in command was Diarmuid Hurley, Captain of the Midleton Company. About four hundred men from the Battalion were out on duty on the night in question. The great majority of these men was engaged blocking roads and cutting telegraph wires in a wide area around Cloyne, in order to delay the advance of any relief parties of British troops from Cobh, Youghal, Fermoy or Cork, which might be sent to the relief of the garrison to be attacked in Cloyne. I have no definite details as to the disposition of our men engaged in these operations as I was one of those who took part in the actual attack on Cloyne that night. The village of Cloyne is about five miles south of Midleton. On the night (Sunday), following the attack, the Gaelic League were staging a play in the schoolhouse, Cloyne. I and others of the Midleton Company were members of the Gaelic League and were taking part in the play. 'Props' and scenery were moved by us to the schoolhouse at Cloyne early in the evening of Saturday 10th May, 1920 and, under cover of these 'props', guns and ammunition were brought to the schoolhouse which was the point of assembly for those

---

186   The reference to the 10th May should possibly read 8th May.

of us engaged in the attack on the barracks later that same night. The schoolhouse in question was about three hundred yards from the R.I.C. barracks. Pretending to be engaged in preparing the stage for the play to be held next night, a party of about fifteen of us 'drifted' into the schoolhouse in ones and twos on that Saturday night about 8.30 p.m. or so. Amongst those whom I remember being present were Diarmuid Hurley, Tadg Manly, Joseph Ahern, Tomás Hourihane, D. Ring, Mick Desmond, Paddy Whelan and Mick Keaney all from the Midleton Company. We expected a stiff resistance from the R.I.C. in Cloyne following the successful captures of Carrigtwohill and Castlemartyr barracks. The building had been specially strengthened against attack by the addition of steel shutters on all the barrack windows and we expected the garrison to be on the alert. The plan of attack was, therefore, as follows:- The two houses (public houses) on either side of the barracks were to be occupied by us after closing time (10 p.m.). Parties of our men stationed in a grain store across the street from the barracks and others at the rear, would open fire with rifles, while those in the houses adjoining the barracks would blast breaches in the party walls, thereby effecting an entrance from two sides to the barracks. Meade's public house was on the south side of the barracks and Power's on the north. Shortly before 10 p.m. three of our men were told to go down the village and into Meade's public house; similarly in the case of Power's: the idea was that these men would remain on in the pubs after closing time and open the doors to those of us who would come along to be admitted after 10.30 p.m. At about 10.30 p.m. I left the schoolhouse with Diarmuid Hurley, Manly, Joseph Ahern, Tom Hourihane, D. King and Mick Desmond. I carried a revolver and a quantity of gelignite. When we approached Meade's public house we found that Mrs. Meade would not allow our lads to remain on the premises up to the time of our arrival, with the result that the door was closed and we couldn't get in. We were debating what to do (for a very few moments as the barracks was next door) when Hurley decided to smash in the door with an iron bar that was across the window. This was done and we entered the house. The R.I.C. now suspected something was afoot and opened fire from the loopholes in the steel-shuttered windows. Our lads across the street and at the rear of the barracks replied with rifle-fire, and the R.I.C. garrison began firing up verey lights to summon assistance. Meanwhile, Mrs. Meade and her maid were removed to a place of safety in a house in the village. D. Ring, Desmond and I now went to a sitting-room on Meade's first floor and prepared to lay the gelignite into the wall adjoining the barracks. Diarmuid Hurley, Tadg Manly and a few others proceeded to a room upstairs, the idea being that they should start tampering with the wall up there to distract the attention of the R.I.C. from us downstairs. When we had placed the gelignite into a recess in the wall we informed Hurley that all was ready. He came downstairs and gave orders to ignite the fuse and withdrew out of the room. When the explosion occurred we discovered that the breach was only about two feet square and not large enough to admit even one man. The R.I.C. now started to fire from the adjoining barrack room through the breach we had made. Hurley then gave orders for six men to line up behind him on the landing. I had some gelignite left which, on Hurley's orders, I tied up in a handkerchief and lit a fuse. Hurley then ran with us alongside the wall of the room in which we had blown the hole and fired with his revolver through the breach. I ignited the fuse and flung the bundle of gelignite through the breach and into the barracks. The explosion˙ which followed drove the R.I.C. from the adjoining room to an upstairs compartment. We had a tin of petrol handy and poured the petrol into a ewer and then flung it (the petrol) through the breach. Hurley next got a piece of cloth, lit it and flung it after the petrol. A sheet of flame immediately burst both in the barracks and the room in which we were. The curtains in our rooms took fire and soon the place was untenable. We cleared out on to the street and saw that half of the barracks was on fire. All this time heavy rifle fire was proceeding both from the R.I.C. garrison and our men attacking front and rear. Our lads in Power's public house had breached the barrack wall on their side, but were unable to affect an entry by reason of the flames started on our side by the petrol. The next move from the garrison was a white cloth fluttering from one of the upstairs windows as a token of surrender. Orders were given to cease fire, and Mick Leahy and some of his men in Power's public house entered the barracks. The door was opened and the garrison walked out with hands up and were placed under armed guard. We rushed into the burning barracks and grabbed all the guns we could lay hands on. Ammunition was exploding all over the place and very little of it was captured. In all we got about eight or ten police carbines and some revolvers. These were taken away to a safe destination. The engagement at Cloyne began about 10.30 p.m. and lasted (until we took the surrender of the police) until close to 12.30 a.m. Our only casualty was Diarmuid Hurley who suffered burns on the arm from flaming petrol. His injury, which was treated by a local doctor, was not serious. A couple of the R.I.C. men were, to the best of my recollection, wounded in the fight. We withdrew from the village about 1 a.m. when we heard from our scouts that the military were approaching in force from Cork City; in fact, the noise of military lorries was heard by us on the roads not far from Cloyne as we crossed the fields on our way northwards to Midleton. After the Cloyne attack, the R.I.C. garrison of about ten constables and a sergeant was dispersed to other barracks Castlemartyr, Killeagh and Youghal in the East Cork area.

Some of those who took part in the attack on the barrack were later killed in the Clonmult Ambush.

At the end of 1920 another event took place in Cloyne. The East Cork Column, I.R.A. under Commandant O'Hurley escaped successfully from a house in the town which was surrounded by British troops.[187]

The Clonmult Ambush took place in February, 1921. Volunteers occupying a farmhouse in Clonmult were surrounded by a force of British Army, Royal Irish Constabulary and Black and Tans. In the action that followed, twelve IRA volunteers were killed, four wounded and four captured.[188] *Rebel Cork's Fighting Story* states that there were three wounded and six unwounded prisoners. Of these Edmund Terry, who was wounded, and Jack Harty were from Cloyne parish. Both were sentenced to death but this was later commuted.

---

187   Rebel Cork's Fighting Story, Anvil Books, pp 187-189.
188   https://en.wikipedia.org/wiki/Clonmult_Ambush; Rebel Cork's Fighting Story, Anvil Books, p195.

1936

In February of 1936, the Ballycotton lifeboat *Mary Stanford* performed the notable *Daunt Lightship* rescue.[189]

1937 Funeral of Canon Lynch

7.6 Funeral of Canon Lynch 1937
(Courtesy: Bunty Cahill)

On the left hand side of the photograph there are six doorways to houses as far as where the coffin is being carried. At the first (nearest) door Bridget Kenneally is standing. At the second is Jack Geary's house. At the third, with the group

189   https://en.wikipedia.org/wiki/RNLB_Mary_Stanford_(ON_733)

of people, is Mrs John Kenneally. The fourth doorway is the house of Jim Geary. The fifth is May Canavan and family. The sixth is the doorway to the British Legion.[190] Next is the Olympia Ballroom.

Church Income – 1930s and 1940s

Income for running the church comes from various sources. An important source in the 1930s was card-playing. In September, 1935, an entry of £33 is shown for the proceeds of a whist drive. In 1939 income from whist is shown as £39 and a separate entry of £130 from a card drive in Shanagarry. In 1940 an entry is shown of £88 and 5s from a whist drive. In 1942, the total income was £1300 and the total expenditure was £1685. It would seem that the local economy was in better shape in the first years of the 2nd World War compared with the end of the War and the years following it. By 1947 income and expenditure had shrunk to £939 and £837 respectively.

1946

Christy Ring captains the Cork senior hurling winning team.

The Chapel Gate

The chapel gate was a focal point for countrymen who lingered after Sunday mass to discuss politics, the weather, hurling and the events of the previous week when they had all the time in the world. If the weather was bad at harvest-time and the farmers had fallen behind, they would wait at the gate to get permission from the priest to continue harvesting on Sunday. In those days 'unnecessary servile work on a Sunday' was a mortal sin.

---

190   Information supplied to Margaret Hartnett.

Before the era of television and mass media, the chapel gate was also the very best place for electioneering. During the canvas it was normal to come out of mass and hear a booming voice delivering an impassioned political speech from the bonnet of a car parked opposite the church gate. In that way the political hopeful could achieve what he has to do nowadays door to door. He needed to be fairly quick-witted as heckling could and did take place.

Collections of all sorts were made at the chapel gate. Some people were very partisan as regards political collections and would only support their own beliefs, but business people usually made some gesture to all, as their customers came from all political shades. Collections would also be made for the local school. Maurice Stack and Johanna O'Connor ran a free school in the mid 1800s with 183 males and 138 females on roll. The average daily attendance was 300 and increasing. The instruction consisted of Reading, Writing, Arithmetic, Roman Catholic Catechism and Needlework for the girls. Their main source of support was collections made at the chapel gate (Commission of Public Instruction Ireland: 1835). At one time the church entrance collection was made at the upper gate, all other gates remaining closed. Tommy John Geary and his father were collectors for most of their adult lives, the former for over fifty years.

Goods were sold. If you were passing the chapel gate after Sunday morning mass in the late 1800s you might have seen Jude Wharton from Ballyandreen selling the periwinkles that she had picked that very morning.

And of course, plans were hatched outside the chapel gate. Once a priest from Cloyne was transferred to Buttevant. Two

Cloyne parishioners hatched a plan after mass to give him a call on their way to Cahermee Fair. The priest was not at home so the Cloyne boys left the following note in poetic form (this verse was given to a local child by her grandfather in the 1950s).

> *Two men from Cloyne whose time is scant*
>
> *Have just arrived in Buttevant.*
>
> *His Reverence they called to see*
>
> *And are off on the spot to Cahermee.*[191]

Visit of Eamon de Valera

7.7 Eamon De Valera in Cloyne
(Courtesy: Cloyne Literary and Historical Society)

Eamon De Valera held an election rally in Cloyne in the early 1950s.

---

191   Aisling Lyons worked on putting this piece together.

1953/4

Christy Ring captains the Cork senior hurling team winners in both 1953 and 1954.

New Liturgy

The new liturgy came into force in March, 1965 and was well received.[192] The altar facing the people in the church was erected in 1969. The reredos that was backing the altar when the priest celebrated mass with his back facing the congregation is now mounted on the east boundary wall in front of the church.

7.8 Pre Vatican II Reredos

---

192   Liber Chronicus Cloyne (unpublished).

1979 Tribute to Christy Ring

One of the biggest funerals in Cloyne was that of Christy Ring, its most famous son, who died in 1979 at the age of 58. The coffin was draped in the colours of Glen Rovers and the GAA. The funeral cortège took over three hours to make its way from Cork City to Cloyne, where he was laid to rest.

7.9 Christy Ring
(Courtesy: Mrs Philomena Hurley)

The final prayers were led by the Bishop of Cloyne, Dr Ahern and the oration at the graveside was given by the Taoiseach Jack Lynch.[193]

193   Dermot Keogh, *Jack Lynch*, Gill & Macmillan, 2008, p416;www.rte.ie/
      archives/2014/.../508129-high-profile-**funeral**-for-**christy-ring**

60,000 people lined the streets of Cork for his cortege. Ring's coffin was shouldered into St Colman's churchyard by renowned sporting celebrities from Cork and other counties. 'We carried him at last' was Ring's former team-mate Paddy Barry's remark, in reference to Ring often saving the Cork hurlers from almost certain defeat.

Ring's graveside oration in Cloyne was delivered by a former team-mate and the then Taoiseach, Jack Lynch.

'Before we leave this hallowed spot let us bide just a few moments longer and cast our thoughts back over the years through which so many of us had the honour to know, to play with or against Christy Ring. What more can be said of him, of his prowess, of his competitiveness, that has not been said already?...'

Lynch finished by claiming that:

'As long as young men will match their hurling skills against each other on Ireland's green fields, as long as young boys swing their camáns for the sheer thrill of the feel and the tingle in their fingers of the impact of ash on leather, as long as hurling is played the story of Christy Ring will be told. And that will be forever.'

It was also related that Professor Seán Ó Tuama heard an old Cork lady say at his funeral: *It was an awful shame to bury that man.*[194]

---

194 glenrovers.ie/contentPage/56135/**christy_ring**

Pope John Paul II visits Ireland

In 1979, Pope John Paul II visited Ireland. A group from Cloyne travelled to Limerick to see him.

Church Facelift 1980s

In the early 1980s the church got a facelift. It required some urgent remedial work in the towers on front where the water was coming through part of the roof and into the gallery. The front wall of the church was altered with two towers being demolished and replaced by weather slating. The work was expensive and a fundraising committee was established.

The Catholic Fireside News at that time was read nationwide and the secretary of the committee wrote to it requesting help of any description to aid the fund. The secretary, the late Babs Daly, Rock St., received many messages offering the contents of houses, such as furniture, glassware, pictures, floor coverings etc., but they would have to be collected.

A day for pick up was arranged and Maurice Griffin Snr and a helper set off with a lorry borrowed from Joe Dolphin. The first stop was Bandon, then onto Clonakilty, Skibbereen, Baltimore and finally Castletownsend. Some of the items donated were restored and repaired by members of the committee. Later an auction was organised and Billy Dunne, Auctioneer, sold off almost every item and it was a great success.

Next on the list was a Garden Fete in the school grounds; this event was held annually for a good many years. There was always something of interest for young and not so young. It was very well supported by many and one could find anything at the Cloyne Garden Fete. For example, one man on his own cut and broke a full tractor trailer of firewood blocks and sold them all off per bag. This brought in quite a bit of money.

There was a cake sale at the Church gate every Sunday and Church Holiday. These plus door collections, a concert, fashion show etc. all contributed. [195]

A big effort was put in by the committee and the wider community.

The then parish priest sought to have mass said in the cathedral while refurbishment work was underway. Permission for this was granted by the Church of Ireland bishop. However, it was not used; instead the schoolhouse was brought into service.[196] In recent decades other remedial work was also carried out.

7.10 Church Refurbishment
Left to right, front: Fr Anthony Cronin,
Canon O'Driscoll, Joe Dolphin, Ann Casey
Back: Ned Foley, Kevin Brosnan
(Courtesy: Joe Dolphin)

---

195 Information supplied by Maurice Griffin.
196 Donal O' Driscoll, *Parish to Parish*, OnStream Publications Ltd, 2002, p76.

Icon of St Colman

7.11 Icon St Colman

In December 1997 an icon of St Colman, the patron Saint of the Diocese was unveiled in the Church. This was commissioned by former parish priest, Dr O' Driscoll. St Colman came to the town of Cloyne in the middle of the 6th century and there founded his first church.[197] The parish priest of Cloyne is bound to say mass on St Colman's feast day, 24th November. In the icon St Colman is painted in a stylised way. He is depicted in the robe of a bishop, holding in his left hand, which is draped with a cloth out of respect for the Gospels, the gold-covered book of the scriptures, while his right hand is raised in blessing. The presence of the scriptures in his hand indicates that his role as bishop is to be teacher and bearer of the word of God. The fingers of his right hand also have a reference to Christ because they are so placed that they form the letters of Jesus' name and title in Greek: IGXC. The face is painted in a stylised way to indicate his nature as a saint in heaven. The facial lines, high cheeks and inflated neck are used to indicate the gifts of wisdom and the presence of the Holy Spirit. His wide ears indicate that he is also to be a hearer of the word as well as a teacher. The aim of the icon is to depict a heavenly reality or sacred personality.[198]

The iconographer was Fr David O'Riordan.

---

197   Liber Chronicus Cloyne (unpublished)
198   Donal O'Driscoll, op. cit. pp95-96

CHAPTER 8

Devotional Practice

First Communion and Confirmation

8.1 First Holy Communion Children 2015
St Colman`s National School, Cloyne
(Courtesy: Mary O'Brien)

8.2 Altar Decoration for First Holy Communion Children

Two events are very important in the life of the Church for young children. These are First Communion and Confirmation. In terms of the life of the church, while it was still under construction, Bishop Coppinger confirmed about 800 in 1818.[199] For just this year a photo of the First Communion group from St Colman's National School is shown in 8.1 and the altar decoration for the event in 8.2. It should be noted that the church has been very beautifully decorated with flowers by Kitty Cahill for a number of decades. Prior to this people brought flowers from their gardens and they were artistically arranged on the altar by Ms Joe Ryan, Mrs Keane and Ms Anne Cuddigan.

8.3 Confirmation – Anna McCarthy
(Courtesy: Mrs McCarthy)

In photo 8.3 a confirmation from the 1930s is shown. In the photograph are: standing up, Anna McCarthy, Miss Jo Motherway, Mary McCarthy; seated, Mrs Anna McCarthy and Betty McCarthy.

House Stations

The Station list was called out from the Altar twice yearly. We grew familiar with the names of the townlands and, as children, we were able to memorise the combinations:

---

199   Eric A. Derr, *op. cit.*

Sheenliss, The Wood, Carrigatogher, Knockasturkeen; Ballybranagh, Kilmacahill, Commons East and West, Ballyduff and Ballyonane; Scarrif, Knockgorm, Kilva, Knocknamadree, Sculleen and Ardavilling. What a wealth of history, culture and tradition lies behind these names. In Cloyne there is a high incidence of Cill names. This is attributable to the Celtic monastery there which owned most of the parish, its termon lands. These names must all predate the year 1000AD.[200]

Station Masses nowadays are celebrated in private houses in the various townlands of the parish and, in some areas, in the churches. These station masses are held twice a year during Lent and in the autumn. This custom of house masses originated in Penal Times when the celebration of Mass publicly was forbidden and priests had a price on their heads and had to go into hiding. But Irish Catholics remained faithful to the celebration of the Mass. Consequently, Masses were celebrated in secret on Mass Rocks, in glens and isolated places. The faithful gathered in the open country near the rock which the priest used as an altar. The priest, who usually arrived in disguise, celebrated Mass while certain locals kept watch for any approaching militia. There are many Mass Rocks around the country which are still regarded as sacred places. The Irish poem *Anseo I Lár an Ghleanna* by Seán Mac Fheorais gives a vivid picture of a Mass being said and, just as Pobal Dé were going about their business, the militia was approaching. The poem tells of an old man called Brian Ó Laoi who came up from the crowd and ordered the priest to swap clothes with him. So the old man in priest's clothes was hanged and the young priest escaped.

200   Paul McCotter article in Pat Lynch's Book of Cloyne.

Do ghabh na Sasanaigh Brian Ó Laoi,

Is d'imigh saor an sagart;

Do chroch siad Brian ar chrann caol ard

Anseo i lár an ghleanna.[201]

In Penal times Mass was also celebrated in people's homes. Since it was considered unsafe for the priest to carry the sacred vessels and vestments with him on his journey, local people took care of the 'Mass Kit' and passed it from house to house as it was needed. This Mass became known as the station Mass on account of the random movement from place to place. Some houses which became regular venues for Mass became known as Mass houses.[202] Even when the Penal Laws were repealed there were more Mass houses in use. By degrees during the beginning of the nineteenth century, many churches were built around the country: Shanagarry in 1814 and Cloyne in 1815 .

When the Mass was over, those in attendance stayed for refreshments. In most cases the hospitality was shared with their neighbours. After the priest had gone, the festivities often continued for the day with dancing singing and merriment. Obviously, some priests remained on to take part in festivities. The excesses in the merriment after the station Mass were a cause of concern to the church authorities which led to the following regulations by the bishops of Munster at a meeting held in Cork on 23rd of August 1808:

No.3: Re. Station Dinner "Our clergy are now strictly forbidden

---

201   Anseo i lár an Ghleanna *Sean Mac Fheorais.*
202   Catholic Diocese of Cork & Ross website.

to partake of such entertainments in any house whatever on the day they shall hold a public or private station".[203]

After the Penal Law Era the Catholic Church needed to reorganise. Catholic Emancipation in 1829 was a victory for the Catholic Church but the Great Famine presented a further obstacle. In 1850 it was decided to hold a National Synod of bishops. This was held in Thurles where the bishops of the country assembled. The state of the church was examined. After such a long period of persecution, it was found that many abuses had crept into the life of the church because of poverty, lack of education, lack of mobility etc.[204] Dr Paul Cullen, the Primate of Ireland, wanted to make drastic changes but other bishops did not want to move too quickly. Baptisms and marriages often took place in houses during Penal Times and at the Synod it was decided that as soon as churches were available this practice would change. Dr Cullen wanted to put an end to the Masses in the houses completely. However, many of the other bishops did not agree. Among them was Bishop Keane, then bishop of Ross, who had been parish priest of Midleton for ten years (1840-1850) and who later became bishop of Cloyne. He argued strongly in favour of house stations so it was decided that each bishop would regulate his own diocese.[205]

Canon Troy, in the weekly parish newsletter 26th. September 2004, stated Bishop Keane was convinced that the stations had great pastoral value both for the priests and people. Besides providing an opportunity for the people, especially the elderly, to receive the sacraments of Penance and Holy Communion, he saw the stations as a good opportunity for

---

203   Cloyne Diocesan Archives.
204   Midleton Parish Newsletter 26 September 2004 *(Canon   B. Troy, decd.).*
205   Ibid.

people to cultivate friendship and charity, to discuss local problems and settle them amicably.[206]

As the years went by and the penal laws were repealed, the custom of having the stations continued. Having the stations was a big event. Preparations often started months in advance. It was an impetus to get on with home improvements, to paint and clean the house from top to bottom. The Mass was said in the kitchen with the kitchen table as the altar. Confessions were heard in another room, usually the Parlour. The best china was brought out and the best linen cloths. The priests had the breakfast in the Parlour, while those who attended stayed in the kitchen.

The station Mass was held usually in the morning. In the past there was a rota of parishioner families who hosted the stations in each station area. Nowadays, people simply volunteer and the station mass time is the choice of the host family. In this parish there is a set rule about refreshments. Keep it simple. The station Mass today is an opportunity for the faithful to contribute to the support of their pastors and for the priest to keep the people informed of the financial state of the parish.

Dr O'Driscoll who was parish priest in Cloyne from 1985-1996 introduced a simple group healing ceremony which he had started in his previous parish.[207]

Many parishioners can recall the occasions when, the station masses having concluded in the area, the priest read the list of contributions from each household during Sunday Mass. The list started with the largest amount and so on down to the smallest. Thankfully this is no longer the case. As times

206   Ibid.
207   Parish to Parish - 2002. *Very Rev. Canon Donal O'Driscoll.*

have changed, there is no longer a need for the priest to call out the station areas. Now the parish newsletter informs us of this.

The Holy Wells

The Holy wells-the living wells-the cool, the fresh, the pure
A thousands ages rolled away, and still those founts endure[208]

In his essay on the Holy Wells of Ireland the Most Rev. Dr John Healy Archbishop of Tuam (1903-1918) says Ireland from time immemorial has been celebrated for its Holy Wells and healing fountains. He says that an appropriate reverence of a religious character can be paid to the Holy Wells, especially to those sacred fountains that have been especially blessed by some great saint. He lists many examples from scripture of similar veneration to be found in the Bible. [209]

It is generally believed that those Holy Wells have been in existence since prehistoric times. The Celts had a strong religious influence on the native Irish people and had a strong belief in the power of place. The earth centred religion of the Celts believed that certain places possess power that is curative. The power of place in Ireland is an intrinsic element of the sacredness of the holy well. After Patrick the pilgrimages and practices associated with the holy well were christianised.[210] The pagan tree took on the symbolism of Christ. Water from Holy Wells cured certain ailments. A very old well in Harty's land at Killmacahill used to cure the ague. People used to make rounds there and drink the water.[211]

---

208 *John de Jean Frazer* 1804 – 1852.
209 Irish Essays – Literary & Historical. *John Healy.*
210 The Holy Wells of Ireland. *Suzanne Barrett.*
211 Folklore of the parish The Book of Cloyne 2nd edition.

St Colman's Well

St Colman's well is located in an area of Cloyne known as Kilva. The name is thought to derive from Macha one of Colman's sisters.[212] Remains of a church are still visible.

St Colman is remembered in folk memory and many tales survive about him. One story concerns the building of the round tower by the saint which according to the story was built in one night. As he was nearly finished and the dawn was breaking, he was asked by a woman what he was doing. He did not like her tone so he got into a rage and he jumped from the tower and landed in Kilva.[213] There in thirst the saint prayed to God to provide water whereupon a spring gushed forth where no spring had been before, the origin of St Colman's Well. Many people visited the well seeking a cure for bad eyesight. Paul MacCotter in his history of St Colman states there was a cure for rheumatism in the waters of the well. A pattern was still held here on the octave of the saint's feast day in the 1930s.[214] Bunty Cahill recalls visiting St Colman's Well in his youth, with his mother and his aunt.

The word pattern is a corruption of patron as in patron saint. In Irish Roman Catholicism a pattern refers to devotions which take place on the feast day of the patron saint or the nearest Sunday.

Before the Reformation, festivities for Pattern Day began with religious devotions in the church. This ceased with the confiscation or destruction of Roman Catholic churches between 1540 and 1690. By 1700 very few churches remained under Catholic control so public religious

---

212 A History of the Medieval Diocese of Cloyne. *Paul MacCotter.*
213 Another version has St Colman landing in Lurrig.
214 Colman of Cloyne – A Study. *Paul MacCotter.*

ceremonies almost disappeared .[215]

During the Penal Laws, with no churches and few clergy and since the centre of worship had gone, people found other ways to honour the saint's feast day.[216] These prescribed rituals were laid down for the pilgrims who came seeking favours, Most devotions took place near a Holy Well celebrated for its curative power. Patterns attracted large crowds. People would walk round the well in a clockwise direction reciting prayers and stopping at various "stations" on the way. They drank the water and often left a piece of cloth tied to the tree near the well. The belief was that, after drinking the water the illness was transferred to the piece of cloth and left behind. When the religious devotions were complete, people often engaged in activities such as singing, dancing and horse racing. Some patterns lasted for days. Often these forms of devotions became quite rowdy and were a cause of concern for the clergy.

In the late eighteenth century the bishops issued edicts forbidding such wild festivals. A meeting of prelates in Kilworth on 15th and 16th October 1777 came to the following agreement:

No. 6   Patterns on Sundays and Holy days, dancing schools and balls at night, profanations at wakes to be hindered by exhortations and exemplary punishments and are reserved.

No. 7   All riots and quarrels to be punished most severely, part of which punishment is to come barefoot to the superior or vicar to receive proper penance and to stand three Sundays in albis where they gave scandal.

---

215   Pattern Day in Old Ireland. *Bridget Haggerty.*
216   Ibid.

No. 10. Those who are guilty of rapt are not to remain excommunicated as before in this diocese, but salutary penance both public and private is to be imposed till ordinary or vicar thinks proper to relieve them.[217]

Not many paid attention to these decrees or even the penal laws of the early 18th century; not even the Act to prevent the growth of popery which prohibited the riotous and assembling together of many thousands of Papists to the said wells and other places. Fines were prescribed on those who assembled and on the vendors of ale, victuals and other commodities. There were strict penalties on all who broke this rule. This law caused the removal of all emblems from wells, but it was completely ineffective in ending Pattern Days.

These patterns were a common part of rural life until the 19th century. In 1850 Cardinal Cullen called a Synod of bishops. Edicts were issued forbidding people to take part in these wild festivals. The excesses - fighting, drunkenness and immorality which became part of these patterns were opposed by the clergy from then on. Pilgrimages to these places did in fact decline but this was due to the famine and social change, a decline in the Irish Language and Gaelic Culture. Sir William Wilde laments the fact that these traditions and rituals were disappearing.[218]

Canon Kelleher was parish priest of Cloyne from 1995 to 2006 and a person who had a deep love of nature which was often reflected in his homilies. A meeting was called to decide how the millennium would be celebrated in Cloyne and a decision was taken that the revitalisation of St Colman's Well would be a laudable project for the parish in the year

---

217   Cloyne Diocesan Records 1791/1/1771
218   Popular Irish Superstitions. *Sir William Wilde*

2000. Two energetic volunteers, Bunty Cahill and Michael Dilworth, together with Canon Kelleher found the location and cleared the area round the well, laid flag stones which were donated, got the place ready for Mass which, with the permission of the Woods family, was celebrated there in June 2000. Many people walked up Kilva through the fields to mark the millennium. As I recall, it was very well attended and a ritual which linked the present with the past. This ritual has continued and Mass is celebrated annually since then in the month of June. This year, the bicentennial year is extra special. Sadly, Canon Kelleher passed away in July, 2015.

8.4 St Colman's Well

**8.5 Kitty Cahill – Reading at Bicentenary Mass,
St Colman's Well**

8.6 Tree Planting Ceremony –
David Cahill, Mick Dilworth, Fr Joe Rohan, Bunty Cahill

Going to the Well

At the beginning of the 20th century the then parish priest of Cloyne, Fr O'Riordan made new copies of the old church registers which were not in a good state.

Vol. 1 Old Register August 1812 states.

A register of Christenings for the Parishes of Cloyne, Churchtown and Kilteskin.[219]

It is thought that the parish of Kilteskin was removed from the parish of Cloyne grouping circa 1835. The Holy Well or Our Lady's Well in Kilteskin was a place of pilgrimage until recent times. Going to the Well was a devotional exercise, a ritual which was very important in the mid and late 1900s.

Written evidence testifies to active devotion at the well at least from 1731 to the present time. Even without written testimony, it is certain it was venerated since medieval times. It is significant that the stone was inscribed in 1731 when all the priests of Cloyne were on the run under Penal Laws. The remarkable stone gives a formula of seven Paters, seven Aves and one Gloria. A ritual practice dating from prehistoric times and which continued into the Christian era when the Celtic spring became Lady's Well was that of circumambulation or making structured rounds of the well always in a clockwise direction.[220] That was how it was in Kilteskin. The Well was open for one week before August 15th and for one week after. People did the rounds many times and when they finished they knelt and made a sign of the cross on the large stone with a smaller stone. One always took water home in a bottle. Many made three trips during

---

219   Cloyne Parish Records.
220   The Holy Wells of Ireland. *Suzanne Barret.*

the period and walked. Parishioners from Cloyne went to 'The Well' in large numbers.

Travelling from Cloyne and the surroundings those going to the well often walked the short cut down through Lurrig past Hayes's thatched house which was so pretty with lovely geraniums around the walls and then to Crocane. When you reached Barrakilla you knew you were nearly there. The places one walked echoed history. Lurrig was where legend had it, St Colman left a footprint (Lorg) when he jumped from the Tower in Cloyne. Another piece of folklore. A short trip down the hill took you down into the well field. There was always a crowd. There is quite a lot of documentation extant on the Pattern in Kilteskin.

In Smiths History of Cork 1893 edition there is the following note:

Titeskin Sunday 18th August, 1878 .

I visited the ancient church of Titeskin, about two miles from Aghada, and saw the pattern of the adjacent holy well. There were between 200 and 300 people there – all the blind, lame, and crippled men and women in the county, beggars innumerable, generally handsome young women with children in their arms. The people were drinking water out of the well, which was handed to them in tumblers by a woman who stood within the enclosure. Over the well was a tree, on which they were placing small bits of rags – there were hundreds of bits. Near the well was a stone, like a tombstone, around which were a number of blind men praying, and boys who used to kiss a rude figure cut on the stone in relief. Beneath this figure was an inscription stating how many and what kind of prayers were to be said. Round about the well, on the rising ground, were great numbers of people praying with beads and walking round it, who used to stop at intervals, kneel and again pray. Outside the well where the surplus water flowed off, women were washing children in the water, others bathed their legs, arms, eyes, hand etc. Some children, nearly naked, were almost immersed in the water. A plaster figure of the Virgin Mary, to whom the well was dedicated, was fixed to the tree by a string. Nothing was sold but cakes, of which there were three or four large stands, in great variety, with a covering[221]

There was an interesting sequel to the Pattern at Kilteskin on August 15th 1852 when at Cloyne Court a number of publicans were summoned for selling spirits and porter there, contrary to an act of parliament which only authorises the erection of booths at fairs and races. The evidence having been gone into, the bench ruled convictions in the mitigated penalty of 10s in each case.[222]

Over one hundred years ago people from Waterford made a long and difficult journey by horse and car to Our Lady's Well. 'They arrived on 15th of August and made their first round. They stayed in Russell's yard that night, had a sing-song around the fire and slept in the barn. Early next morning they made their second round, attended early mass, returned for a meal, made their final round after which they headed home for Dungarvan.'[223]

People still continue to come to Our Lady's Well in Kilteskin during the period from 8th August to the 22nd. Mass was celebrated there on August 15th 2014.

---

221 Midleton Parish Newsletter. 3 October 1999. *(Canon B.Troy. decd.)*
222 Midleton Parish Newsletter. 13 January 2002. *(Canon B.Troy decd.)*
223 Aghada -Echoes of the Past. *Aghada Historical Society.*

8.7 Tobar Muire (Lady's Well) Kilteskin
(Photo: Eddie Tucker)

**8.8 Carved stone representing the Crucifixion,
Lady's Well Kilteskin**
(Photo: Eddie Tucker)

**8.9 Carved stone representing the Crucifixion,
Lady's Well Kilteskin**
(Photo: Eddie Tucker)

A carved stone representing the Crucifixion, which is located nearby, probably dates from Penal times. It carries the words 'Seven Pater Nosters and seven Ave Marias - the Honour 1732'. Over the years the practice of rubbing the inscribed cross with a stone in order to trace the shape of a cross on it has worn away.

The Confraternity

In 2007 at NUI Maynooth, a conference was held on the theme 'Honouring God and community: confraternities and sodalities in modern Ireland'. From that meeting came the idea of a project aimed at documenting and studying the contribution of parish confraternities to the religious and social history of modern Ireland. The first phase of the project was to locate, collect and document as many records of confraternities and sodalities as possible from the late eighteenth century onwards.[224] There are no records of the Confraternity in Cloyne Diocese in existence and there are no parish records either.

Religious groupings of lay men and women have been in existence in Ireland since the Middle Ages. They have been called Fraternities, Religious guilds, Confraternities or Sodalities. The Sodality of the Sacred Heart flourished until the 20th Century. The momentum for the founding of the Sacred Heart Sodality came from Cardinal Cullen who desired to inspire a devotional renaissance in his diocese. As a result there was a great surge in the number of branches through Ireland from the late nineteenth century.[225] Although the clergy were fully in charge of the establishment and overall regulation of confraternities, many laymen and women were chosen to occupy supervisory positions as prefects who had responsibility for maintaining records of membership, contributions and attendance. The routine organisation of the branches of the Confraternity was in the hands of lay people.

In Cloyne the left side of the church was for the women, the right side for the men. Each side was divided into guilds and each guild had a prefect who collected the money each first Sunday night. Small but regular monetary contribution gave members a sense of belonging. The fee was 2d. and the prefect took the money, put it into a small red bag attached to a pole and ticked off the names in a slim red attendance book. Each guild was marked by a pole which was inserted into a circular crook attached to the end of the seat. On top of the pole was an emblem of the Sacred Heart. In an age of little

224   Confraternities and Sodalities in Ireland. *Colm Lennon*.
225   Flowering of Confraternities and Sodalities. *Colm Lennon and Robin Kavanagh*

social opportunity the Confraternity membership offered the companionship of like minded people and an opportunity of social interaction as did the practice of attending The Stations of the Cross during Lent or the October Devotions. I can remember the prefect in my guild 8 was Miss Maher who owned a pub in Rock Street. Mick Stafford Rock Street was a prefect at the men's side.[226] Prayers were said, a sermon given, followed by Benediction. A daily routine of prayers and meditation was enjoined on all.

The duties of members:

8.10 Confraternity Medal
(Courtesy: Michael Cuddigan)

There was a requirement by all to recite morning and evening prayers. Daily Mass and communion became a desire for many. The public face of the Confraternity was shown when men and women and young people assembled in the Parish Church with their guild shields. Attendance at the monthly meeting was a duty for all members who were required to wear their medals – an oval shaped medal attached to a red ribbon which was worn round the neck. When a parishioner was asked to recall his memories of the Confraternity his reply was *All I can remember was, the church was thronged.*

Members of the Confraternity derived many spiritual benefits from their participation in these prescribed religious

226   Margaret Hartnett.

activities. The indulgences or graces derived from the faithful fulfilment of the appropriate conditions provided a safety net for men and women in their quest for salvation.[227]

Of course there was a social aspect to going to the confraternity meetings. Besides the spiritual benefits of membership, the Confraternity afforded material advantages to members. Small regular monetary contributions together with a joining fee which helped to defray costs of sacred objects such as scapulars and medals afforded members a sense of inclusion.

The important role of sacramentals in the culture of Irish Catholicism was very evident in the confraternity movement. Members initially were conferred with a medal of membership and were required to wear these medals at all the confraternity meetings. Like other sacramentals there were very specific rules governing the meaning and the wearing of medals.[228] Sacred material culture was very important to the running of any Catholic organisation. There occurred in the 19th century, alongside devotional exercises, the introduction of a wide range of religious objects. These religious objects were primarily on sale at the Parish Mission. Many can recall these being blessed at the closing of the parish mission.

Members of the Catholic Young Men's Society were constantly encouraged to join the Confraternity and the records of Cloyne Catholic Young Men's Society show that this was so in Cloyne.

For almost a century from 1860 on, the religious lives of most Irish Catholics revolved around the Confraternities. What was remarkable about the Confraternities was they

227   Ibid.
228   Display Sacramentalism and Devotion. *Lisa Godson*

reached out to the whole community: men, women, youths and children.[229] The church today has been described as an aging church and one dominated by women. Yet men were strongly represented in the confraternity movement. What was it that attracted and focused men's energy then? The Confraternities had a much wider influence as a social outlet and a sense of involvement in an age where in the words of Bishop Primeau, Manchester, New Hampshire at a debate on The Second Vatican Council, the lay person's role was none other than to believe, pray, obey and pay.[230]

By the 1950s it appeared that the influence of the Confraternity movement in Ireland had reached and had passed its zenith. From the mid 20th Century, liturgical changes such as evening mass and profound social changes called into question traditional forms of pious organization – the Confraternities faced the ultimate challenge. The records show that the Confraternities and Sodalities limped on until the 1970s when the radical new thinking which emerged from the Second Vatican Council was to spell the death knell of Irish Catholic devotional life as it had been experienced since the latter half of the nineteenth century .[231] One of the main aims of The Vatican Council was to re-centre devotion to the liturgy and it did not concern itself with popular devotions.

The devotional aspects of the Confraternity no longer had any appeal for youths and adults in a changing landscape. It seems in a swiftly changing world the Confraternity had lost its past and couldn't find a future.[232]

---

229   Confraternities, decline, background analysis and review. *Louise Fuller.*
230   Debates and Decrees of Vatican Council II. *Xavier Rynne.*
231   Confraternities – their decline. *Louise Fuller*
232   Confraternities Social Capital and Civil Society. *Nicholas Terpstra*

The Devotional Revolution

We have seen the part the Confraternity played in the lives of Catholics in Ireland for almost one hundred years from the middle of the 19th century. This was an element of what Emmet Larkin called the devotional revolution in Ireland. In a 1972 article the historian Emmet Larkin argued that, in the third quarter of the 19th century, Irish Catholicism underwent a 'devotional revolution' that made practising catholics of the Irish people.[233] But devotions to the Sacred Heart and the Blessed Virgin were already known in Ireland. It is still generally accepted that Cardinal Cullen (1803-1878) spearheaded the consolidation of this 'revolution'. Several additional devotions - litanies, novenas, confraternities, sodalities, holy pictures, scapulars, retreats and missions - became the hallmark of Irish Catholicism.[234]

Cardinal Cullen was guided by an overriding desire, as he saw it, 'to rescue this Catholic country from the religious inferiority in which it now lies.[235] To this end he summoned a synod of bishops in Thurles in 1850. Throughout the religious decade before the famine, the religious practice of the great majority of Irish Catholics remained severely limited, in frequency of attendance, in range of observance and in the degree of ceremony. Attendance at Mass pre famine for the whole of Ireland was 40%. Analysis of 1834 religious census states that universal, weekly-mass attendance was confined to the affluent areas in the south east of the country.[236] Larkin attributes the reversal of this to the determined efforts of Paul Cullen, Archbishop of Dublin and later Cardinal.

233 Encyclopaedia of Irish History and Culture.
234 Cardinal Cullen and his world; review Donal McCartney Irish Catholic 2011.
235 Cardinal Paul Cullen and his world .Daire Keogh and Albert McDonnel eds.
236 Landscape and religious Practice ;A study of Mass attendance in pre-famine Ireland, David Miller.

The Parish Mission

Emmet Larkin has described the parochial mission movement as 'the single most important factor in making and consolidating the devotional revolution'.[237] Paul Cullen (1803-1878) used his influence in Rome to ensure the appointment of reforming bishops, promote parish missions and introduce a variety of new devotional practices

Between 1850 and 1880 some 1000 parishes were visited by missionaries of the various religious orders including Vincentians, Rosminians, Jesuits, Redemptorists, Passionists, Dominicans etc. By 1880 most of the parishes had been visited again. The effect of these two thousand missions, renewals and many other apostolic works by regular and secular clergy, in the forms of retreats, tridua, novenas, stations of the cross, benediction of the Blessed Sacrament was a remarkable religious revival which profoundly affected the character of the Irish People and their history.[238] The mission became a regular feature of parish life. Growing up in Ireland in the mid 20th century, the high point of Catholic life was the Parish Mission.

In Cloyne, a mission was held every five years. Three priests stayed in the parish for a week and ministered to the whole parish. There was early morning Mass at 7.30 for those going to work followed by a later Mass; an evening ceremony which consisted of a sermon in which the missioners preached, often proclaiming hell-fire and damnation on the unrepentant sinner, followed by Benediction. Homes were visited by the missioners. It was also an opportunity to go to confession. It

---

237 The Parish Mission Movement 1850-1880 Emmet Larkin.
 Eds. (Brendan Bradshaw and Daire Keogh).
238 Ibid

was essentially a time to consider the big issues of Catholic life: the Mass, the family, the afterlife, marriage etc.

The mission ceremonies were always well attended.

8.11 Parishioners at the Mission - 2015

8.12 Mission Leaflet 1940
(Courtesy: Kevin Terry)

The first sign of the impending event was the erection of the stalls. These structures remained for the duration of the mission. On sale were rosaries, miraculous medals, statues, prayer books. John Sharp states that at missions 'prayer was facilitated by the cultic artefacts of the Church, such as rosaries, scapulars, holy pictures … and medals'.[239] Many can recall these being blessed at the closing of the parish mission.

October Devotions

These devotions were a significant part in the life of the parish in the mid 20th century. Pope Leo XIII personally started the practice of devoting October to the Rosary devotion. In a letter of September 1st 1883, he admonished the faithful to dedicate the month of October to the Blessed Virgin through the daily recitation of her Rosary in the presence of the Blessed Sacrament, in order to obtain through her intercession the grace that God would console and defend His Church in her sufferings. Going to the October Devotions was also a social occasion. These were held in Cloyne every night during the month of October. They consisted of the recitation of the rosary followed by benediction of the Blessed Sacrament. Children commonly found something quite amazing in the incense which was an essential part of Benediction.

Stations of the Cross

It is one of the most popular devotions for Roman Catholics. The devotion consists of meditating on 14 events of the passion of Christ which make up the 14 stations of the cross. The purpose of this devotion is to focus on the Passion of Jesus Christ. Making the stations privately was a popular exercise during Lent in Cloyne. The stations of the cross

---

239   John Sharp, Reapers of the Harvest: Redemptorists in Great Britain and
        Ireland

were held in Cloyne church every Wednesday and Friday during Lent. The Stabat Mater was sung as the priest moved from station to station.

Devotion to Our Lady of Lourdes

Devotion to Our Lady of Lourdes grew during the1930s and there have been many pilgrimages from the parish since then.

Since the Second Vatican Council

The second Vatican Council closed 50 years ago this year having started in October 1962. One of the major changes brought in was the saying of the Mass in the vernacular languages. The priest would now face the people. A member of the Latin Mass Society of Ireland has described the old rite as *the Mass which in its essentials, inspired the saints of the western church for well nigh 1500 years from Pope Gregory the Great up to and including Therese of Lisieux and Padre Pio.*[240]

Two parishioners in Cloyne were talking about the changes in the Mass. One of them said, *'Isn't it great that we can understand the language, not like the Latin?'*. To which the other person replied, 'But *sure wasn't that the mystery of it?'*.

In Cloyne the altar rail was also removed and so was the pulpit. There were many other changes to the liturgical year.

- Elimination of Ember Days

- Elimination of Rogation Days (which date from at least the 400s and 500s and which the saints participated in). The farmers coming to mass on those three days.

- Changes of Friday Abstinence regulations.

---

240   Brian Maye. Irish Times 2015.

- Constant change in the liturgy.

- Communion in the hand and under both species.

- Confessionals changed to reconciliation rooms.

- Dropped feast days.

- Female Altar Servers.

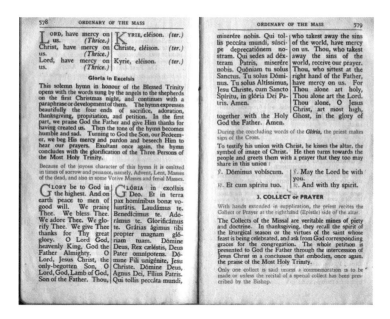

8.13 The Latin Mass[241]

---

241   from the Roman Missal revised by Very Rev J Canon Rea.

Cloyne Catholic Young Men's Society

Richard Baptist O'Brien was a remarkable priest. Born in Carrick on Suir in 1809, he and his widowed mother moved to Limerick. He graduated from Maynooth College with distinction in 1839. After spending time in England, he returned to Limerick in 1847 as a curate in the parish of St Mary's and was made a Monsignor. Two years later he founded the Catholic Young Men's Society. The society was founded to promote the religious, intellectual, social and physical welfare of its members and, in due course, its constitution and rules received the approval of Rome.[242] It took a further 35 years for a branch of the society to be established in Cloyne. The first written report on the establishment of Cloyne CYMS appeared in *The Cork Examiner*.

The Cork Examiner October 1884.

> *A Young Men's Society under the patronage of Saint Colman has been established in Cloyne. On Saturday a public meeting for that purpose was held. The men of the townland and its vicinity having long felt the want of such a society expressed to their clergymen, a wish that such should be furnished and the meeting on Saturday was the outcome. A large number of the inhabitants of the town interested in the success of the society attended. Amongst those present were: The Very Rev. Canon O'Brien, P.P., Rev. Fr. O'Riordan, Rev. Fr. Norris, Dr. O'Riordan; Messrs Cronin, Sisk, Walsh, Forest, Collins and Ahern.*

---

242   Glimpses of Limerick: Limerick Leader .1985 *Willie W. Gleeson.*

8.14 CYMS Hall

Dr O'Riordan was moved to the Chair amidst applause. In addressing the meeting, he said, *I thank you heartily for calling on me to preside on so important an occasion and I trust it will prove an auspicious occasion. As you are all aware, we have assembled for the purpose of establishing in this ancient town a Catholic Young Men's Society. The mere name of the Society to a great extent proclaims the object – A Catholic Young Men's Society is one intended to elevate and improve, to raise and unite Catholic young men of the town as well as those of the parish.* Dr O'Riordan's address was long. There was much praise for the Rev. Fr O'Riordan, the spiritual director.

Dr O'Riordan noted that there were many highly intelligent and nationally minded young men in the area. He said one of the great tasks of the society would be to give to the young men a habit of reading and that there was more to this habit than might appear on the surface, to find an ever welcome companion in a great book and not be burdened with the task of *killing time*. He impressed on them that *knowledge is power*. He told them reading was like any habit; the more they indulge the stronger it grows and the more the mind becomes informed. He said that 'education levels all distinctions and makes the humblest the equal of the highest in the land'. He said 'they were Catholics and Irishmen and as such they should maintain a society on which religion was the foundation. A civilization without religion is barbaric. A man that is false to his God cannot be true to his country.' He reminded them of the struggle their forefathers had for their country and their God. He gave a very emotional reference to the culture of the Irish, the Golden Age when other nations of Europe were at war. He urged the youth to join the society so that they could get to know each other and be more tolerant of each other's weaknesses and be a benefit to the society.

On November 1st the hall was opened as a Catholic Young Men's Society Hall.

The following report appeared in *The Cork Examiner* on October 13th 1886.

The Second Anniversary of the above was celebrated in the beautiful Hall of the Society which has been vastly improved. The Spiritual Director, Rev. J. O'Riordan, presided and gave an eloquent résumé of the good work done by the Society in the town and neighbourhood for the past two years and exhorted the members to continue the good work in the future. The treasurer, Mr D. Cronin, drew up an excellent statement of the accounts of the Society since its inception.

Receipts:	£	s.	d.
Local Subscriptions	24	3	11
Cash from Committee	17	2	0
Concerts and Lectures	54	13	1
Weekly Subscriptions	44	12	0
Billiard Table	17	2	9
Total:	167	14	5

Expenditure:			
Shop Accounts	47	13	10
Tradesmen Bill	37	3	8
Books & Newspaper	24	3	3
Expenses of Concerts	14	12	1
Billiard Table	15	11	0
Room Keeper	13	15	0
Rent of Room	11	0	0
Coals Account	19	10	0
Cash on Hand	2	15	9
Total:	167	14	5

The number of books given out to the members for home reading has quadrupled this year.

The librarian, Mr N. Walsh, was highly praised for the regularity and order with which he has conducted this department of the Society.

The address and financial business over, a number of choruses, songs and recitations were given in a very credible manner by a few members of the Society. Miss O'Donovan and Miss O'Brien gave some excellent songs for which they received great applause. The brave band attended and performed some national airs in splendid styles which brought a very enjoyable evening to a close.

As is true today, fundraising was a problem for the society so they had to think of novel ways of making money. To this end a lecture was given on Daniel O'Connell by Mr George Crosbie. The following is an extract from *The Cork Examiner.*

Saturday Morning – April 21st 1888

St Colman's Young Men's Society, Cloyne

A lecture on O'Connell was delivered in St Colman's Hall on Monday 16th April, 1888 by Mr George Crosbie, Cork, before a very large and appreciative audience.

Rev. J. O'Riordan, C.C. presided on the occasion and, in introducing the lecturer, spoke of the improvements effected within the Hall within the last three years; improvements of £150 having been spent for said purposes. The library which at first only contained a few dozen books now contains several hundred volumes, but is still insufficient to meet the increased demands of the readers. The proceeds of the lecture were to be applied for the purpose of increasing the library. He also referred to the great improvement of the young members in attending the classes of Irish and general history. The Society was in receipt of Honorary Subscriptions from members of the Church of Ireland and from people from outside the area. 1907: Most Rev. Dr Cotter Aux. Bishop of Portsmouth: Mr C.F.P. Creed. Cloyne House: Mr M Russell, Kilteskin: Mr Andrew Rowland: Mr P. Heron, Rock St.

The minute books remaining give a clear picture of the activities of the society.

We learn from the entry of December 1899:

The room-keeper was paid 3s per week,

McGregor's shop was paid 4d for a water jug.

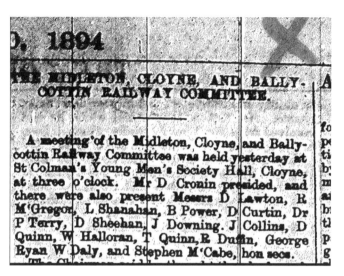

8.15 The Midleton, Cloyne and Ballycotton Railway Committee[243]

The January 1900 meeting revealed that The Christy Minstrel's entertainment of St Stephen's Night 1899 netted £15 14s 6d. James Power was paid 1s 6d in 1900 for cleaning the chimney. Cash in for billiard table for September was £2 5s 11d and from May 6th 1900 to November 6th 1900 the billiard table netted £7 4s 7d.

The income from the billiard table was a constant source of revenue. In 1903 two members of the society attended the golden jubilee of the Cork Branch of the CYMS by invitation and one, Mr G. Ryan, received first place at the bishop's table at these festivities.

The minute books reveal the true spirit of Catholic Action in as much as the Society was involved in fund raising for the victims of the Ballingrane tragedy in 1901.

At the annual meeting held on November 15th 1903 the

243   *The Cork Examiner* 30th July 1894.

secretary announced that the finances of the society were in a healthy state, that much work was carried out during the year renovating the hall, and the pretty appearance of the hall was second to none. The following members of the billiard Tournament 1903 were: Joseph Collins, Timothy Sheehan, Thomas O'Brien, James Barry, Jeremiah Rohan, William Forrest and Edmond Costine. Fr Foley chaired a meeting on March 20th 1904 and informed the committee that Gaelic League classes were to be established in the hall that week and urged those present to attend the first meeting of the class. A meeting presided over by the Very Rev. Canon O'Riordan, now P.P. in Cloyne, on January 31st 1904 discussed the matter of introducing a game of cards to those games already within the Society. Fr O'Riordan said gambling of every description should be condemned and so the matter was dropped.

In 1905 it was recommended that members of the committee would prepare a paper on a historical topic, and we read that in Jan. 1905 Mr Timothy Walsh gave an excellent talk. Patrick's Day 1904 saw a small variety entertainment in honour of Saint Patrick. This was reported in The Cork Examiner on March 23rd 1904. The Examiner reported that 'what proved to be a very successful concert was held on St Patrick's Night. The members of the C.Y.M.S. availed of the opportunity to celebrate in a proper and fitting manner the anniversary of Our National Apostle. The programme was opened by the boys of the National School neatly attired and displaying the green immortal together with green rosettes with a harp in the centre. They very creditably rendered The Dear Little Shamrock. This was followed by songs from individuals and a recitation from Mr John Duggan N.T. There were other items among which were a violin recital and a production from the gramophone which caused much laughter. The programme closed with the singing of the National Anthem "God Save Ireland" after which Rev. Fr O'Riordan thanked the performers and the audience.'

The state of the stove gave cause for concern and was referred to on many occasions until a new one was purchased. Fr O'Riordan purchased same and was paid £3 5s 6d on March 11th 1906. We learn that at the meeting of 3rd October 1947 a decision was taken to raise the subscription to 3d.

There are many references to the Spiritual Director Fr Fitzgerald. On 4/11/1949, Fr Fitzgerald addressed the members and reminded them of their obligations from the point of view of Catholic Action. Membership of the CYMS entailed much more than merely attending the hall and playing games, he said. He also reminded them that it was incumbent on them to be members of some other religious society such as The Confraternity.

On 4th Jan. 1906 Bishop Cotter handed in his subscription of 10s. A rather interesting item concerns fundraising in 1922. A raffle was to be held for money prizes only. The secretary was directed to send in the order for 1500 tickets to The Eagle Printing Co., the printing to be done on paper of Irish Manufacture only. The ban on card games must have been lifted as card games were mentioned in 1922.

The original aims of the society seemed to be adhered to as is evident in 1948 when the library features on the agenda regarding opening hours and terms of borrowing. Members of the CYMS were asked in 1958 by the Very Rev. Canon Fitzpatrick to take over the church collections. It was agreed to appoint six collectors each month. The attendance to this duty was commended, as was the counting of the money.

The meeting always ended with a prayer. The members were encouraged to say the Family Rosary and constantly reminded that the CYMS was an arm of Catholic Action and the members had certain responsibilities. In 1952 it was decided to purchase a picture of The Sacred Heart and get the hall consecrated.

That year it was decided to redecorate the hall with voluntary labour. The annual meeting of 1950 said membership topped the one hundred mark. In 1954 membership started falling and by 1955 there were only 35 members but it had reached 60 by 1959. Card Drives were a major take in the 1960s and the annual 45-drives were very successful and were the main source of income. In the 1960s, it was decided not to have suit lengths anymore as prizes, only money - £30 in cash. Pete Morrisson attended a 45-drive, the night President Kennedy was shot in 1963. In 1955 we learn that the Whist Drives held in aid of parochial funds were a huge success.

For 1957 the following were the agreed charges: - Snooker: 4d for 20mins and 1d for every 5 mins. extra; Billiard charge 6d per half hour; Table Tennis: 2d for 3 games and 5d for 5 games. Other activities were held in the hall. The local branch of Macra Na Feirme was given permission to hold Question Time as were other organizations.

The last remaining minutes of a meeting are dated 01 / 10 / 1962.

The Irish Independent reported on Monday October 9th 1972 from the 41st annual meeting of the National Council of the CYMS held in Youghal, opened by the Most Rev. Dr J.J. Ahern bishop of Cloyne. The bishop said, *Those today charged with guiding the destinies of the Catholic Young Men's Society should examine again its aims and the work it was doing and have the courage to make changes where these were necessary.*

Bishop Ahern continued and said that there was a tendency to look down on old institutions and to think that they were no longer of value. He reminded the delegates that *it is well to remember that even in the world of 1972 tradition has its place. The CYMS has a long and honourable tradition of quiet but effective work, but it must look to the future and be open to change when change is seen to be necessary.*

In 1971, when Archbishop McQuaid was informed that a branch of CYMS in his diocese had been disintegrating over the past decade, his written reply was. *We must bow to the inevitable. The CYMS even more than Confraternities and Sodalities has melted away. And nothing can restore it in our time.*[244]

The CYMS hall served the men of Cloyne for almost eighty years and was the centre of their recreation. The hall is now turned into apartments. Thankfully the beautiful engraving of the name Catholic Young Men's Society is still in good condition. But 'the old order changeth' and the Cloyne CYMS is no more. This is now and time is the measure of change.

Society of St Vincent de Paul

The first Conference of St Vincent de Paul was in 1833 at which Conference distributed food and fuel to the poor of Paris.

A year after its foundation in Paris the society began to spread throughout France and later throughout the world. It is now established in 132 countries with almost one million members in 50,000 conferences.

---

244   *McQuaid to Mgr.R.J.Glennon,* 4 Feb.1971 DDA, McQuaid Papers (A/8/b/ XXI/30).

The first Conference in Ireland was established in Halston Street parish in Dublin in 1844 by Dr Woodlock, President of All Hallows College. Redmond Peter O'Carroll was its first president. It had nineteen members, including John O'Connell, MP, and son of Daniel O'Connell, the Liberator and John O'Hagan, an active member of the Young Ireland movement.

The St Colman's Conference of the Society of St Vincent de Paul was founded in 1988 by the late Dr Canon O'Driscoll PP of Cloyne in conjunction with the area president at that time the late Liam Allen of the Cobh Conference. The first Conference meeting was held in the sacristy of the Cloyne Church and had volunteer members from all areas of the parish. Meetings were held every Monday evening there after throughout the year followed by visitation to the many people which had requested assistance, no mobile phones in those days.[245]

The Society of St Vincent de Paul is a lay Christian voluntary organisation working with those in need and the disadvantaged. Inspired by its principal founder, Fredric Ozanman, and its patron St Vincent De Paul, it seeks to respond to the call every Christian receives to bring the love of Christ to those we serve in the spirit of the gospel message *I was hungry and you gave me to eat.*[246]

No work of the charity is foreign to the society. It is involved in a diverse range of activities characterised by:

  - Support and Friendship,
  - Promoting Self-Sufficiency,
  - Working for Social Justice.

---

245   Information provided by Dominic Neville.
246   Matt.25

St Colman's Conference Cloyne is generously supported by the people of the parish by way of contributions to the monthly collections taken up after all Masses on the second weekends of the month and other donations received, especially at Christmas. The Conference depends on volunteers who give their time and support to its objectives. Successive priests of the parish have given whole-hearted support to the Conference.

Eucharistic Congress

The 50th International Eucharistic Congress was held in 2012. The bell shown in Photo 8.17 when it was in Cloyne, was a key symbol of the Congress.[247]

8.16 The Eucharistic Congress Bell
(Courtesy: Cloyne Parish Office)

Remembering the Faithful Departed

The practice of praying for the dead is rooted in Christian belief in life everlasting. The feast of the Holy Souls is on November 2nd. Before the Blessing of the Graves ceremony became the standard devotion for the dead, most of us can

247 www.iec2012.ie/bell

remember going to church on All Souls' Day. We did the 'rounds' all day long and made as many visits as we could and each time said certain prayers for the dead which gained an indulgence for the Souls in Purgatory. Now the Blessing of the Graves is held in Cloyne New Cemetery in early November and in the Old Cemetery later in the month.

8.17 Memorial Place

It was a bright crisp Sunday in November 2014. We had gathered in the New Cemetery for the annual blessing of the graves. As is usual, the cemetery was packed. The prayers started at three pm. After the initial readings, Canon O'Mahony proceeded to bless the graves accompanied by the altar server who carried the Holy Water. Up and down each row the graves were blessed and sprinkled with Holy Water with the palm in his hand. Relatives gathered in groups at graves throughout the cemetery. For some, who recently lost a loved one, it was the first time they attended the ceremony and for them the grief was very raw. For others, whose relatives were long gone, this was an annual visit.

This was a day for memories and each had his own. While Canon O'Mahony blessed the graves, the rosary was lead by Fr Joe Rohan and hymns were sung.

After the prayers had finished, the congregation retired into the church for benediction. This was a very poignant ceremony. Everyone sang. The final hymn was *How Great Thou Art*. It was especially touching for those of us who, perhaps, have autumn or maybe winter in our souls.

Mass is celebrated annually during the summer months in the New Cemetery and in the Old Cemetery. In 2015, Mass in the Old Cemetery was celebrated by the Rev. Fr Joe Rohan on a lovely August evening with a touch of autumn in the air. Twittering swallows circled overhead, breaking the stillness of this ancient place. All around were many gravestones marking the final resting places of so many Catholics before the new cemetery was enclosed around the present Catholic Church in 1935. This sacred space is fifteen hundred years old. For the past 25 years three people voluntarily have kept this cemetery in fine condition: Bunty Cahill, Maurice Griffin, Paddy Cahill.

The photograph shows the McCarthys, Ross and Anne, with their son Sam, 6 months, coming to pray for Ross's deceased father Dave, from the town of Cloyne, who passed away in 2005.

8.18 The McCarthy family, 2014

The Grotto

Thirty years ago, in 1985, the grotto to Our Lady was opened in St Colman's Terrace. This was a result of the inspiration and dedicated work of the local residents. Every year since it opened there has been a May procession to it in honour of Our Lady.[248] Geraldine O'Brien's grandmother, Mary Daly, had a bird's eye view of the 'ring', as it was affectionately known by the terrace residents, from her upstairs bedroom window. She often spoke of her love of Our Lady and her dream of building a grotto. The opportunity for its construction arose when the new housing estate, Berkeley Court, was being built. Through the work and credit of the residents the opportunity was seized upon and the grotto was built.

**8.19 Preparation of Grotto,
Mrs Mary Daly, Mrs Cusack**
(Courtesy: Geraldine O'Brien)

---

248   Information supplied by Geraldine O'Brien.

8.20 Grotto Opening
(Courtesy: Geraldine O'Brien)

Photo 8.20 shows Fr Corkery, P.P., Cloyne, Fr Troy and Fr Halliden together with altar boys Thomas O'Brien, Gerard Ring and Tom Kelly.

8.21 Grotto Mass July 2015
– Mrs Ring & Mrs O'Shea

In the photo showing some of the attendees at the Grotto mass in July 2015 are Mrs Ring and Mrs O'Shea, original committee members.

CHAPTER 9

Bicentenary Year in Photographs

9.1 Opening Night

9.2 Celebrating the Mass, Opening Night

9.3 Celebrating the Mass, Opening Night

9.4 Exposition of the Blessed Sacrament

9.5 The Choir

9.6 Parish Mission:
Sr Briege McKenna, O.S.C.

9.7 Parish Mission Group: 12ᵗʰ March, 2015

9.8 Holy Saturday – Polish Community
(Courtesy: Kitty Cahill)

9.9 Easter Garden
(Photo: Aoife Terry)

As well as decorating the church with beautiful displays of flowers, Kitty Cahill also prepared this wonderful Easter garden.

9.10 The Bishop and the Cardinal

Cardinal Murphy O'Connor examining a presentation made to him by Bishop William Crean.

9.11 St Colman's National School Choir – Bicentenary Mass
(Courtesy: Mary O'Brien)

9.12 Altar servers

9.13 Presentation to Muireann O'Brien Kelly, past organist

Muireann's family is an example of the significant contribution many families, made to the parish and community.

William O'Brien and Kathleen O'Driscoll - a remarkable family contribution

From his appointment as principal of Churchtown South in 1917 until his death in 1966, Liam as he was always affectionately known locally, lived in Cloyne. In his application for the post of principal of Cloyne Boys' National School in December 1949, he stated: During my time in Cloyne I have acted as secretary or treasurer of every organisation for the welfare of the people of the parish. He served in Cloyne BNS until his retirement in 1962.

The O'Brien family have memories of the stress caused to their father by the counting, recording and banking of the church-door collections each week. The Christmas and Easter dues brought extra pressure on a kind man who felt that the widow's mite was just as valuable as the offering of the rich man, and all deserved to be entered in copperplate handwriting to be read out at Mass, a custom he abhorred! Kathleen came to Churchtown in 1925 as a JAM (Junior Assistant Mistress) and taught the lower classes there until she moved to Cloyne Girls' National school in 1951, where she became the teacher of junior and senior infants.

At that time a half an hour a day was allotted in schools for religious instruction. Liam and Kathleen would have spent that time teaching prayers and catechism with a sprinkling of stories from Schuster's Bible. The children's proficiency was examined once a year by the Diocesan inspector who gave a grade for every pupil: E for excellent, VG for very good and so on. A VG or worse stuck out like a sore thumb in a column of Es on a document that was there for posterity. As well as this work the teachers were expected to prepare the pupils for the sacraments, where their religious knowledge was again examined.

After four years with the girls, Mrs O'Brien moved across town to join her son Michael, who had succeeded his father, in the Boys' School. Any more than her husband, her service to the community did not finish when she left school in the evening. Mrs O'Brien trained and conducted the church choir for many, many years, which meant always being present whether it was practice of Latin hymns and Gregorian chant, benediction, confirmation, the sung Mass at Christmas, or the Easter liturgy which was the pinnacle of the choir's endeavour.

9.14 Mission 2015: Rev. Kevin Scallon, C.M., Sr Briege McKenna, O.S.C., Canon Donal O'Mahony, P.P.

Appendix A

Letter from Treasury Chambers to the Rev. Mr Rogers 1849[249]

20.563 ⁹/10

Treasury Chambers.
23ʳᵈ October. 1849

Sir,

The Lords Commissioners of Her
Majesty's Treasury having had under
their consideration your letter
dated the 1ˢᵗ instant, requesting
that an answer may be given to
your prior memorial, in which
you prayed that My Lords
would authorize the Trustees
for the Irish Reproductive
Loan Fund in the County of
Cork to stay their proceedings, until
after the present harvest, against
yourself and other parties who
had become Sureties to the
Trustees for a sum of £400 advanced
by them to a Loan Association at
Cloyne, and that My Lords
would be pleased to direct the
Trustees

The Rev. W. Rogers
Kilmahon Glebe
Cloyne

---

249   Source Find My Past Data set.

Trustees to remit so much of the Balance as cannot be recovered.

I am commanded by their Lordships to inform you that My Lords have not received from the Trustees in County Cork the information respecting the state of their trust to 30th September last, which they are required to transmit pursuant to the 6th Section of the Bye Laws of the Fund in force under the Act 11 and 12 Vic: Cap: 115; and without such information My Lords are not able to consider the Memorial referred to by you nor interfere in any proceedings which may be taken by the Trustees against the parties liable to them.

I am, Sir,
Your obedient Servant.

Appendix B

Signatories to the Address to
Fr O'Riordan, 1904[250]

(MISS) Nora Aherne

Richard Barry KNOCKGURM.

Garrett Barry CASTLEMARY.

Thomas Connell SHANAHEE.

James Costine CLOYNE,

(MISS) Bridget Costine, CHURCH STREET, CLOYNE.

Charles J. P. Creed CLOYNE HOUSE, CLOYNE.

Daniel Cronin CLOYNE.

James Collins SHEENLIS.

Michael Cronin BALLYRUSSEL, CLOYNE.

Thomas Crotty MONEAY.

Walter Crotty, ROCK STREET, CLOYNE.

John Cuddigan CLOYNE.

William Daly CLOYNE.

John Daly ROCK STREET, CLOYNE.

Patrick Dempsey BALLYCOTTON.

A Donelan M.P.

Patrick Dorgan ROCK STREET, CLOYNE.

Daniel Duffin BALLYCOTTON.

Michael Higgins BALLYROBBIN.

Edmond Hoare TULLAGH.

Michael J. Ivers CHURCHTOWN.

John Kenna CLOYNE.

Mrs Kearney BALLYCRENANE.

Thomas Kelleher SCARIFF.

John Kenefick SHANAGARRY.

James Kenefick BALLYBRENAGH, CLOYNE.

John Kenefick BALLYCATOO, CLOYNE.

Mary Kennelly MAIN STREET, CLOYNE.

James Lahiive CASTLEMARY.

C. C. Crooke-Lawless KILCRONE, CLOYNE.

W. R. Crooke-Lawless KILCRONE, CLOYNE.

David Lawton CLOYNE.

Jeremiah Leahy WOOD, CLOYNE.

William Litchfield BALLYMALOE.

Robert Mackrym CLOYNE.

Edmond Mahony BALLINVOHER.

Matthew McAuliffe
CARRIGATOGHER, MIDLETON.

Thomas O'Brien
CHURCH STREET, CLOYNE.

William McCarthy
BALLYCRONEEN.

Thomas O'Brien
ROCK STREET, CLOYNE.

Michael J. MacCarthy

Jeremiah O'Brien
ROCK STREET, CLOYNE.

John McGrath
BALLINVOHER.

Michael O'Brien
CHURCHTOWN.

(MRS.) Margaret Meade
CLOYNE.

Daniel O'Connell
COOLBAY.

John Moreen
KILVA.

James O'Neill
BALLYBRENAGH.

Daniel Joseph Murphy, M.D.
CLOYNE.

Bartholomew Power
TULLAGH, CLOYNE.

Michael Murphy
THE DEMESNE.

Michael Power
CHURCH STREET, CLOYNE.

Michael Mullany
BALLYBANE, SHANAGARRY.

Ellen Power
BALLINVOHER, CLOYNE.

John Duggan
CLOYNE.

Mrs Hankard
TULLAGH.

William J. Dunne
CLOYNE.

John Harty
BALLYROE.

Edward Fleming
RIVER STREET, CLOYNE.

Jeremiah Healy
LISANLEY, CLOYNE.

W. H. Forde
BALLYGEANY.

John Hegarty
KILSHANE, CLOYNE.

James Forrest
ROCK STREET, CLOYNE.

Philip Hegarty
BALLINVOHER, CLOYNE.

Robert Garde
BALLINAMONA, SHANAGARRY, MIDLETON.

Maurice Hegarty
KNOCKGURM.

Redmond Geary
CLOYNE.

Thomas Hennessy
CHURCHTOWN SOUTH, CLOYNE.

John Grace
CLOYNE HOUSE, CLOYNE.

Robert Heron
CLOYNE.

Joseph Grogan
MONAGURRA.

Mrs Higgins
MAYTOWN.

320

John Smyth, TULLAGH, CLOYNE.

William Spillane, KNOCKACRUMP.

J. Wilson Strangman, KINOITH, SHANAGARRY.

Patrick Sullivan, SHANAGARRY.

John ay Terry, BALLINGRANE.

Charles Terry, KILVA.

John Terry, IVY COTTAGE, BALLYLANDERS.

Robert Walsh, MAIN STREET, CLOYNE.

Thomas Walsh, BALLYLONGAN, SHANAGARRY.

Thomas Walsh, BALLINGRANE.

Timothy Walsh, CLOYNE.

William Walsh, CHAPEL STREET, CLOYNE.

William Walsh, CHURCH STREET, CLOYNE

Thomas Williamson, CLOYNE.

Mrs. McCarthy, BALLYMACANDERICK.

Select Bibliography

Suzanne Barrett, *The Holy Wells of Ireland*.

J.A. Coombes: *A Bishop of Penal Times*, Tower Books, 1981.

Mark Cronin, *To the Blackpool Front,* The Collins Press, 2014.

Eric A. Derr, *Episcopal visitations of the diocese of Cloyne and Ross, 1785-1828 [with index],* Archivium Hibernicum, LXVI 2013, The Catholic Historical Society of Ireland, 2013.

Sean Horgan, *Famine and Politics in Midleton Poor Law Union 1845-1851*, Litho Press 2012.

Dermot Keogh, *Jack Lynch*, Gill & Macmillan, 2008.

Colm Lennon, *Confraternities and Sodalities in Ireland,* Columba Press, 2012.

Samuel Lewis' Cork, a topographical dictionary of the parishes, towns and villages of Cork City and County, The Collins Press, 1998.

Padraig O'Loingsigh (Editor), *The Book of Cloyne.*

Diarmaid Ó Catháin: *An Irish Scholar Abroad : Bishop John O'Brien of Cloyne and the Macpherson Controversy* (in 'Cork History and Society' eds Patrick O'Flanagan and Cornelius G. Buttimer).

Breandán Ó Conchúir: *Scríobhaithe Chorcaí 1700 – 1850*.

Paul MacCotter, *A History of the Medieval Diocese of Cloyne,* The Columba Press, 2013.

Paul MacCotter, *Colman of Cloyne* – A Study, Four Courts Press, 2004.

Donald M. MacRaild, *Irish Migrants in Modern Britain, 1750-1922,* Macmillan Press Ltd., 1999.

Michael A. Mullett, *Catholics in Britain and Ireland, 1558-1829*, St. Martin's Press Inc., New York, 1998

Nicholas Terpstra, *Confraternities Social Capital and Civil Society*.

Gerry White and Brendan O'Shea, editors, *A Great Sacrifice Cork Servicemen who died in the Great War*, Echo Publications (Cork) Ltd, 2010.

Index

Daly, Michael, 241

Daly, Mrs, 214

Darrara, 57

Daunt Lightship, 255

David Walsh, 53

Davis, John Francis, 67

Davis, Mr, 76

Davis, Rev Charles, 76

Dawkins, George, 243

Dawkins, Nathaniel, 241

De La Rue, Thomas, 240

de Lacey, Peter

Count, 23

De Valera, Eamon, 95,197,240, 258

Delany, William

Bishop, 66

Devon Commission, 70

   devotional practice, 265

   devotional revolution, 286

Dillon, Author, 23

Dilworth, Michael, 275

Diocesan Inspectorship

   of schools, 87

Diocesan Statutes, 63

Doneraile, 32, 65, 73, 137

Donovan, Bridger, 230

Donovan, M., 86

Donovan, Michael, 92

Donworth, Rev P., 35

Dorgan, Betty, 208

Dorgan, John, 232

Downing, Mr, 69

Downing, Mr., 238

Doyle, Bishop, 47

Drinan, Thomas, 234

Driscoll, Daniel, 241

Driscoll, William, 241

Duane, John, 112

Duffy, Gavan, 71

Duhallow, 48

Dunboyne establishment, 65, 76, 83

Dunn, W, J., 86

Dwire, Michael, 232

Eager, John, 117

   buried in Bruges, 118

Eager, Rev John, 238

Earl of Thomond'

   claim to title, 25

East Cork, 9, 212, 227, 246, 254

Easter garden, 312

Easter Rising, 1916, 245

Eaton, Eileen, 208

   economic

   activity, 10

Edinburgh, 86

   education, 237

Egypt, 244

   emigration, 3, 8, 45, 229, 230

Emmet, Robert, 51

Esbon, 101

Eucharistic Congress Bell, 303

Eugenie, 237

   famine, 2, 8, 55, 64, 227, 229

1820s, 45

Cloyne, 113

   famine period, 227

   population decline, 228

Feiritéir, Piaras, 28

History, 246

Rome, 19, 24, 28, 46, 53, 66-67, 71-73, 77- 78, 227-230

Rostellan, 1, 7, 37, 243

Rourke, Michael, 241

Rowland, Mr F, 116

Russell, Fr, 227

Russell, Fr Jeremiah, 176

Russell, Fr John P.P., 64

Russell, John, 112

   appointed parish priest, Cloyne, 113

   nominated as Bishop, 116

Ryan, George, 86

Ryan, John, 244

Ryan, Mrs George, 88

Sacred Heart Sodality, 282

Salamanca, 58

Scallon, Rev Kevin, 208

Scanlan, Rev J., 48

Scanlon

Rev. John, 14

Scanlon, John, 109, 111

Scanlon, Rev John, 3, 15-16, 21, 200, 204

Scannell, Bishop

   birth, 101

   bishop of Concordia, 101

   early priesthood, 101

Scannell, Hanora, 233

Shanagarry, 3, 7, 10, 12, 43, 88, 198, 225, 228, 238, 256

Shanagarry Church, 268

Shanagarry Guild ICA, 204

Shanballymore, 65

Shannon, Earl of, 68

Sheehan, Canon, 87, 137

   serving in Scotland, 138

Sinn Fein, 240

Sirius, 229

Sisk, Canon, 165

   fundraising for Cobh cathedral, 166

Sisk, Fr James, 78

Sisk, John, 244

Sisters

   born in Cloyne, 183

Skibbereen, 52, 53, 55, 56

Sliney, James, 234

Smart, Jack, 246

Smith-Barry syndicate, 80

Smith-Barry, Mr., 238

Smyth, Canon, 163

   Creamery in Ballyarra, 163

Smyth, Fr Nathaniel, 145

Society of Antiquarians, 107

Society of St Vincent de Paul, 301

Southampton, 87

Spain, 23, 26

Spike Island, 35, 40

   dispute over, 36

Spital Cottages, 244

Spital Lane, 19

Spy Hill, 66

St Colman

   icon, 264

St Colman's College, 65, 73, 83, 87, 95, 102

St Colman's

338